THE MUSIC GUIDE TO GREAT BRITAIN

Elaine Brody
Claire Brook

THE
MUSIC
GUIDE TO
GREAT BRITAIN

England
Scotland
Wales
Ireland

Dodd, Mead & Company · New York

Library of Congress Cataloging in Publication Data

Brody, Elaine.
  The music guide to Great Britain.

    1. Music—Great Britain—Directories.   I. Brook,
Claire, joint author.   II. Title.
ML21.B78   780'.2541   75–30809
ISBN 0-396-06955-X

Preface

This book, conceived in frustration, was born into a world besieged by unprecedented economic problems. It was originally planned as one mammoth volume covering eighteen European countries, but like so many grandiose projects, has fallen victim to our current recession. The result is a series of self-contained fragments—each book treating a specific country or area and each one available at a negotiable price. However, this necessary compromise has moved us far from our original intention.

How did it all start?

We both travel as much as our professional responsibilities will allow. We are both trained musicians married to men whose work requires them to spend some part of each year in Europe and we try to accompany them whenever possible. Too often, however, we have found ourselves in the right city at the wrong time or—worse still—in the right city at the right time without being aware of it until it was too late.

Often when faced with the delightful prospect of a few weeks abroad, we have been astonished at how difficult it is to acquire sufficient information to make these visits as fruitful as possible. The musical traveler has no central source of data on a multitude of questions practical, historical, or theoretical. There are those who want to be sure that if they are in Bayreuth on a Tuesday, they can visit the theater even though there is no performance; others may try for weeks to isolate the moment when the Musée d'Instruments of the Paris Conservatory receives visitors and allows them to play the instruments on display; the curious amateur may wish to locate the Brahms House in Baden-Baden, while others may have heard that there is an interesting music festival in Fishguard without being able to guess exactly where it is and when it is held. Graduate students seeking to avail themselves of the resources of the Gesellschaft der Musikfreunde in Vienna will be grateful for precise information concerning the visiting hours and credentials requirements; the opera lover enjoying a performance at La Scala would have to be aware of the proximity of La Scala Theater Museum in order to explore it during an intermission. The young scholar arriving in Rome on a two weeks' summer leave, only to find that all the libraries are closed and there is no one within miles to provide a bit of assistance, could have been forewarned had schedules been available to him. And so on and so on and so on.

The idea for the *Music Guide* came to us in recognition of the need for a handbook which could provide to the widest range of people—from the musical dilettante to the highly motivated specialist—a compendium of information of a practical nature. The idea seemed so straightforward and obvious that we could not understand why such a guide did not already exist. Once we had embarked on the project, we understood only too well; it had not already been done because it was utterly impossible!!!

But we are getting a bit ahead of ourselves. The *Guide,* once we began to classify and organize the areas for investigations, began to shape itself. Certain editorial decisions concerning the geographical limitations of this volume had to be made arbitrarily. In addition, we would not know just how to treat individual cities until enough information had been gathered to determine the extent of the musical activity and resources in each place. Questionnaires were prepared in five languages for five categories. With the invaluable cooperation of the official cultural offices in each of the eighteen countries we had decided to discuss, we amassed lists of places and people that formed the basis of a large initial mailing. So the process of information-gathering began. As the responses came in, most of our questions concerning inclusion, exclusion, format, and style were answered. The results are to be found in the volumes that follow.

Within each country, the physical, political, and musical organizations indigenous to that nation determined the ordering of the material. In some instances, a chapter consists of a series of short essays on individual cities; in others where there is only one important urban center, additional information applying to cities outside that center is provided by categories: i.e., miscellaneous opera houses and concert halls, libraries, conservatories, etc. We have taken it upon ourselves to enter the lists editorially by making evaluative judgments.

In addition to decisions of qualitative merit, we have had to take cognizance of length and usefulness. We have tried to maintain a reasonable level of consistency in approach and depth of information. Although we sent the same questionnaires to each country, the responses were incredibly uneven. In some cases information was unavailable because we received no replies and it was impossible to pursue the matter personally. In other instances one of us did the necessary legwork to ferret out answers when the official sources were uncooperative. Very often, however, we received invaluable help from many of the Music Information Centers (CeBeDeM in Brussels, Donemus in Amsterdam, the Music Information Centers of Finland and Sweden, to mention but a few) as well as from individuals whose professional affiliations enabled them to provide us with precise details in addition to general information.

Subject to geographical variations, the information we have prepared is organized under the following general headings: Opera Houses and Concert Halls; Libraries and Museums; Conservatories and Schools; Musical Landmarks; Musical Organizations; Business of Music; Miscellaneous. At the conclusion, there is a section devoted to Festivals and Competitions.

Opera Houses and Concert Halls: we have tried to include the information necessary for the reader's use in determining season, program, and hours of performances. Although we mention some churches in which concerts usually take place, we have not attempted to be overly comprehensive, since almost every church will house the odd public concert from time to time and this does not automatically qualify it as a site for musical entertainment. There has been an increasingly prevalent tendency to present concerts, opera, and chamber music in castles, courtyards, parks, and gardens. The reader is therefore advised to consult a local newspaper or concert guide, which will be indicated at the beginning of most city segments, for details of the unusual events taking place in the unexpected places.

Libraries and Museums: to facilitate practical reference to specific collections, we have attempted to give library and museum names in their original languages. We wish to acknowledge here and now our gratitude for the scholarship and generosity of Rita Benton, whose *Directory of Music Research Libraries* constituted the basic foundation of our investigations in this category. (Hence Ben. 1, 2, etc. found in our volumes refer to Dr. Benton's numbering system.) We are particularly grateful to Dr. Benton for permission to see the third volume of this important work while it was still in manuscript. For more detailed information about the institutions mentioned in this present volume, please consult her book. Where our questionnaires contained information at odds with hers, we assumed that we had the more recent data.

For the most recent and most comprehensive coverage of archives, collections, libraries, and museums, consult the cumulative index (vols. I-V, 1967–1971) of RILM (acronym for the *International Repertory of Music Literature*), an absolutely essential reference work available at most libraries.

Established in 1966 by the International Musicological Society and the International Association of Music Libraries to attempt to deal with the explosion in musicological documentation by international cooperation and modern technology, *RILM,* a quarterly publication of abstracts of books, articles, essays, reviews, dissertations, catalogues, iconographies, etc. is available in the USA through the International RILM Center, City University of New York, 33 West 42nd Street, New York 10036. European subscriptions are available from RILM Distributor for Europe, Bärenreiter Verlag Heinrich-Schütz-Allee 31–37, D-3500 Kassel-Wilhelmshöhe, West Germany.

Institutes of Musicology are to be found under different headings according to their function within the host country. In France, for example, the Institute is part of the university and is found under Schools and Conservatories. In Spain, it is a library and publishing organization and will appear under Libraries.

Schools and Conservatories: we have had to eliminate ruthlessly all but the major musical institutions in the interest of keeping this book portable. Because course offerings and degree requirements differ from country to country, we have eschewed program descriptions and instead supplied an address from which the interested reader may obtain further information. Summer courses are included in this section, except where they are clearly allied with a festival, in which case they can be located through a cross reference. A cautionary word: those planning to attend seminars or master classes in European universities should bear in mind that no housing arrangements are made by the university. The administration will supply the names of private persons who take in boarders, but these arrangements should be made well in advance of arrival. A list of organizations with special services for the English-speaking student abroad can be found in the Appendix.

Musical Landmarks: after an enthusiastic beginning, it became apparent that it would not be possible to include every commemorative plaque and graveyard that concerned a musician or musical event without rivaling the telephone directory in size. Therefore, we have usually restricted ourselves to establishments which are open to the public but do not qualify as museums. Occasionally the address of such a place seems to differ in alternate descriptions of the same place. This is invariably due to the fact that building compounds may have entrances on several streets. Where a mailing address is at variance with the public entrance, we have indicated both.

Musical organizations of international significance have been mentioned and, in some exceptional instances, described in detail. The same criteria were applied to commercial musical establishments.

The concluding section, that devoted to Festivals, Competitions, and Periodicals, brings together a body of material never before found between the covers of a single volume. Because we did not wish to build immediate obsolescence into the book, we have not supplied exact dates or typical programs for Festivals and Competitions. Instead, we have sought to give an accurate name and address to which the reader might address himself for that information. We did attempt, wherever possible, to provide descriptive as well as factual material on the more colorful festivals.

There is always a question, where co-authorship is concerned, about the division of labor in any particular project. We are sure that others have arranged their mode of cooperation in a variety of ways. Once the operational procedures had been established by mutual decision, we found it expedient and practical to divide our work on a geographical basis. Therefore, Elaine Brody supervised the research and wrote up the materials on Germany and Austria, Belgium, the Netherlands, Spain, Portugal, Switzerland, Luxembourg, and Monaco; Claire Brook did the same for Great Britain, France, Italy, and the four Scandinavian countries: Denmark, Finland, Norway, and Sweden.

The problems inherent in this kind of compendium are legion. Having to depend on the cooperation of hundreds of functionaries from

secretaries to cultural ministers—disinterested at one extreme and overly
zealous at the other—as well as on our own researching techniques and
efforts, has resulted in somewhat uneven coverage with somewhat
variable accuracy quotient. Although we have visited almost every one
of the cities discussed in depth and many of those covered more cur-
sorily, we have not attended all the festivals nor have we physically
investigated all the libraries, institutes, and museums. It has been utterly
impossible to check all of our sources personally. We have tried to
circumvent this lapse from scholarly grace by choosing our sources as
carefully as we could.

Three years after we began this Herculean task, we halted the
gathering, collating, checking, writing. It would not be accurate to say
that we "finished," for we are both only too aware of the fact that we
have barely skimmed the surface of the material. But our manuscript
had already become five times the length contracted for, and other
duties called. In those three years we had the good fortune to work with
a group of exceptional people—exceptional not only because of their
extraordinary sense of responsibility and selfless dedication to their
nation's music, but also for the care and precision with which they
answered our questions. We would like to thank the following people—
and to apologize to those whom we have inevitably and inadvertently
overlooked: John Amis (London), Dr. R. Angermüller (Salzburg), the
Comtesse de Chambure (Paris), Ulla Christiansen (New York), Hans
Conradin (Zurich), Adrienne Doignies-Musters (Brussels), Ady Egleston
(New York), Dr. Georg Feder (Cologne), Marna Feldt (New York), Jean
and Mimi Ferrard (Brussels), Prof. Kurt von Fischer (Zurich), Claire
Van Gelder (Paris and Brussels), Dr. Jörn Göres (Dusseldorf), Marlene
Haag (Salzburg), Prof. Edmund Haines (New York), Ernesto Halffter
(Madrid), Dr. Hilde Hellmann (Vienna), Per-Anders Hellquist (Stock-
holm), Maurice Huisman (Brussels), Antonio Iglesias (Madrid), Dr.
Erwin Jacobi (Zurich), Jean Jenkins (London), Newell Jenkins (Giglio
and New York), Prof. Rudolf Klein (Vienna), Kåre Kolberg (Oslo), Dr.
Johanna Kral (Vienna), Dr. Gunnar Larsson (Stockholm), Albert
Vander Linden (Brussels), Anders Lönn (Stockholm), Per Olaf Lundahl
(Stockholm), René de Maeyer (Brussels), Matilde Medina y Crespo
(Madrid), Per Onsum (Oslo), Dr. Alfons Ott (Munich), Pierluigi Petro-
belli (Parma), Henry Pleasants (London), Andrew Porter (New York
and London), Sheila Porter (New York and London), Anders Ramsay
(Stockholm), Albi Rosenthal (London), Dag Schjelderup-Ebbe (Oslo),

Torben Schousboe (Copenhagen), Jarmo Sermilä (Helsinki), Sheila Solomon (London), Anna van Steenbergen (Brussels), Jean Touzelet (Paris), Edmund Tracey (London), Tatu Tuohikorpi (New York and Helsinki), Renaat Verbruggen (Antwerp), Linde Vogel (New York), William Weaver (Monte San Savino), Henry Weinberg (Florence and New York).

We would also like to acknowledge the invaluable help we received from the team of graduate students and research assistants who have supplied so much of the energy and muscle for this project. They include: Asya Berger, Louise Basbas, Lisa Mann Burke, Pamela Curzon, Hinda Keller Farber, Anne Gross, Peter Kazaras, Debbie Moskowitz, and Barbara Petersen.

And, finally, we two very liberated women would like to thank our husbands for their encouragement, patience, and touching faith that sooner or later we would emerge from behind the mountains of colored questionnaires better people for having written the *Music Guide*.

ELAINE BRODY
CLAIRE BROOK

Contents

Introduction

GREAT BRITAIN! By rolling the rrr's properly, one can pronounce these two words in a way that fevers the blood and stirs the imagination—evoking knights in armor and men in green—the Magna Carta and Bosworth Field—beggars in India and Boxers in China. However, the current antipathy to historical sentimentality being what it is, "Great Britain" can best be defined as a geographical designation for England, Scotland, Wales, and Northern Ireland, and a request for some spontaneous reactions to that compound name would undoubtedly elicit "Common Market," Queen Elizabeth, the Beatles (this with at least a touch of wistfulness?), Winston Churchill, and, one hopes, William Shakespeare.

Is it pure accident that our little game of words has turned up so many proper names? Or is it perhaps even more characteristic of British history than of any other that the course of events that shaped the country's destiny may be measured in the lifespans of its great figures?

This is very much the case in English music history—a history both rich and important, which does not lend itself to easy evaluation. For at the time when the European continent was seething with *Sturm* and teaming with *Drang*, nineteenth-century English musical life was very much a spectator sport.

But let us go back a bit. Our capsulated survey of music in Britain begins in AD 596 when Pope Gregory sent his emissary, Augustine of Kent, to Canterbury to introduce Roman Catholicism to southern

England. Augustine became the first Bishop of Canterbury and helped establish Christianity as a viable religion there. We next take note that the art of organ-building culminated in the construction of an enormous organ at Winchester, as early as 950. Another important native phenomenon developed at Salisbury Cathedral, was the *Sarum rite*. It embodied variations of the practices of the Roman liturgy and prevailed throughout the Middle Ages in much of England. As a result of the Norman conquest of 1066, cultural ties with France and The Netherlands were forged. Architecturally, the effects are still apparent in the cloisters and cathedrals constructed in the "new" Norman style. Musical influences, however, developed more slowly.

What has come to be recognized as the first typically English repertory emerged around 1300, but very little of the simple, conductus-like, conservative style has survived. Nevertheless, from the testimony of Chaucer, who refers to a large variety of instruments and musical combinations, we can infer that music was an important part of English life at this time.

The fifteenth century is known, musically, as the Age of Dunstable. John Dunstable (c. 1385–1453) was a versatile composer who had considerable influence, not only on his countrymen, but on many composers working on the Continent. His consonant harmonic idiom and beautiful melodic style are revealed in about sixty extant compositions, principally motets, secular songs, and settings of various liturgical texts. The chief collection of music from this period is the Old Hall manuscript, which contains one hundred and thirty-eight compositions dating from 1400 to about 1430 and consisting, for the most part, of settings of sections of the Ordinary of the Mass. Twenty-four composers are represented, most of them unknown outside of Britain. After Dunstable's death, the War of the Roses (1455–1485) brought about a noticeable decline in musical production, which only began to revive during the reign of Henry VII (1485–1509).

Multi-voiced polyphony, using as many as eight or even eleven parts, and set to a wide range of poetry, characterized the early sixteenth century. King Henry VIII wrote secular songs to humorous, romantic, and satirical texts. The Anglican Reformation (1534) inevitably resulted in a spate of religious compositions with English texts. The three T's of Tudor music—John Taverner (c. 1495–c. 1545), Christopher Tye (c. 1500–c. 1572), and Thomas Tallis (c. 1505–1585)—wrote masses for both the Roman and the Anglican churches, using Latin and English texts, and featuring flowing, vocal melodic lines. Secular songs, primarily madrigals, were based on pastoral poems, and combined expressive and pictorial devices with a decidedly declamatory use of text. The principal exponents of this style were Thomas Morley (1557–1602), Thomas Weelkes (c. 1575–1623), and John Wilbye (1574–1638). The lute *ayres* of John Dowland (1562–1626) and Thomas Campion (1567–1620) also gained great popularity during this time.

The greatest English composer in this Golden Age of English music—without a doubt and without a peer—was William Byrd (1543–1623). He wrote in all the secular vocal forms then current, but his greatest achievements were in keyboard and church music. The great school of keyboard writing in the late sixteenth century was that of the virginalists, so-named for the favored instrument at that time. The *Fitzwilliam Virginal Book*, compiled in 1620 and containing nearly three hundred compositions of the late sixteenth and early seventeenth centuries, stands as eloquent witness to the quality of English writing. The leading composers, besides Byrd, were Giles Farnaby (c. 1560–1640), John Bull (c. 1562–1628), and Orlando Gibbons (1583–1625). Stimulated by the popularity of secular keyboard music with its dance forms and variations, English chamber music in general took great strides forward. And when the Elizabethan composers were all dead, and the seemingly inexhaustable flow of vocal and keyboard music slackened, the progress of chamber music continued. John Jenkins (1592–1678), for example, the leading composer of viol consort music in the mid-seventeenth century, wrote "fancies" for an interesting variety of instrumental combinations; Matthew Locke (c. 1630–1677) wrote contrapuntal fantasias for strings without the traditional basso continuo.

Cromwell and the Civil War (1642–1649) brought about a period of suspended animation for public music-making. The establishment of the Commonwealth (1649–1660) saw, not the total suppression of music as has often been suggested, but the development of two interesting phenomena: first, the emergence of a broadly based practice of amateur music-making in the home, which continues to thrive until today in a most extraordinary and almost unparalleled fashion; and secondly, the appearance of an early form of opera. Because stage plays were prohibited and a play set to music could conceivably be regarded as a "concert," this premature version of what later became opera was permissible under the limitations imposed by the Puritans.

During his exile on the Continent, Charles II had acquired a taste for music as it was practiced in the court of Louis XIV under the supervision of Lully. With the restoration of the Stuart monarchy, a new vogue for those styles, forms, and media common at the French court was introduced. Charles established his own "Royal violins" and modeled his court's musical life after Louis'. The masque, a sort of aristocratic entertainment, first introduced in the court of Charles' father, continued to flourish. In the 1670s, the Franco-Italian influences were apparent in the work of John Blow (1648–1708), pointing the way for Henry Purcell (1659–1695), the last great English composer until the twentieth century in the opinion of many. Purcell was to achieve eminence, not only in the relatively new forms of opera, cantata, and oratorio, but in the traditional English genres of fancy, anthem, masque, and catch. His opera, *Dido and Aeneas,* written for a girls' school in Chelsea, ranks to this day as one of the great dramatic masterpieces of the seventeenth century. He subsequently experimented with a hybrid semi-operatic form which combined opera, ballet, masque, and play as exemplified by *The Fairy Queen* (1692) and *The Indian Queen* (1695), to mention but two. One of his greatest claims to fame rests in the masterful way he set the English language to music.

With the arrival of George Frederick Handel (1685–1759) in 1710, England was able to lay claim to yet another great composer. Although his attempts to impose the Italian operatic tradition on English audiences ultimately met with failure, his operas, oratorios, and organ concertos established him as one of the greatest figures in the late Baroque period and endeared him to his adopted countrymen. His overpowering influence on English music seemed to serve, perversely, to discourage originality. In fact, the subsequent low level of English church music was not raised until the advent of Samuel Wesley (1766–1837), a convert to Catholicism who nevertheless contributed mightily to Anglican church music with excellent services and anthems.

The mid- and late-eighteenth century call into focus the somewhat lesser figures of Thomas Arne (1710–1778), and William Boyce (1710–1779). It should be noted that England enjoyed a very active musical life throughout the eighteenth and early nineteenth centuries, witness the steady increase of music publishing and concert activity which has been extensively documented. It was, however, predominantly imported talent such as J. C. Bach, K. F. Abel, and Joseph Haydn, who were most successful with the avid London audiences. This situation persisted until the strong and delayed impact of nationalism on British musical creativity after a hiatus of two-hundred years. The fact that only two rather slight figures come to mind when we think of British composers of the nineteenth century—John Field (1782–1837), who wrote lovely Chopinesque nocturnes, and William Sterndale Bennett (1816–1875), whose abundant output is virtually unknown today—leads us to reflect on the possibility that the romantic movement with its overstated gesture was uncomfortable and alien to the English character. There is no doubt that the daily concert life of the major urban centers and the university towns of Great Britain was as active as any in Europe and rivalled the best on the Continent. But it was not until Edward Elgar (1857–1934) began to be performed that an English composer once again achieved international prominence. There followed swiftly, at the beginning of the twentieth century, a renascence of British music. Frederick Delius (1862–1934) and Ralph Vaughan Williams (1872–1958) continued the "nationalistic" tendency which had been introduced by Elgar. In fact, Vaughan Williams took an active part in the formal revival of English folk music and its codification. Of the older generation of British composers working successfully today, one might cite William Walton (b. 1902), Michael Tippett (b. 1905), and one of the greatest of the contemporary opera composers, Benjamin Britten (b. 1913). The state of contemporary music in Britain is an enormously healthy one, and one can hear, with very little effort, the works of such composers as Richard Rodney Bennett (b. 1936), Peter Maxwell Davies (b. 1939), and Alexander Goehr (b. 1932), not only in quaint little backwaters of avant-garde fanaticism, but in the major opera houses and concert halls of Great Britain.

In this brief summary, we do not intend to imply that the historical growth of music in Scotland, Wales, and Ireland ran a parallel course to that of England. In all three of these fiercely independent and highly individualistic cultures, music has served a dual purpose—in church services and in the folk tradition. In the former category, while there were very interesting developments at St. Andrews, to name but one Scottish cathedral town, they were not especially innovative; in the latter case, although few folk traditions are as unique and pervasive as the Welsh, it did not travel well and had little influence on other cultures.

It is only in recent times that a clear and constructive course of action has been taken to reinforce and cultivate the musical heritage of each of these three distinct societies through a program of development and subsidy. An American may well look at the state of music in Britain with envy and longing. Despite complaints of many Britons, the British Arts Council, with its members, branches, and subdivisions contributes more than money to the support of the musical life. There is, in the Council and its specialist officers, a knowledge about music, and a concern for the recipients of subsidies and their problems. In the thirties, there were three symphony orchestras struggling in London (the British Broadcasting Company Symphony, the London Philharmonic, and the London Symphony) and they performed in the 2,000-seat Queen's Hall or in the notoriously echo-ridden Albert Hall. (The acoustics were corrected in 1969 by the suspension of large platterlike discs from the ceiling.) Today, there are five flourishing symphony orchestras and four major concert halls. There is no doubt that London has become the center of musical activity, unrivaled in the world. We are not succumbing to the statistics syndrome and assuming that growth is equated with progress. The expansion has been directed with intelligence and an eagle eye on standards of excellence.

Outside of London, there has been a comparable development in musical activity. The four regional symphony orchestras—the Liverpool Philharmonic, the Hallé, the City of Birmingham, and the Bournemouth—now engage their players on a year-round basis with appropriate compensation and ample provision for rehearsal. These orchestras serve not only their own cities, but the surrounding regions as well. Each orchestra presents about two hundred concerts a year. Attendance at these symphony concerts is at about eighty percent of capacity and the figure increases yearly. Concert-giving by choral and chamber groups has also increased considerably, primarily due to the growing activity of local organizations affiliated with the National Federation of Music Societies. In 1956, there were some 444 groups affiliated with the NFMS and they consisted of music clubs, choral, and orchestral societies, each sponsoring a concert series during the winter season. In 1974, there were more than 1,200 affiliates.

The BBC contributes greatly to the lively state of music in Britain. It not only reflects the country's public concert life, but influences and shapes it to a considerable extent. The BBC organizes its own recital series, produces the annual two-month Henry Wood Promenade Concerts (an extraordinary, yet typical London phenomenon supported by the Arts Council). It maintains and supports thirteen performing orchestras, most of them with ad hoc choral groups attached. The music division of the BBC seeks out new performers and new works and encourages them through programming and commissions. It offers over 5,000 hours of serious music annually!

Opera, ballet, and festivals also enjoy the support of the Arts Council. The subventions which have been described for England are duplicated on a proportionate scale in Scotland, Wales, and Northern Ireland. For example, the remarkable transformation of the Welsh musical scene during the 1960s was the result of a great increase in funds allotted to Wales by the Arts Council; a good percentage of this allotment was spent in arranging concerts throughout Wales and in a program of commissions to Welsh composers which has already had a very positive effect on the national music. In addition, the Council has given a substantial grant to the Welsh Amateur Music Federation for the encouragement of amateur music-making through mixed choral societies, brass bands, folk song and folk dance groups. The same intelligent planning has gone into the support of the Scottish Opera and the Scottish National Orchestra, the Edinburgh Festival, and the many other Scottish musical projects which have been flourishing of late. It has been less of a grassroots movement in Scotland, it must be admitted, which, due to its historical closeness to England, was not in as deprived a state as Wales—essentially a non-elitist society.

This brief description of the current state of music in the British Isles should not end as a paean to the British Arts Council. The taxes which support the Council, which in turn supports the arts, are supplied, it must be remembered, by a willing population. The organizational talents which seem to be endemic to the British people are reflected in a very active and capable National Music Council, in functioning British federations and associations whose names are legion, and in well-organized amateur music-making groups which proliferate throughout Britain.

A brief mention of some of the other resources of this musically active country: the number of universities which give advanced degrees in music is extraordinarily high in relation to the total population of the islands. The number of libraries and collections which are, for the most part, well-catalogued and intelligently organized, is remarkable. The number of interesting, regularly-held and well-attended festivals and the number of competitions so beloved of tenors, bagpipe blowers, and male quartets, is astonishing. In fact, to throw caution to the wind while going all the way out on a limb (a most acrobatic finale for a modest essay), we would venture to say that the resources, activities, and variety which characterize the state of music in Great Britain today would compare favorably with those of any country in the world, and in most cases and on most counts, come out ahead!

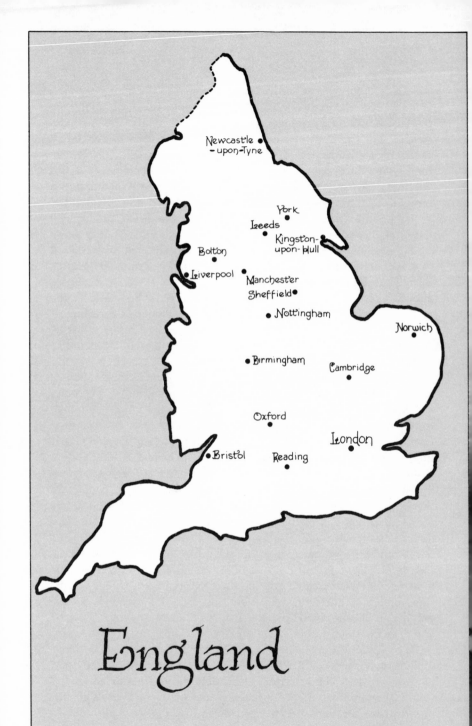

Newcastle
-upon-Tyne

York
Leeds
Kingston-
upon-Hull
Bolton
Liverpool
Manchester
Sheffield
Nottingham
Norwich
Birmingham
Cambridge
Oxford
London
Bristol
Reading

England

England

Guides and Services

The Tourist Information Centre of the British Tourist Authority
64 St. James's Street, London SW1.   Tel: (01) 629 9191

British Events

Published annually by the British Tourist Authority. A calendar of events throughout Britain, including festivals, theater, and music, ceremonial occasions, and old customs, sports, exhibitions and trade fairs. Available without charge from the British Tourist Authority. See address above.

In Britain

Published monthly by the British Tourist Authority. A superb picture magazine which appears regularly from April to September, and only once between October and March. Each issue contains a list of coming events, shows, tournaments, royal occasions, and festivals. Feature articles. Apply to the British Tourist Authority for copies.

NATIONAL HOLIDAYS

January	1	New Year's Day (Scotland)
March	17	St. Patrick's Day (Northern Ireland)
March	*	Good Friday
April	*	Easter Monday (Not in Scotland)
May	31	Bank Holiday
December	25	Christmas
December	26	Boxing Day (Not in Scotland)

* = movable

LONDON   Tel. prefix: (01)

It is very difficult to avoid confusing London with Great Britain. One is
continually assured that Paris is not France and that New York in no way
resembles the vaster reaches of the United States of America, but the reasons
that pertain for Paris and New York are not necessarily applicable to London.
London represents, to a much greater extent, the tastes and tendencies that
prevail throughout Great Britain. The confusion exists because of degree: the
intensity of activity, the richness of resources, and the diversity of musical
possibilities in London and its environs are infinitely more appropriate for a
country rather than a city—even a city as large and special as this one.

There are many countries that do not have as many as five full-force
symphony orchestras running full season. There are a number of nations that
do not have three fully-equipped opera houses, two independent opera companies, and several chamber opera groups, two ballet companies and seventeen
permanent chamber orchestras. There are, admittedly, several performance
complexes throughout the world comparable to the South Banks Arts Center
(total seating capacity 4,478), but not many of them boast some form of musical
activity virtually every night of the year and an average attendance of seventy-
five percent in each of the three halls in the complex. Are there many cities
with as many as seven daily newspapers with staffs (please note well the plural)
of music critics? The numbers game is tempting and one could go on almost
endlessly, compiling figures about clubs and singing societies, amateur opera
groups, concert organizations, schools of music, libraries, instrument collections,
concert halls, record shops, music publishers, and music antiquarian bookshops.
The results would be as staggering as they would be tedious.

In truth, there are an almost infinite number of musical delights in this
great city: St. John's, a lovely church in Smith Square, a pleasant residential
neighborhood, originally designed by Christopher Wren and bearing the
unmistakable mark of his genius, is now a concert hall devoted to midday
concerts, evenings of avant-garde music, and organ recitals. Innovative concert
locations are matched by innovations in concert procedures: the abandonment
of evening dress for orchestra members has suddenly become an accepted
practice. Opera in English is no longer controversial at the recently rechristened
English National Opera (formerly Sadler's Wells). Newly released statistics
show that twenty-five percent of the audience for the Royal Philharmonic is
under twenty-five years of age. Stockhausen and his singers lie on large cushions
while they perform at the Elizabeth Hall, and the exploration of the Baroque
continues side by side with the expansion of the contemporary.

Londoners flock to the Proms every summer and vie for tickets to the
closing night performance, an annual ritual not to be missed. There are perhaps
as many mediocre performances in this musical paradise as anywhere else, but

the involvement of the audience, their willingness to queue up for a gala at Covent Garden, the availability of inexpensive tickets, and the well-organized method of disseminating concert information, make for a musical life that is at once available, multifaceted, and exciting.

Guides and Services

This Month in London, The British Tourist Authority's Official Guide to London
64 St. James's Street, SW1.   Tel: 629 9191
Available at all BTA offices, at airports, and upon mail order.
Excellent and very comprehensive, running to well over one hundred pages a month, this compact booklet lists current shows at art galleries, ballet and dance events, as well as concerts and recitals, folk singing clubs, jazz clubs, opera, and all the standard tourist information, such as walking tours, late-night London, eating out in London, etc. Programs for concerts are included— also starting hours and box-office telephone numbers.

Complete concert listings, not only current, but advance notices, are to be found in the Saturday edition of the major London newspapers. In the case of *The Sunday Times,* there is a weekend review section which lists per-formers and where they are playing. Several of the music periodicals readily available at W. H. Smith & Sons Bookstalls and described in greater detail on pp. 148–153 following, contain carefully itemized musical diaries for London and environs; among them, special mention should be made of *The Musical Times, Musical Events,* and *Music and Musicians.* (The last-mentioned publication also contains, as an insertion, a brochure called *Twentieth-Century Music in London,* a chronological listing of concerts in which at least one composition pro-grammed was written in the twentieth century.)

Tourist and Information Bureau (British Tourist Authority)
64 St. James's Street, SW1.   Tel: 629 9191
Hours: Monday to Friday, 9:00 AM to 6:00 PM; Saturday, 9:00 AM to 2:30 PM; closed Sunday.

London Tourist Board
4 Grosvenor Gardens, SW1.   Tel: 730 0791
Hours: Monday to Friday from 9:15 AM to 5:30 PM.
Branches at:
Victoria Station. Inquiry office opposite Platform 9, SW1.   Tel: 843 3700
BOAC Terminal, Buckingham Palace Road, SW1.   Tel: 843 3750
International Students House, 1 Park Crescent W1.   Tel: 636 9472
(April–September)

City of London Information Center
St. Paul's Churchyard, EC4.   Tel: 606 3030.

Teletourist: Brief details of daily activities are given over the telephone:
    246 8041.
        For the same service in French: 246 8043; in German: 246 8045; in
Spanish: 246 8047; in Italian: 246 8049.

London Information Service: a telephone inquiry service set up to provide
    information about London or for people living in London. The hours are
    Monday to Friday, 9:00 AM to 6:00 PM. At other times there is a recording
    service.   Tel: 928 0303.

Opera Houses and Concert Halls

The Royal Opera House
Covent Garden, WC2.   Tel: 240 1200
Season: Mid-September through the end of July. Visiting companies sometimes
    perform during August and the beginning of September, which is officially
    the holiday period for the house companies.
Box Office: mail orders to Royal Opera House, P.O. B. 6, London WC2.
    Advance Box Office: 48 Floral Street, WC2. Tel: 240 1066
    Hours: 10:00 AM to 7:30 PM, Monday to Saturday.
    Performance Box Office: main theater foyer. Opens one hour before curtain
    for the sale of tickets to that performance only. Forty standing room places
    sold three hours before curtain time.
Booking System: several alternatives are available. There are four booking periods
    for each season. These are clearly indicated in all repertory literature. The
    following booking system alternatives apply to each booking period:
    1. Booking in person: on the opening days of general booking, a queue
       system operates. No one may get on line before midnight on the evening
       before booking opens.
    2. Booking by mail: applications should be submitted separately for opera
       and ballet and should not arrive earlier than the booking date opening.
    3. Booking by telephone: all seats other than the least expensive (the
       amphitheater), may be reserved by telephone. However, these reserva-
       tions will be held for three days only by which time they must be picked
       up and paid for. Reservations made within three days of a performance
       will be held at the box office only until one and a half hours before
       curtain time. The least expensive seats may be purchased at the theater
       the day of the performance. Curtain time is usually at 7:30 PM for

evening performances and 2:15 PM for Saturday matinees. There are no performances at all on Sunday.

Seating capacity: 2,115

Presents ballet and opera by the resident companies, the Royal Opera and the Royal Ballet (see pp. 37 ff.).

Dress is quite informal except on first nights and galas.

The first of the three theaters on the site of the present Royal Opera House was built by John Rich in 1731–32 under a Royal Patent allowing him to construct a theater or playhouse within the boundaries of London and Westminster. The theater opened with Congreve's *Way of the World,* followed shortly by *The Beggar's Opera.* The Handel seasons began in 1735 and *Ariodante, Alcina, Atalanta, Arminno,* and *Berenice,* to mention a few, were written especially for Covent Garden. The house was destroyed by fire in 1808, and with it the scenery, costumes, music, and dramatic libraries, including original manuscripts by Handel and Arne as well as Handel's organ. The documents and house records from the opening up to that moment were reduced to ashes.

A new theater was designed by Richard Smirke and opened in September 1809 with a double bill: *Macbeth* with Mrs. Siddons and Kemble, and the musical entertainment entitled *The Quaker.* The next event of interest to us here was the establishment in 1847 of the Royal Italian Opera Company at Covent Garden. However, at the end of the 1855–56 season, the house was once again destroyed by fire and this time all the scenery, costumes, the musical and dramatic library, including Weber's score of *Oberon* and the original manuscript for *School for Scandal,* went up in smoke with it.

The present theater, designed by Edmund Barry, was opened in May of 1858 with a performance of *Les Huguenots.* From then until 1939, except for the duration of World War I, opera was given at Covent Garden every year during the season. During the Second World War, the Royal Opera House was used as a dance hall, but reverted to its original use to become the permanent home of the Sadler's Wells Ballet (now the Royal Ballet) as well as the Royal Opera Company.

Today the splendid building with its massive Corinthian portico sits in the middle of London's flower and vegetable market. Upon leaving a gala performance, the opera or ballet buff will find himself in the midst of a covey of enormous trucks hovering broodingly over the as-yet-unopened wholesale stalls. Later on the sidewalks will be heaped with sacks and crates, and in the early morning hours the entire area will be crawling with robust activity. Despite vague gestures in the direction of a conveniently located and modernized market, there has been no serious attempt to break with tradition and move the Covent Garden market elsewhere. It was the site of the vegetable garden for Westminster Abbey in medieval times. The square was designed by Inigo Jones on the plan of an Italian piazza—and remain it will, as long as Londoners revere tradition and bow to custom.

South Bank Arts Centre
Belvedere Road, SE1.   Tel: 928 3641

The South Bank Arts Centre is situated, not surprisingly, on the south bank of the Thames River between the Waterloo and Hungerford bridges. It is a clutch of buildings which bids fair to be the practical and actual center of London's musical life. Better known by the name of one of its constituents, Royal Festival Hall, the Centre has been carefully planned to provide convenient access to public transportation, parking for automobiles, protected walkways, exhibition space, and dining facilities, as well as expansive public areas for easy circulation during intermissions.

A monthly calendar of events is published under the auspices of the Greater London Council, called *Music on the South Bank*. It is available at the Information Desk in the lower main foyer of the Royal Festival Hall (open Monday to Saturday, 10:00 AM to 8:00 PM and Sundays from 1:30 PM to 8:00 PM) or by subscription, by writing to the Mailing List Department at the Hall. All concerts scheduled for the Royal Festival Hall, the Queen Elizabeth Hall, and the Purcell Room are listed together with artists, program details, price schedules, and times. The individual management for each event is also given. The monthly diary is indispensable for the more than casual visitor to London.

Royal Festival Hall was built in 1951 for the Festival of Britain. It is the only structure remaining from that celebration. When its career as a concert hall started, the Hall was under the management of the London County Council which promoted (i.e., acted as manager) the concerts presented there. As time went on, the role of the Council decreased. By 1960–63, Festival Hall was its own landlord, renting out space for concert events. The Council, now called the Greater London Council, promotes a small number of events annually—twenty or thirty at most. In 1964 the building was closed down for eight months for a complete overhaul and reconstruction. Administrative space, office space, and changing facilities were added at that time. In February 1965 a new entrance, cafeteria, and administrative offices were added for a total of seventy feet of additional building. Work was begun at that time on two new halls. The Queen Elizabeth Hall and the Purcell Room became operative on March 1, 1967, and the Hayward Gallery one year later. The entire compound is administered by the Arts Council. Exhibitions related to concert activities are held in the Riverside Terrace and the Main Foyer of Festival Hall.

Royal Festival Hall
South Bank, SE1.   Tel: 928 3641

Box Office: located to the left of the motorists' entrance on the ground level.
Open weekdays from 10:00 AM to 9:00 PM; Sundays and bank holidays from 1:30 PM to 9:00 PM. Closed when there is no performance.

Tickets are placed on sale one month before the event concerned. Orders by mail should be addressed to the Box Office, Royal Festival Hall, London SE1 and clearly marked with the name of the hall for which you are seeking tickets. Telephone reservations will not be accepted on the first day of booking nor within forty-eight hours of the concert. Tickets booked by phone must be claimed within forty-eight hours of booking them. Tickets cannot be exchanged or returned after purchase. There is absolutely no standing room anywhere in the Centre.

Seating capacity: between 2400 and 3140

Symphony concerts (New Philharmonia, London Philharmonic, London Symphony, and the Royal Philharmonic orchestras perform here regularly), choral concerts, major solo artists. Organ recitals in the afternoons.

There is a restaurant on level three of the Royal Festival Hall, overlooking the Thames. Open for lunch and dinner Monday to Friday, dinner only on Saturday. Closed on Sunday. The cafeteria is on the ground floor near the box office foyer. Open from 10:00 AM Monday to Saturday for light refreshments, and from noon for full meals. Open Sunday and holidays from 1:00 PM. Coffee and sandwich bar on level two, main foyer open daily from 6:00 PM. There is also a bookstall on level two of Royal Festival Hall. An information desk has been set up in the lower main foyer. Open from 10:00 AM to 8:00 PM, Monday to Saturday, and from 1:30 PM to 8:00 PM on Sunday to deal with all inquiries and sales of monthly diaries.

Queen Elizabeth Hall

Box Office: there is only one box office for advance bookings, the box office of the Royal Festival Hall. The Queen Elizabeth Hall box office opens forty-five minutes before the commencement of concerts when tickets go on sale for the current concert only.

Seating capacity: 1106

Solo recitals, chamber concerts. The adjustable stage is designed to accommodate an orchestra of thirty-five and a choir of fifty.

The hall itself has cinema and projection facilities. There is a coffee-sandwich buffet and licensed bar open to concert patrons only, forty-five minutes before commencement of concerts. The restaurant and cafeteria in the Royal Festival Hall are also available to the Queen Elizabeth Hall visitor.

The Purcell Room

Box Office: same as Queen Elizabeth Hall.

Seating capacity: 372

Facilities: same as Queen Elizabeth Hall.

Chamber and solo recitals, concerts of a highly specialized nature with a more limited audience (harpsichord recitals, poetry readings, folk concerts, contemporary music, and experimental music events).

Note: tickets for all events in the South Bank Arts Centre are sold at all legitimate ticket agencies such as Keith Prowse, Ibbs & Tillett, etc.

The London Coliseum

St. Martin's Lane, WC2.   Tel: 836 0111

Season: from July until March. Usually closed in June. Rented to visiting companies in April and May while the resident company tours.

Box Office: located in the main foyer of the theater.

Hours: Monday to Saturday, 10:00 AM to 8:00 PM. Closed Sundays.

Telephone numbers: for bookings held for three days: 836 3161
recorded information on ticket availability: 836 7666

Booking system very much resembles that of the Royal Opera House in that the season is divided into booking periods. Postal booking opens in advance for mailing list subscribers. General booking opens one month in advance of the booking period. Tickets are also available at all ticket agencies. Performances begin at 7:30 PM. There is no standing room.

Seating capacity: 2,358

Since August 1968, the permanent home of the Sadler's Wells Opera Company, now called the English National Opera.

Dress is informal.

The Coliseum was opened on December 24, 1904 as a variety theater. It was designed by Frank Matcham, who years later helped to design the Sadler's Wells Theatre. During its heyday as a vaudeville showcase, it saw such stars as Lily Langtry, Ellen Terry, and Sarah Bernhardt grace its stage. Since it was the largest theater in London, Diaghilev's Russian Ballet gave its seasons at the Coliseum between 1918 and 1925. After 1931 the weekly repertory drudged along unconvincingly. The era of the American musical began after World War II, and the Coliseum housed one after another until 1962. From 1963 to the time when the English National Opera Company moved in, renovated it, and made it its own, the theater was used as a first-run cinema (see also p. 38).

Fairfield Concert Hall

Park Lane, Croydon, Surrey.   Tel: 681 0821

Box Office: Hours from 10:00 AM to 8:00 PM. Closed on Sundays. Tel: 688 9291

Seating capacity: 1,850

Opera, symphony concerts, recitals by international artists.

In the same concert compound, generally called the Fairfield Halls, but used for smaller events (much like the Queen Elizabeth Hall and the Purcell Room in relation to the Royal Festival Hall), there is the Arnhem Gallery (capacity 350) and the Ashcroft Theatre (capacity 750).

Royal Albert Hall

Kensington Gore, SW 7.   Tel: 589 8212

Season: open throughout the year except for a short period at Christmas.

Box Office: hours Monday to Saturday from 10:00 AM to 6:00 PM and until
the intermission of an evening concert when there is one. Sunday booking
only for the concert that day.

Seating capacity: 6,606 to 8,000

Classical concerts, rallies, and displays, religious services, political meetings, wrestling and other sporting events, popular and folk jamborees, the
Henry Wood Promenade Concerts (see p. 139).

Built in 1867–71, the Royal Albert is an oval-shaped amphitheater sur-
mounted by a glass cupola. Long known for the inadequacies of its acoustics,
the hall has undergone several serious renovations and a system of baffles
installed resulting in considerable improvement in sound fidelity.

Sadler's Wells Theatre

Roseberry Avenue, EC1   Tel: 278 6563

Seating capacity: 1499   *Box Office:* Tel: 837 1672

Primarily used by visiting opera companies, the Handel Opera Society,
and visiting dance and ballet companies.

The Sadler's Wells Theatre in Islington got its odd name in 1683, when
workmen digging in the grounds of a Mr. Sadler's newly-erected "Musick
House" unearthed a well which had been closed after the Reformation on the
grounds that it encouraged superstition since its waters were supposed to be
endowed with healing properties. Sadler exploited the medicinal properties
of the spring and established a fashionable resort where patrons drank the
waters and listened to the music. In 1756, a Mr. Rosoman put up a larger
brick building and continued in business as a "music and dancing place."
Under the direction of Samuel Phelps, Sadler's Wells enjoyed a period of
prominence from 1844–62, when no fewer than thirty of Shakespeare's plays
were produced there. After Phelps' time, the theater underwent a decline. It
changed hands many times and was used for competitions, circuses, a skating
rink, a music hall, and a cinema. After World War I, the theater remained
empty until January 6, 1931 when the present house opened with a performance of *Twelfth Night* with John Gielgud and Ralph Richardson. Until 1934
the drama and opera companies interchanged between Sadler's Wells and the
Old Vic, but eventually Sadler's Wells became the home almost exclusively
of opera and ballet, with theater and drama only at the Old Vic. From 1931
until the beginning of World War II, opera and ballet thrived at Sadler's Wells.
When the theater reopened in June 1945 with the world premiere of Benjamin
Britten's opera *Peter Grimes,* the event attracted worldwide attention. The Ballet

was transferred to the Royal Opera House and the opera company continued at this location until it totally outgrew the premises and moved in 1968. Today the Sadler's Wells is used for visiting and touring companies of both opera and ballet and continues in its tradition of fine entertainment.

Wigmore Hall
36 Wigmore Street, W1.   Tel: 486 1907

Season: mid-September to mid-July. Closed from mid-July to mid-September and at Christmas and Easter.

Box Office: open weekdays from 10:00 AM to 8:00 PM; Saturday from 10:00 AM to 12:30 PM and half an hour before each performance. Seven standing room places are available. Tickets sold through all ticket agencies.

Tel: 935 2141

Seating capacity: 544

Concerts, recitals, chamber music, singers, soloists, etc.

Opened in 1901 as the home of the instrument manufacturers Bechstein, Wigmore Hall enjoys the reputation as the finest chamber music hall in London. Traditionally, this was the debut hall for young artists starting their careers.

The Round House
Chalk Farm Road, NW1.   Tel: 267 2564

Seating capacity: 700

Formerly a railroad storage shed, this shabby, but interesting building was converted into an art center in 1967. Under its circular roof, it now houses a theater, movie house, library and art gallery. In the short history of its existence, the Round House has established a firm reputation as the home of avant-garde music and experimental musical theater.

There are hundreds of theaters and concert halls all over London where music is sometimes, often, or frequently performed. Each borough has a Town Hall where special events are scheduled, either in connection with a borough-sponsored festival, as part of a local concert series, or as an isolated visiting attraction. There are seasonal events: summer concerts of music in the open air at the Festival Pleasure Gardens in Holland Park (Kensington), at Kenwood in Hampstead Heath, and in parks all over the city. For the less than solvent, there are Sunday evening chamber music recitals at Conway Hall in Red Lion Square, afternoon concerts at St. Martin-in-the-Fields and at the converted-church-into-concert-hall, St. John's in Smith Square (SW1). The art lover will enjoy the concerts in the lovely Raphael Cartoon Gallery of the Victoria and Albert Museum where there is an exhibition area available to the stroller during the interval, or at the Horniman Museum in Forest Hill, where the free Friday evening concerts are performed on instruments from the collection for which the Horniman is justly renowned. A record buff may well find a kindred spirit at one of the series of lectures, soirees musicales, and record recitals which are frequently and inexpensively held in the 120-person auditorium of the British Institute of Recorded Sound. The number of churches and abbeys where organ recitals and concerts of sacred music are given ranges from Westminster Abbey to St. Paul's Church in Covent Garden and from the Brompton Oratory to Bloomsbury Central Church on Shaftesbury Avenue. (In Arthur Jacobs' indispensable *Music Yearbook,* there is a chapter written by Bernard Newman entitled, "Music in Places of Worship," in which denominations, names, times of services, addresses, telephone numbers, and choirmasters, organists, or cantors are exhaustively listed.)

London is a very large city and her musical life is fairly centralized. Nevertheless one can find many interesting concerts of an experimental or offbeat nature in out-of-the-way places like the Cockpit Theatre (Gateforth Street, NW8) where the Focus Opera Group performs avant-garde works or The Place (17 Duke's Road, Euston Road, WC1) where Peter Holman conducts the Ars Nova Ensemble. It would be quite impossible to describe the one o'clock concerts at Bishopsgate Hall (230 Bishopsgate, EC2) and not mention the Crystal Palace Concert Bowl. In brief, there are literally hundreds of locations where musical performances take place; all we have sought to do here is detail the most prominent.

In describing only that handful mentioned earlier, we have nonetheless accounted for the major portion of the concert life of London. A quick survey of the *Times,* the *Observer,* or the *Daily Telegraph* on Saturday (where all the weekly events and many of those in the month ahead are listed) will show that all three halls of the South Bank are occupied every night during the season and often there are two tenants on Saturdays and Sundays. You will find that the opera and ballet seasons at the Royal Opera House, Covent Garden, and the Coliseum are long and full. Furthermore, the frequent recitals and chamber concerts at Wigmore Hall and the mammoth brouhahas at the Royal Albert Hall continue unabated, summer and winter.

There are in addition two unique series which offer a very happy marriage of musical entertainment, architectural satisfaction, and historical interest. The National Trust for Places of Historic Interest or Natural Beauty (usually mercifully shortened to The National Trust) runs a series called the Trust House Concerts each year. Ranging far outside of London as well as within her boroughs, they will sponsor a concert at Fenton House in Hampstead, or at Leighton House in Holland Park (for more information, see p. 42). Another organization, this one privately run, is called Residence Recitals (see p. 43) and features music recitals, poetry and letter readings, and dramatic renderings in houses where famous composers, writers, and artists lived and worked.

Libraries and Museums

British Broadcasting Corporation, Central Music Library
[Ben. 53, Long 55]
Yalding House, 156 Great Portland Street, W1.   Tel: 580 4468, ext. 4880
Hours: Monday to Friday, 9:30 AM to 5:30 PM, Saturday from 9:30 AM to noon.
Closed on bank holidays.
Credentials Required: libraries of the BBC primarily for BBC personnel or artists.
Collections not available to general public, but reference facilities are
extended to visitors upon presentation of authentic identification. Appli-
cation in writing is advisable.

British Broadcasting Corporation, Popular Music Library [Long 56]
Aeolian Hall, 135 New Bond Street, London W1.
Hours: Monday to Friday, 9:30 AM to 5:30 PM.
Collection covers popular music from circa 1850 to date.

British Broadcasting Corporation, Television Music Library
Television Center, Wood Lane, Shepherds' Bush, W12.

British Council Music Library [Ben. 54]
Regents Arcade, second floor, 19–25 Argyll Street, W1.   Tel: 499 8011
Hours: Monday to Friday from 9:30 AM to 5:30 PM. Closed Christmas, Easter.
Credentials Required: Advisable to phone for permission to use library.
British music only.

British Institute of Recorded Sound
29 Exhibition Road, SW7.   Tel: 589 6603/4
Hours: Monday to Friday from 10:30 AM to 1:30 PM and 2:30 PM to 6:00 PM.
Description of the Collection: this is the national sound archive of Great Britain and
it has one of the largest public reference collections in the world, the
average monthly intake being 1,000 discs. The total collection as of 1970
was 200,000 items including discs, tapes, and cylinders. The range of music
thus preserved includes classical music, works rarely heard in concert or on
radio, popular music, British music, non-European music and other folk
music, performances of great artists, etc. There is an extensive library of
written material about records, record catalogs of all periods, and discographies, as well as recitals. Has recital schedule (see p. 11). Publishes
quarterly journal (see p. 153) as well as its own discographies. Listening
facilities on premises.

The British Museum, Music Room [Ben. 56, Long 57]

Great Russell Street, WC1.   Tel: 636 1555, ext. 260

Hours: Monday, Friday and Saturday, 9:00 AM to 5:00 PM; Tuesday, Wednesday
and Thursday, 9:00 AM to 9:00 PM. Closed Christmas Day, Boxing Day,
Good Friday, and the first full week in May.

Credentials Required: admission to persons over 21 years of age; a ticket of
admission is obtainable at the Director's office.

Description of the Collection: the Museum collections are divided between the
Department of Printed Books and the Department of Manuscripts (see
below). The Music Room collections comprise the collections of printed
music plus two special collections: the Paul Hirsch Music Library and the
Royal Music Library. There are, exceptionally, some important manuscripts, notably the Handel autographs, in the Royal Music Library. Books
on music and musical theory are kept in the Department of Printed Books
and are consulted in the main reading room of that department. All
printed music from the Music Room is sent to the main reading room
when it is requested for consultation. Manuscripts in the Hirsch Music
Library and in the Royal Music Library are consulted in the Music Room
itself.

The British Museum, Department of Manuscripts [Ben. 55]

Great Russell Street, WC1.   Tel: 636 1555, ext. 372

Hours for Manuscripts Students' Room: weekdays from 10:00 AM to 4:45 PM,
including Saturdays and bank holidays. Closed on Good Friday, Christmas
Eve, Christmas Day, Boxing Day, and the last complete week in October.
Exhibition galleries (which include a small section of music manuscripts)
open until 5:00 PM daily and on Sunday from 2:30 PM to 6:00 PM.

Credentials Required: application in writing to the director of the Department of
Manuscripts, specifying the particular purpose for which admission is
sought, and a permanent address. Application must be made at least two
days before admission is required and must be accompanied by a written
recommendation from a person of recognized position. Tickets of admission are not transferable and must be produced upon entering the department. Readers' tickets are not issued to people under 21 years of age. The
Students' Room is restricted to purposes of research which cannot be
carried on elsewhere.

Description of the Collection: music manuscripts from medieval to the twentieth
century (see article in *Grove's Dictionary* under "Libraries and Collections"
for summary description).

The British Museum, Department of Western Asiatic Antiquities

Great Russell Street, WC1.   Tel: 636 1555, ext. 308

Hours: weekdays 10:00 AM to 5:00 PM and Sunday 2:30 PM to 6:00 PM. Closed
   only on Christmas Day, Boxing Day, Good Friday.
Credentials Required: application for admission to the Students' Room of this
   department should be made in writing to the Keeper. There are no
   credentials necessary for admission to the exhibition galleries, however.
Description of the Collection: antiquities of the Near East from Neolithic period to
   the advent of Islam. The musical materials are not all together in one
   place.
Note: there are other departments in the British Museum which do have some
   material on music, of a highly specialized nature. To mention a few, there
   are the Department of Egyptian Antiquities, the Department of Greek and
   Roman Antiquities, the Department of Prehistoric and Romano-British
   Antiquities and the Department of Ethnography.

British Music Information Centre [Ben. 57, Long 58]
10 Stratford Place, W1.   Tel: 499 8567
Hours: Monday to Friday from 11:00 AM to 5:00 PM.
Description of the Collection: published and unpublished music by twentieth-
   century British composers, particularly living ones. Ten thousand scores,
   two hundred LP recordings, one thousand tapes. Catalogs of music by
   living British composers on sale. Biographic material and discographies
   available for study. Special section for music suitable for schools, including
   operatic, orchestral, choral, instrumental, and piano works.
   Established by the Composers' Guild of Great Britain (president: Sir
Arthur Bliss) and opened in November 1967 on grants from the Arts Council,
the Gulbenkian Foundation, and the British Performing Rights Society, its
objectives are to encourage the performance of British music and to develop a
national showcase for all new British works, published and unpublished.

The British Piano Museum
368 High Street, Brentford, Middlesex.   Tel: 560 8108
Hours: March to November, Saturday and Sunday from 2:30 PM to 6:00 PM.
Description of Collection: private collection of automatically-played keyboard
   instruments including pianos, orchestrions, nickleodeons, old musical
   instruments, and automatic violins, carefully restored and operating. Some
   of these instruments play music exactly as recorded by the greatest
   performing artists at the turn of the century.

Central Music Library [Long 446]
Westminster City Library,
160 Buckingham Palace Road, SW1.   Tel: 730 8921/0446
Hours: Monday to Friday from 9:30 AM to 8:00 PM. Saturday from 9:30 AM to
   5:00 PM. Closed on all usual British holidays.

Admission Requirements: anyone who is a member of the Westminster libraries or who has a current ticket issued by any public library in Great Britain may borrow music for a period of twenty-one days. Renewals may be made by telephone. Music may also be reserved for a nominal fee.

Description of the Collection: the national music lending library and the largest collection of music in the city. It consists of about 78,000 items including sheet music, miniature scores, parts, periodicals, music books, and reference books. It houses the Oriana Madrigal Society collection and the Edwin Evans Library.

Charing Cross District Library
4 Charing Cross Road, WC2.   Tel: 930 3274 (Renewals: 240 2989)
Hours: Monday to Friday, 9:30 AM to 7:30 PM; Saturday 9:30 AM to 4:00 PM.
Admission Requirements: as Central Music Library.
Description of the Collection: one of the largest public gramophone record collections in the country. Includes almost every type of serious music which has been recorded. The major art-music forms are thoroughly represented, as well as folk-idioms and language records. The collection comprises some 13,000 records. Miniature scores are available in most cases for loan with the appropriate record.

Many public library branches in various boroughs of London contain outstanding music collections. In all cases these libraries offer lending facilities free of charge to residents of the area. For details concerning admission requirements, see Central Library (above). Branches worthy of special mention include those at Bromley, Enfield, Greenwich, Hackney, Hammersmith, Haringey Park, Islington, Lambeth, Marylebone Road, Porchester Road, Southwark, Tower Hamlets, and Waltham Forest.

The English Folk Dance and Song Society
Vaughan Williams Memorial Library [Ben. 69, Long 146]
Cecil Sharp House, 2 Regents Park Road, NW1.
Hours: 9:30 AM to 5:30 PM every day except Sunday and public holidays.
Contains the Vaughan Williams collection of folk music (books and recordings).

Fenton House
Hampstead Grove, NW3.   Tel: 438 3471
Hours: weekdays except Tuesday from 11:00 AM to 1:00 PM and 2:00 PM to dusk. Sunday from 2:00 PM to dusk. Closed Good Friday, Christmas Day.
Late seventeenth-century house, now part of the National Trust. Collection of porcelain, pottery, and the Benton Fletcher collection of musical instruments.

Goldsmiths' College Library, London University [Long 255]

New Cross, SE14.

Hours: term, Monday to Friday, 9:15 AM to 9:00 PM; Saturday 9:15 AM to noon. Vacation: Monday to Friday 9:15 AM to 5:00 PM.

Admission Requirements: membership.

Collection: 1,500 books on music and 2,600 scores. A new music, art and audio-visual department is planned.

Guildhall Library [Ben. 59, Long 254]

Basinghall Street, EC2.   Tel: 606 3030

Hours: Monday to Saturday, 9:30 AM to 5:00 PM. Closed bank holidays and the second week in November.

Description of the Collection: acquired Gresham College Library in 1958. Not related to the Guildhall School of Music, the music collection is contained within the general reference library which emphasizes London history. Music holdings chiefly from the eighteenth century. Includes the library of the Concentores Society.

Horniman Museum

100 London Road, SE23.   Tel: 699 2338

Hours: weekdays from 10:30 AM to 6:00 PM; Sunday from 2:00 PM to 6:00 PM. Closed only Christmas Eve and Christmas Day.

Description of Collection: approximately 5,000 instruments from all parts of the world, of which about 1,600 are on display. Divided into ethnic (exotic and folk) instruments and art instruments. Includes several famous collections such as the Adam Carse Collection of European Wind Instruments; the Percy A. Bull Collection; the ethnographic instruments from the Engels catalog of the Victoria and Albert Museum. Instruments are often lent out for special exhibits (such as displays related to specific occasions at the Royal Festival Hall) or for special performances (see also page 18 about Concert and Lecture Series).

Kenwood House

Hampstead, NW3.

Hours: Monday to Friday, 10:00 AM to 7:00 PM; Sunday, from 2:00 PM to 5:00 PM.

Presented to the nation by the first Earl of Iveagh including his collection of eighteenth century instruments. Open air concerts are held each evening from June until October.

King's College Library, University of London [Ben. 60, Long 256]

The Strand, WC2.

Hours: Monday to Thursday, 9:30 AM to 8:45 PM; Friday 9:30 AM to 7:15 PM;

Saturday from 9:30 AM to 12:45 PM. In vacation, Monday to Friday 9:30 AM to 4:30 PM; Saturday 9:30 AM to noon. Closed for one week at Christmas, Easter.

Collection: general music reference collection in general library.

Lambeth Palace Library [Ben. 61]

SE1   Tel: 928 6222

Hours: Monday to Saturday, 10:00 AM to 4:45 PM. Closed Christmas, Easter, and public holidays.

Private collection of manuscripts and printed church music available to bona fide scholars upon application to the Director for admission.

London Museum

Kensington Palace, Kensington Gardens, W8.   Tel: 937 9816/9

Hours: weekdays from 10:00 AM to 6:00 PM; Sunday from 2:00 PM to 6:00 PM. October to March, open only until 5:00 PM.

Public Entrance: near Orangery.

Collection of stringed, keyboard, and wind instruments.

Morley College Library [Long 282]

61 Westminster Road, SE1.   Tel: 928 6863

Hours: Monday to Friday, 11:00 AM to 9:15 PM.

Primarily available to staff and students, but visiting scholars are admitted upon application in writing.

Royal Academy of Music Library [Ben. 62]

York Gate, Marylebone Road, NW1.   Tel: 935 6580

Hours: Monday to Friday, 9:30 AM to 5:00 PM during term. Closed Christmas, Easter, and summer vacations.

Admission Requirements: the library is primarily for use of staff and students, but visitors are also admitted upon application in writing.

Collection includes the Sir Henry Wood library of orchestral music and the English Bach Society library.

Royal College of Music, The Parry Room Library [Ben. 63]

Prince Consort Road, South Kensington, SW7.   Tel: 589 3643

Hours: Monday through Friday during college terms from 10:00 AM to 5:00 PM. Closed during college vacations.

Admission Requirements: applicants who are not registered students or faculty at the College should write a preliminary letter of introduction to the Keeper (Director).

Description of the Collection: basically that of the former Sacred Harmonic Society with some later additions. Valuable early printed music, books on music, and manuscripts. The libraries of Sir George Grove, Sir Hubert Parry and Sir Malcolm Sargent.

Royal College of Music, Donaldson Collection
Prince Consort Road, South Kensington, London SW7.
Hours: 10:00 AM to 3:00 PM daily during term.

Collection of historical musical instruments is housed in an exhibition hall in the east courtyard.

Royal College of Organists Library [Ben. 64]
Kensington Gore, London SW7.   Tel: 589 1765
Hours: Monday to Friday, 10:00 AM to 5:00 PM.

Primarily for the students and members of the College, but bona fide scholars may gain admission by writing in advance. Collection includes the Organ Club holdings.

Royal School of Church Music, The Colles Library
Addington Palace, Croydon, CR9 5AD.

A comprehensive collection of English church music as well as the Frost Collection of Metrical Psalters.

Royal Society of Musicians of Great Britain Library [Ben. 65]
10 Stratford Place, London W1.
Hours: Monday, Wednesday, and Friday. Closed during Secretary's vacation.

St. Paul's Cathedral Library [Ben. 66]
Holborn, London EC4.
Hours: Tuesday to Friday. Closed holidays and during services.
   Important ecclesiastical collection.

Sion College Library [Ben. 67]
Victoria Embankment, London EC4.
Hours: Monday to Friday, 10:00 AM to 5:00 PM. Closed religious holidays.
   Includes sixteenth- and seventeenth-century music prints.

Trinity College of Music, Frederick Bridge Memorial Library
11 Mandeville Place, W1.   Tel: 935 5773/5
Hours: Monday to Friday, 10:00 AM to 5:00 PM.

Collection includes sixteenth- and seventeenth-century music prints and a large collection of musical literature and records.

University of London, Music Library [Ben. 68]
Senate House, Malet Street, WC1.   Tel: 636 4514

Hours: October to July, Monday to Friday, 9:30 AM to 8:45 PM; Saturday 9:30
   AM to 5:30 PM July to October, Monday to Saturday, 9:30 AM to 5:30
   PM; closed Christmas, Easter, August bank holiday. For admission to
   non-University visitors, apply with credentials to Librarian.
Description of the Collection: strong reference collection plus Tudor and Jacobean
   church music, Royal Musical Association library, American music, plainsong, and Gregorian chant collection of the Plainsong and Mediaeval
   Music Society. Libraries of the Oxford and Cambridge Musical Society
   and of George Elvey, the United States Embassy, and A. H. Littleton.

Victoria and Albert Museum

The Cromwell Road, SW7.   Tel: 589 6371
Hours: Monday through Saturday, 10:00 AM to 6:00 PM; Sunday 2:30 PM to
   6:00 PM. Closed Boxing Day.
Description of the Instrument Collection: accent on the decorative aspects of musical
   instruments and on craftsmanship. Strong keyboard collection, notably
   in sixteenth-century Italian. Undoubtedly one of the most important
   instrument collections in the world, it includes the earliest dated harpsichord, a set of virginals that belonged to Queen Elizabeth I, and a
   Stradivarius, as well as many other highly important items.

Department of Prints and Drawings: theater section.
Hours: Monday to Friday, 10:00 AM to 5:00 PM; Saturday by appointment.
   Closed on Good Friday, Easter Monday, Christmas Eve, Christmas Day,
   Boxing Day, and other public holidays.

Special collections of interest

The Gabrielle Enthoven Collection: a day-by-day history of the London stage and
   the important English centers and festivals from 1700 to the present.
   Playbills, engravings, designs, music sheets, libretti, modern programs,
   newspaper cuttings and illustrations, modern and nineteenth-century
   photographs are on display and arranged chronologically under the name
   of each theater.

The Harry R. Beard Collection: similar to the Enthoven collection but smaller.
   Special emphasis on the history of opera, the life and work of the singers.
   Records of modern productions in European opera houses, programs,
   engravings, photographs are also available.

The Guy Little Collection: contains photographs dating from 1855 to 1900 of
   opera, theater, and ballet personalities.

The London Archives of the Dance: a library and collection of photographs and
   other materials related to dancing.

Westminster Abbey Library [Ben. 70]
The Cloisters, SW1.   Tel: 222 4233
Hours: Monday to Friday, 10:00 AM to 4:00 PM. Closed August.
    Sixteenth- to eighteenth-century manuscripts and music prints. Admission by written application for permission.

Miscellaneous Musical Monuments

Like so many important cities with a healthy sense of historical continuity, London boasts a system of commemorative plaques used to mark the places where famous figures of the past lived, slept, or supped. The Greater London Council, which supervises the installation of these objects, also has published a catalogue of "Blue Plaques" which is available from the County Hall, London SE1. Among the statesmen, innovators, musicians, and writers immortalized in this manner may be found a diverse group of composers and performers, including such names as Hector Berlioz, Dame Clara Butt, Muzio Clementi, Jenny Lind, George Frederick Handel, Franz Joseph Haydn, Marie Taglioni, Richard Wagner, and Carl Maria von Weber.

    In Westminster Abbey, the tombs of John Blow, Handel, and Dr. Isaac Watts may be found among the mighty. In St. Pancras' churchyard, alongside Johann Christian Bach, son of Johann Sebastian and often called the London Bach, we see the tombstone of another eighteenth-century composer, Karl Friedrich Abel.

    In the National Portrait Gallery at St. Martin's Place, WC1, a marvelous museum not to be missed even by the most casual visitor, you will find portraits of many musicians, including Frederick Delius, Dr. Charles Burney, Sir William Gilbert alongside Sir Arthur Sullivan, Dr. Ralph Vaughan Williams and many others.

Conservatories and Schools

Hundreds of music schools of all sizes, shapes, and flavors flourish in London. These schools fulfill many special requirements (for instance, compulsory education for professional musical performers of school age), concentrate on specific instruments (International Cello Centre or the Ealing Spanish Guitar Studio), feature the pedagogical techniques of a particular person (Tanya Polunin School of Pianoforte Playing or the Mayer-Lismann Opera Workshop), or simply fill a neighborhood need for musical instruction (Chiswick Music Centre, Croydon and Purley Academy of Music or the Blackheath Conservatoire of Music). In the pages which follow, we will restrict ourselves to mentioning only those internationally prominent institutions of music which are responsible for the major part of advanced musical training, both practical and theoretical, of the largest number of British musicians today. The information supplied concerning each of these institutions will be minimal. The reader is advised to write directly to the school in which he is interested for all specific details concerning admission, curriculum, and faculty.

Goldsmith's College, Department of Music
University of London, Lewisham Way, SE14.   Tel: 692 7171
Note: all courses offered are for academic qualifications only and minimum
    requirements are essential for admission to the College. The complete staff
    is listed in the prospectus available from the Academic Registrar, Gold-
    smith's College.

Guildhall School of Music and Drama
John Carpenter Street, Victoria Embankment, EC4.   Tel: 353 7774
    The Guildhall School was founded in 1880 on premises adjoining Guild-
hall but the accommodation soon proved inadequate, and in 1887 the School
moved to its present site. Annexes have been added as required by increases
in the student body. Originally the School was named The Guildhall School
of Music but by 1935 the growth of the drama department warranted the
inclusion of that discipline in the title. A new building was scheduled to be
opened sometime in 1974 as part of the Barbican Arts Centre and includes,
in addition to the School, a theater (to be the home of the Royal Shakespeare
Company in London), a concert hall, library and art gallery.
Foreign Students: When it is possible, arrangements are made for auditions by
    the School's representative in certain countries. When this is not possible,
    applications will be considered provided the registration form is accom-
    panied by satisfactory testimonials from present or former teachers and
    a recently made tape of the applicant's performance also accompanies the
    request for admission. For further details apply to the Registrar.

King's College, Faculty of Music, University of London
152–153 Strand, WC2.   Tel: 836 5454
    Music has been taught at the University of London since it was granted
its charter in 1900, but for a long time the faculty was part-time. It was not
until 1964 that music was established as a subject in its own right on equal
footing with its seven sister faculties. In setting up its criteria and regulating
itself, the faculty decided that ten was the maximum number of full-time
students to be admitted to the undergraduate course of study each year.

However, the staff does help with the teaching of music to a fairly large number of B. Mus. students registered at the other schools of the University, the Senate Institutes, or the Music Colleges. The prevailing view of music as a university subject differs somewhat at King's College from other and longer-established departments. They do not believe in teaching instrumental performance or singing or conducting, believing that these are more properly the province of the conservatory. The core of undergraduate study consists of surveys in breadth and depth of the literature and materials of music belonging to the mainstream of Western European traditions and viewed in their historical, social, and cultural contexts.

The facilities of the College library are available to the student of the music faculty. The music section is housed in the general library and consists mainly of works on the history of music, and general background interest, together with some works of reference and periodicals. Music students also have at their disposal a working collection which is maintained and administered by the faculty of music in the music building. Also available are a wide variety of instruments, tape recorders, and phonographs. The music library of the University constitutes the third resource at the disposal of the student of King's College. Details of this will be found in the University Guide published annually.

Foreign Students: application form may be obtained from the Universities Central Council on Admissions, P.O. Box 28, Cheltenham, Glos. GL50 1HY. The UCCA handbook is useful for overseas candidates.

London College of Music

Great Marlborough Street, W1.   Tel: 437 6120

Founded in 1887, the London College of Music offers full-time tuition for students intending to become professional musicians. They offer a Graduate Diploma Course leading to a G.L.C.M. and a School Music Course leading to the L.L.C.M. Diploma. Examinations for Certificates and Diplomas take place three times a year. Apply to The Secretary for particulars.

London Opera Centre for Advanced Training and Development

490 Commercial Road, E1.   Tel: 790 4468

The London Opera Centre was established as a result of a recommendation to the Arts Council of Great Britain that there was a need to provide training for opera singers, repetiteurs (rehearsal pianists), and stage managers in order that the proliferating opera companies be kept supplied with qualified personnel. The Centre is financed primarily by the Arts Council. A close association with all the national opera houses is maintained. The general administrator of the Opera Centre, for example, is also the general administrator of Covent Garden (John Tooley). Technical assistance and cooperation is forthcoming from Covent Garden, Sadlers' Wells, and Glyndebourne. End of term performances at the Centre are given at the Sadlers' Wells Theatre. Close touch is maintained with the various British Colleges of Music, five of which are represented on the Board by their respective heads (those of the Royal Manchester College of Music, Royal College of Music, Trinity College of Music, Royal Academy of Music, and the Guildhall School of Music and Drama). The London colleges give invaluable help in that they supply, in rotation, the orchestras for end-of-term performances. Related activities include a summer school held in a different location each year and an opera organization called Opera for All (see p. 37). The entire operation represents a triumph of cooperation and correlated efforts which is admirable in principle and successful in operation.

Royal Academy of Music
Marylebone Road, NW1.   Tel: 935 5461
    One of the British Colleges of Music, conferring the L.R.A.M. Diploma (Licentiate of the Royal Academy of Music) in music, speech, drama, or mime.

Royal College of Music
Prince Consort Road, SW7.   Tel: 589 9498
    The Royal College of Music was founded by the Prince of Wales, later Edward VII, and incorporated by Royal Charter in 1883. From modest beginnings, the number of pupils increased rapidly and a new building, the gift of Mr. Samson Fox of Leeds, was erected in 1894 on a site immediately behind the Albert Hall. Subsequently the concert hall and opera theatre were added, the latter in memory of Sir Hubert Parry, a former director. The concert hall, one of the most beautiful in London, seats between 700 and 800. Its organ, presented by Parry, was rebuilt in 1938. Many concerts are given there during the term and are open to the public. Concerts of special interest are advertised in the music pages of the *Times* and the *Daily Telegraph* on Saturdays for the following week. In addition there are informal concerts on most Mondays during term at 11:00 AM.

Royal Holloway College
Englefield Green, Surrey.   Tel: 389 4455
    Offers an advanced degree in music combined with mathematics or with French, as well as a B. Mus.

Royal School of Church Music
Addington Palace, Croydon.   Tel: 654 7676
    The Royal School of Church Music (College of St. Nicolas) was founded in 1927 to encourage the study, practice, and improvement of music, speech, etc., in the services of members of the World Council of Churches and the Roman Catholic Church. It provides full-time training of church musicians,

aids affiliated churches, colleges, and schools, organizes festivals, residential courses, and publishes anthems and handbooks as well as items of choir equipment. The School has accommodations sufficient to house thirty-six students at Addington Palace. They publish a quarterly journal, *Promoting Church Music.*

Trinity College of Music
11–13 Mandeville Place, W1.   Tel: 935 5773

Originally planned as a school for the study and practice of music for the church, Trinity's activities were extended early on to all fields of music. From 1872 (when it was founded) to the present, the College has grown in size, scope, and standing in the academic and musical community. It is an acknowledged teaching school in the University of London with internal students registered as undergraduates. Courses are also available for external students. In addition to a complete curriculum in Renaissance and Baroque music, there are lectures, recitals, and concerts weekly. Students who are sufficiently advanced take part in chamber music and ensembles. The instruments at Fenton House (see p. 23) may be used by special arrangement.

On Saturdays the College facilities are reserved for the education of selected children from the Greater London area.

Summer Courses

Of the many summer courses which are organized for the teaching of music, many originate in London but take place in the country—for example, the Ernest Read Music Association [ERMA] organizes extensive children's music holidays in Berkshire, Hertsfordshire, and Brighton. (Their headquarters is in London.) We have chosen to list these under Summer Courses by the location in which they take place. You will find this list beginning on p. 122. Of the few that remain in London throughout the summer, we might mention:

Holiday Course for Organists
Royal Academy of Music for five days in July.

Apply: Dr. D. Hopkins, St. Marylebone Parish Church, Marylebone Road, London NW1 5HT.

Society for the Promotion of New Music (SPNM)
29 Exhibition Road, SW7.   Tel: 584 6716

Composers' weekend at Goldsmith's College, London. July. Also one day workshop.

Musical Organizations

Performing Groups

As the acknowledged center for Great Britain's professional performing groups, London houses, on a permanent or temporary basis, thousands of performing groups of a permanent or temporary nature. Orchestras (symphony, chamber, jazz), choruses of all shapes and hues, amateur choirs, music societies, opera groups, are enumerated in careful detail by Arthur Jacobs in his *Music Yearbook,* an annual publication which dazzles the reader with its completeness and the message implicit in its bulk.

We will mention very briefly in the pages which follow, the performing groups and organizations which lie at the heart of British performance today, transcending fad and currency.

British Broadcasting Company
156 Great Portland Street, W1.

BBC Choral Society: 150 amateur singers organized each year primarily to participate in Prom Concerts.

BBC Chorus: professional chorus employed year-round.

BBC Concert Orchestra: fifty-four professional instrumentalists perform light music, operettas, etc.

BBC Symphony Orchestra: ninety-eight musicians. Winter season at Festival Hall on Wednesday evenings; tours; guest conductors. One of the best orchestras in London. Tickets for Festival Hall winter series obtainable from the Royal Festival Hall box office and the usual agents. Booking opens one month prior to each concert.

BBC Workshop: available for hire, this elaborately-equipped electronic studio produces all soundtrack for the BBC requiring special effects.

Bridget D'Oyly Carte Ltd. •
1 Savoy Hill, WC2.

Richard D'Oyly Carte (1844–1901) formed a comic opera company to produce the works of W. S. Gilbert and Arthur Sullivan. The collaboration between impressario, composer, and librettist began with *Trial by Jury* in 1875. In 1881, D'Oyly Carte opened the new Savoy Theatre, the first London theater with electricity. The Savoy also gave the operetta company its nickname, Savoyards, and the group which performs G & S is called that to this day. The touring and resident companies founded by D'Oyly Carte secured the copyright to all Gilbert and Sullivan operettas and they continue to perform in the United States and Britain.

English Chamber Orchestra
14 Hamilton Terrace, NW8.

Sponsored by the English Chamber Orchestra and Music Society, a promoting body which, in addition to presenting a London season by this group, commissions works and gives opportunities to young artists to play and conduct.

English Opera Group Ltd.
Royal Opera House, Covent Garden, WC2.

The English Opera Group was formed in 1946 and made its auspicious beginning with a performance of *The Rape of Lucretia*, by Benjamin Britten at Glyndebourne. The Group was made up of top-flight professionals who saw the necessity for an economic unit geared for traveling, yet capable of musical variety, expression, color, and style. The initiators were primarily Britten, Peter Pears, Joan Cross, the singer and director, and John Piper, the painter. In the first ten years of its existence, the English Opera Group performed and commissioned seventeen new operas by eight different English composers. When the Aldeburgh Festival was initiated in 1948, it was, of course, very natural for the newly-formed chamber opera company to make Suffolk its summer home. It has been essentially an ad hoc company—assembled in the spring and existing until October with crack singers and orchestra composed of instrumentalists of soloist caliber—eminently mobile and intended for festival work. When Covent Garden took over the administration of the English Opera Group in 1961 it was felt that this could be of great value to both organizations. Covent Garden would have more employment for the singers in its company, some of whom do not always have sufficient work during the season, and the English Opera Group would be relieved of administrative expenses and would have rehearsal facilities in London. The smaller group does a season of repertory in London at the Sadler's Wells Theatre every other year, tours, and, in addition to the regular season at Aldeburgh, does a season of Opera at the Maltings at the end of August (see p. 128).

Handel Opera Society
Flat 3, Medwar Street 26, SW1. Tel: 222 6505

When Edward J. Dent, the well-known English musicologist, persuaded Charles Farncombe to conduct a single performance of the little-known *Deidamia*, at St. Pancras in 1955, that was the beginning of what is now known as the Handel Opera Society. The Society, which today has an annual London season, tours the major festivals such as Llandaff, Oxford Bach, and Camden, and travels abroad to Sweden, Germany, and Belgium to give performances. It has established over the years a more or less stable pattern of programming. Each year the Society produces a new Handel dramatic oratorio and one Handel "Italian" opera, edited by Mr. Farncombe from the original materials.

The Handel Opera Society Chorus stay together all year and, in addition to their above-mentioned performances, sing works by other composers as well. The prestigious company has become a permanent feature at the Wells each fall. Box office: priority booking begins two months in advance of the programs.

London Philharmonic Orchestra Ltd.

53 Welbeck Street, W1. Tel: 436 9771

Season: September through May. Touring of the festivals during the summer as well.

Box Office: London concerts are given at Royal Festival Hall. Tickets go on sale one month prior to each concert at the Hall. They are also available at the usual concert ticket agencies, such as Chappell & Co. and Ibbs & Tillett (see p. 48).

As one of the five major symphony orchestras based in London, this 89-member, first-rate ensemble has traveled extensively in recent years in addition to a very full London season. (During the 1970–71 season, for example, the LPO, as it is commonly known in London, gave some fifty-one concerts in London, including the regular concert series at Royal Festival Hall, a specially prepared series for school children, and a series for commerce and industry at Royal Albert Hall. The LPO is the official orchestra of the Glyndbourne Festival and does a twelve-week season of opera each summer. In addition, they perform at Promenade Concerts and at the Edinburgh Festival as well as other festivals in a guest capacity. To encourage a close relationship between the audience and the performers, the LPO has established a London Philharmonic Society which features a membership plan offering open rehearsals, priority booking, and a bimonthly newsletter to its members. Details and information may be obtained from The Secretary, London Philharmonic Society at the address above.

London Philharmonic Choir

37 Eagle Street, WC1. Tel: 242 3102

The London Philharmonic Choir is made up of non-professional singers who devote one or two evenings a week to rehearsals. The time and energy they spend working on oratorios, operas, and other choral works is rewarded by the experience of singing frequent public concerts in one of London's finest choirs with internationally-famous conductors.

In order to maintain its high standards, the Choir is continually in the process of building up its membership. People are welcome who have a keen love of music, combined with a natural singing voice, though not necessarily a trained one.

London Sinfonietta

33 Cholmley Gardens, NW6. Tel: 435 4285

Thirty-member chamber symphony group which presents a highly specialized season from September to June of contemporary music for small combinations. Concerts at the Queen Elizabeth Hall. Guest conductors such as Luciano Berio, Pierre Boulez, Sir Michael Tippett, and John Tavener. This group was the first to abandon traditional dress clothes for performing.

London Symphony Orchestra
1 Montague Street, WC1.   Tel: 636 1704
Season: September to July

Founded in 1904 under the baton of Dr. Hans Richter, the LSO is today acknowledged as one of the world's leading symphonic organizations. Pierre Boulez described some of the attributes which contribute to the continued success of this organization as "the LSO's alertness of response, brilliant virtuosity and buoyant enthusiasm." The alchemy that transforms individual talents and creative personalities into an effective team is hard to describe. However, one thing may be agreed upon: the musicians of the LSO are fiercely jealous of their artistic standards and the democratic practices of this cooperative body. The difficult working conditions and the lack of a permanent rehearsal facility or concert hall require a mutual respect and individual discipline that are rare and hard to come by. By all accounts, the LSO has achieved these interior qualities as well as the high musical standards it maintains. Under such legendary figures as Beecham, Elgar, Hamilton Harty, and Pierre Monteux, the LSO established its reputation through the years, augmenting its concert season with film music recording sessions and touring. Today, recording is a major portion of the LSO activity. In London, the LSO traditionally does an important season at the Royal Festival Hall as well as a stint at the Prom Concerts at the Royal Albert Hall. In addition, there are guest visits in the London area and to the important urban centers of Great Britain and the Continent. The Orchestra has the basic complement of 89 musicians which is augmented as the occasion demands. For the Royal Festival Hall concerts, tickets are available at the traditional outlets and booking begins one month before the concert dates.

New Philharmonia Orchestra of London
61 Carey Street, WC2.   Tel: 242 5026
Season: September to July.
Box Office: bookings at the Royal Festival Hall and the usual ticket agencies.
Tickets go on sale one month before the concert event. As with all South Bank events, there is no standing room.

As one of the five major symphonic organizations based in London, the 90-man NPO presents a major portion of its London season at the Royal Festival Hall. But as with the other London orchestras, the Hall is not its permanent home and it is allocated a certain number of dates each year for which it hires the hall from the Greater London Council in order to promote its own concerts.

Opera for All

London Opera Centre, 490 Commercial Road, E1.   Tel: 790 4468

    In 1949, inspired by the success of a tour of northeast England by a small group of Lithuanians giving operatic extracts accompanied by piano, John Denison and Mona Tatham of the Arts Council Music Department launched a group of four singers, a pianist, and compère (Douglas Craig), who toured continuously, performing operatic excerpts on bare platforms, music club rooms, and school auditoriums throughout Britain. In 1952, at the repeated request of the audiences, a Mozart opera was staged, and in 1955 another one added. Although the changeover to staged and costumed complete perform-ances made it impossible to perform in some of the village halls which had previously been on the group's route, it did come closer to the ideal, of which the previous presentations had been the merest approximation. Opera for All was formed primarily to introduce opera to new audiences, but it has also carried with it the important corollary of providing professional work for beginning artists. Three equal groups now tour concurrently in order to cope with the nationwide demand by civic theaters, civic halls, music clubs and arts clubs, technical colleges and colleges of further education. One group is provided by the Scottish Opera (Group S), one by the Welsh National Opera (Group W), and Group E is provided by the London Opera Centre. The tours are all booked through the Arts Council's three offices.

Royal Opera Company

Royal Opera House, Covent Garden, WC2.   Tel: 240 1200

Season: mid-September to early June. From April to the beginning of June the Opera does not alternate with the Ballet, since this is the time when the Ballet tours. In general the Opera does not tour as it is too cumbersome. Guest companies appear at the Royal Opera House in July and August.

Booking: season is broken up into four to six booking periods (details are given on p. 12 in the discussion of the Royal Opera House).

Standing Room: the line for standing room begins at 8:00 or 8:30 AM. You will receive a number telling you when to come back for your standing room ticket. Number of places limited to forty or so. Four PM is the official time when the SR office opens. When the house is not sold out, there is no standing room.

    The Royal Opera Company is characterized by a firmly traditional, wide repertory. The company receives support from the Arts Council and there is also an organization called the Friends of Covent Garden, which offers certain booking advantages and a publication called *About the House* in return for a membership fee.

One British premiere a year is commissioned by the Friends of Covent Garden or revived from the repertory and freshly produced. Singers come from all countries. This is the London showcase for great stars. There is a coordinating committee with Sadler's Wells to obviate the obvious.

The Royal Opera received its official name and regal adjective in 1968 when Queen Elizabeth II approved the recommendation of the Home Secretary that the Covent Garden Opera should in future be so designated. In being thus honored, the Royal Opera joined its sister arts of ballet and drama, the Royal Ballet and the Royal Shakespeare Company. Colin Davis is the fourth musical director of the Opera Company since it was established in 1946; Karl Rankl (1946–51), Rafael Kubelik (1955–58), and Georg Solti (1961–71) preceded him. But the figure who presided over the Royal Opera House and supplied the patience and common sense needed to continue throughout the years, was Sir David Webster, who will surely be remembered as one of the great opera administrators of all time.

Royal Philharmonic Orchestra
70 Wigmore Street, W1.   Tel: 935 5465/6
Season: September to August; there is usually a two-week break during August.

The Royal Philharmonic Orchestra (RPO), the final organization of the alphabet soup which is the London symphonic scene (LSO, BBC, NPO, LPO, and RPO), consists of eighty-four permanent members, their numbers being swelled when a particular score calls for an expanded orchestra. They, like their fellow orchestras, have no permanent house, but rent space in the Royal Festival Hall and other halls of suitable size. The Orchestra was founded by Sir Thomas Beecham in 1947. It favors a very solid and conventional repertoire under its present administration, maintaining, however, the high technical standards for which it earned its reputation.

Sadler's Wells Opera Company (English National Opera)
Coliseum Theatre, St. Martin's Lane, WC2.   Tel: 836 0111

The Sadler's Wells Opera dates from 1931. It took its name from the theater in which it was originally housed. In 1959 the company took on the prime responsibility for touring opera in the United Kingdom, and in 1968 the much-expanded company burst the seams of the old house and moved to the London Coliseum, leaving the Sadler's Wells Theatre available to house visiting companies for short seasons. As an ensemble which eschews the star system, Sadler's Wells Opera has been acclaimed throughout Europe, and the first season at the Coliseum saw a fifty percent increase in audience size.

The two companies that comprise the Opera—two orchestras, two choruses, two ballet groups—plus some seventy principal singers—give over 400 performances a year in London and on tour. They employ only singers with British passports and it is company policy that operas are sung in English.

Basically, the underlying philosophy of the Sadler's Wells company (recently rechristened the National Opera Company) is that opera is a form of theater rather than simply music; the emphasis for each production is the unity of design, the sum total of all its parts. Acting is placed on an equal footing with singing, and a performer whose physical attributes deter rather than contribute to a characterization will not be cast in that role no matter how well the voice may be suited to it (there are no 350-pound consumptives here!).

Every season six new productions are scheduled. There are two months between new productions and revivals are interleafed between (each revival nevertheless gets two weeks of solid rehearsal time). There is a healthy emphasis on modern works and an even healthier one on literate translations of libretti into English. A brief survey of some of the works presented in recent years will show a catholicity of selections which will amaze the reader: Wagner's complete *Ring* in a translation by Andrew Porter, *The Makropolous Case* by Janacek, Edmund Tracey's translation of *The Tales of Hoffmann, Gloriana* by Britten, and *Duke Bluebeard's Castle* by Bartok, as well as *Kiss Me Kate* by Cole Porter, and *Cosi Fan Tutte, The Seraglio,* and *Marriage of Figaro* by Mozart. The audiences at the Coliseum tend to be younger, more informal, more vocal, and less status-conscious than at Covent Garden, which is in all respects a more traditional house. The admission prices are on the whole considerably lower, and the entertainment experience, if a little less exalted, is a good deal more relevant.

Musical Organizations

Professional, Official and Concert Societies

Once again in the interest of brevity we have chosen a sampling of the musical organizations which operate within London. We have attempted to include only those groups which occupy an important and policy-affecting position on the British musical scene. We have eliminated trade organizations, unions, promotional, religious, and gramophone societies, as well as concert-sponsoring associations. These are listed, without evaluation and with accuracy, in the oft-mentioned *Music Yearbook* edited by Arthur Jacobs.

The Arts Council of Great Britain
105 Piccadilly, W1.   Tel: 629 9495

The Arts Council of Great Britain is funded by the government and is incorporated under Royal Charter for the following purposes: to develop and improve the knowledge, understanding, and practice of the arts; to increase the accessibility of the arts to the public throughout Great Britain; and to advise governmental departments, local authorities, and other organizations on matters concerning the foregoing objectives. There are no more than twenty members of the Council appointed by the Secretary of State for Education and Science after considerable consultation with the Secretaries of State for Scotland and for Wales. With the approval of both of them, the Council appoints separate committees for Scotland and Wales, known as the Scottish and Welsh Arts Councils (see pp. 170 and 188) respectively. A music director and deputy music director supervise the activities relating to their special areas of competence.

British Broadcasting Corporation

Broadcasting House, Portland Place, W1. Tel: 580 4468
    Television: Television Centre, Wood Lane, W1.
    Broadcasting: Bush House, Strand, WC2.
    Publications: 35 Marylebone High Street, W1.
    Organizations which come under the BBC umbrella include: BBC Symphony Orchestra (see p. 33), BBC Northern Symphony Orchestra (see p. 74), BBC Scottish Symphony Orchestra (see p. 160), BBC Welsh Orchestra (see p. 187), BBC Concert Orchestra (see p. 33), London Studio Players, the Radio Orchestra (fifty-six players under Malcolm Lockyer), BBC Northern Dance Orchestra, BBC Midland Light Orchestra (see p. 53), BBC Scottish Radio Orchestra (see p. 160), BBC Northern Ireland Light Orchestra (see p. 214), BBC Training Orchestra (sixty-nine members under Meredith Davies), and the BBC Chorus (see p. 33).

The British Council, Drama and Music Department

97–99 Park Street, W1. Tel: 499 8011
    The British Council, established in 1934 and given its Royal Charter in 1940, has for its primary aim the promotion of a wider knowledge of Britain and the English language in other countries, as well as the furtherance of cultural relations with those countries. It is funded by Parliament and has representatives in over seventy countries.

British Federation of Music Festivals

106 Gloucester Place, W1. Tel: 935 6371
    Clearinghouse for information concerning the nearly three hundred amateur music festivals, mostly of the competitive kind, which occur annually in all parts of Great Britain. (For more information concerning these festivals, see pp. 127–144.) They also organize summer music programs in the country.

English Folk Dance and Song Society

Cecil Sharp House, 2 Regents Park Road, NW1. Tel: 485 2206
    Established to encourage the performance and enjoyment of English folk

music, in traditional forms, the Society headquarters at Cecil Sharp House has become an international center for folk dance and song, arranging courses, and offering facilities including a library (see p. 23) and a recording studio. The organization publishes books and a quarterly magazine. There are member clubs and branches throughout Great Britain which carry on local activities in an autonomous manner. In the London headquarters, which is open daily except Sunday, from 9:30 AM to 5:30 PM as well as some evenings, there are small halls available and a shop for the purchase of books, records, music, and instruments.

ERMA: (see Read Music Association, p. 43)

Galpin Society
School of Physics, University of Warwick, near Coventry.
Founded in 1946 for the publication of research into the history, construction, and use of musical instruments.

Incorporated Society of Musicians
48 Gloucester Place, W1.   Tel: 935 9791
A representative association for the musical profession, the ISM Council considers all public events affecting music or the interests of professional musicians and takes appropriate action.

London Musical Club
21 Holland Park, W11.   Tel: 727 4440
Twenty-seven rooms for fifty guests and residents; liberal practicing hours. Elegant neighborhood, spacious rooms, and a bar. Reasonable weekly rates. Concerts—jazz on Friday and classical on Sunday—given by residents. Book at least one month ahead.

London Orchestral Concert Board
Royal Festival Hall, Belvedere Road, SE1.   Tel: 928 3641
The London Orchestral Concert Board was established by the Arts Council of Great Britain, and the Greater London Council jointly in 1965. The Board's functions are to review annually the subsidy requirements of the four associated orchestras (LPO, LSO, NPO, and RPO) and to advise the Arts Council accordingly; to allocate such funds as are made available; to attach such conditions to payments as are considered desirable; to report annually on the past year's activities and the financial viability of the associated orchestras; to allocate funds for the promotion of concerts in the Central London area; and to allocate subsidies provided for the performance of British contemporary music by the four associated orchestras.

Robert Mayer Concerts Society Ltd.
22 Blomfield Street, EC2.   Tel: 588 4714
Founded in November 1923, the first program presented by Dorothy and Robert Mayer was conducted by Sir (then Dr.) Adrian Boult. Bearing in mind that most children had never heard, let alone seen a symphony concert, the concert venture thus undertaken was instrumental in securing for music its proper position in British schools and in society. The emphasis has always been on young performers as well as a catholic selection of composers performed.

The Music Society of St. Martin-in-the-Fields
5 St. Martin's Place, WC2.   Tel: 839 1930
Duration of Season: Mondays and Tuesdays all year except for bank holidays.
Chamber music and lunchtime recitals at 1:05 PM. Admission free. Collection is made for charities or St. Martin's Church itself.
Concerts at St. Martin's give an opportunity for recital work to many young soloists and choirs. The concerts are funded entirely by collections. In addition to the afternoon (lunchtime) concerts, there are hymn singing sessions on Sunday evenings at 7:50 PM as well as choir recitals at that hour. Also, choral concerts on Saturday nights at 7:00 PM, as well as a series called Music Without Distraction, on Wednesday evenings at 7:30 PM.

National Music Council of Great Britain
69 Wigmore Street, W1.   Tel: 935 3125
The National Music Council, founded in 1953, represents the UK in the International Music Council. It aims to encourage and coordinate music in Great Britain and consists of some fifty-four member constituent organizations, ranging from the Association of Municipal Corporations, to Youth and Music.

National Trust Concerts Society
Trust Houses Group Ltd., 166 High Holborn, WC1.   Tel: 242 2481
When it became apparent that the Claydon Concerts (see pp. 111–112) were a successful experiment and the idea of concerts in great country houses appealed to many people, the National Trust Concerts Society was founded in 1961 for the purpose of establishing a peregrinating series which would take place in a great variety of famous houses. Many of the concerts are now held in Trust House Hotels—historical monuments which have been taken over and maintained for commercial use. Others are museums, or famous old inns, completely restored. An average concert season will feature chamber music by the Prague String Quartet, or the Galliard Harpsichord Trio, or the English Consort of Viols, presented in such locations as The Dolphin and Anchor in Chichester, Petworth House in Sussex, The Swan in Lavenham, or The Vyne,

a Tudor mansion in Hampshire. A schedule for the year is published and available in early September.

Proms: (*see Wood [Henry], Promenade Concerts [p. 139]*)

Ernest Read Concerts for Children (*ERMA*)
143 King Henry's Road, NW3.   Tel: 722 3020
Season: October to May inclusive.

Presenting orchestral concerts in Royal Festival Hall and chamber concerts in the Purcell Room. Morning concerts at 11:00 AM and afternoon concerts at 2:00 PM. There is also a Holiday Concerts for Young People series during Christmas and again at Easter. These take place at 3:00 PM. Adults are admitted only if accompanied by children.

Participating groups vary: they have included the English Chamber Orchestra, the LPO, RPO, NPO, the London Mozart Players, the Philip Jones Brass Ensemble, and the Thames Chamber Orchestra. Each year four performing organizations are engaged to give the series of children's concerts.

Residence Recitals
34 Hillgate Place, W8.

A membership series of music recitals, poetry and letter readings, held in the houses where famous composers and writers lived or worked. Dramatized presentations staged in great country houses. Founded in 1966, the Residence Recitals are now open to public membership. There are three kinds of membership: Founder, Ordinary and Country. A newsletter is published. Some of the typical events scheduled by the directors include a Barrie Recital at Sir James Barrie's house in Bayswater; a Fanny Burney Recital in the Westminster Library, on the site of Fanny Burney's home for fifteen years; a Berlioz Recital in the home of the composer; a waterborne presentation of "The Life of Handel" on a barge leaving Westminster Pier (a buffet supper is also available at a small extra charge), etc., etc. A program is published annually of the scheduled events for the year.

Royal Musical Association
British Museum, Great Russell Street, WC1.

Founded in 1874, The Musical Association was established for the investigation and discussion of subjects connected with the art, science, and history of music. It is therefore the second oldest musicological society in the world. Publishes *Proceedings* annually; also *R.M.A. Research Chronicle.*

Society for the Promotion of New Music
29 Exhibition Road, SW7.

Gives long series of almost monthly concerts devoted nearly exclusively to contemporary British works; annual concert at the Cheltenham Festival. Public workshop performances and, occasionally, public orchestral rehearsals. Each summer the Society organizes a residential Composers' Weekend, built around leading visiting composers, with seminars and master-classes, workshop rehearsals, and an improvisational group—in effect, a miniature summer school.

Youth and Music
22 Bloomfield Street, EC2.

This organization, founded in 1954 by the same Sir Robert Mayer who is responsible for the Concerts for Children (see p. 42), seeks to introduce young people to music in all its forms. Besides arranging visits abroad for English choirs and orchestras, the organization gives grants to outstanding young performers, administers scholarships for study abroad, sponsors evenings of music and opera for the uninitiated young. Youth and Music is open to anyone between the ages of 14 and 25 and is affiliated with the International Jeunesses Musicales, representing Great Britain in all the regular Jeunesse events. They publish a quarterly magazine, *Youth and Music News.*

The Business of Music

From among the thousands of music businesses in the London area, we have made a very modest selection of reliable establishments in each of the categories listed below. These will serve, we hope, to satisfy the musical needs of even the most imaginative visitor.

Musical Instruments: Manufacture and Distribution

Barnes & Mullins (Wind instruments and guitars)
155 Gary's Inn Road, WC1.   Tel: 278 4631
John Broadwood & Sons, Ltd. (Pianos)
12 Edgware Road, W2.   Tel: 723 7482/3
Peter Coutts (Harpsichord maker)
43 Perryn Road, Acton, W3.   Tel: 743 8727
The Harpsichord Centre
5 Chiltern Street, W1.   Tel: 935 3438
William E. Hill & Sons (String instruments, antique & new, strings, accessories)
140 New Bond Street, W1.   Tel: 629 2175

M. Hohner Ltd. (Accordians, harmonicas, school instruments)
    39–45 Coldharbour Lane, SE5.   Tel: 733 4411/4
T. W. Howarth & Co. Ltd. (Oboes, cor anglais, oboes d'amore,
reeds, canes, etc.)
    31 Chiltern Street, W1.   Tel: 935 2407
Henry Keat & Sons, Ltd. (Bugles, horns, wind instruments)
    32 Clarence Mews, E5.   Tel: 985 5673
G. L. Leblanc (Woodwind and brass instruments)
    144 Shaftsbury Avenue, WC2.   Tel: 836 1021
Louis Musical Instruments Co. Ltd. (Woodwind instruments)
    8–10 Denman Street, W1.   Tel: 437 1649
Noel Mander (Pipe organ building and restoration)
    St. Peter's Organ Works, St. Peter's Avenue, E2.   Tel: 739 4747
Ronald Prentice (Viols, violas d'amore, medieval fiddles,
all string instruments)
    The Violin Shop, 16 The Grangeway, N21.   Tel: 360 2701
Whelpdale, Maxwell & Codd Ltd. (Pianos)
    47 Conduit Street, W1.   Tel: 734 7361

Musical Instruments: Sales and Repair

John and Arthur Beare Ltd. (Repair of rare string instruments
and bows)
    179 Wardour Street, W1.   Tel: 437 1449
J. P. Guiver (Repair and restoration of string instruments;
conductors batons)
    99 Mortimer Street, W1.   Tel: 580 2560
Keith Harding Antiques (Polyphons, barrel organs, collectors' items)
    93 Hornsey Road, N7.
George Howarth & Sons. (Instrument sales and repair)
    28 Montpelier Groves, NW5.   Tel: 267 1191
Philip Leigh (String instruments and bows by appointment only)
    113 Telford Avenue, Streatham Hill, SW2.   Tel: 674 2044
Robert Morley & Co. (Harps, spinets, harpsichords, clavichords)
    56 Old Brompton Road, SW7.   Tel: 589 4743
Paxman Musical Instruments Ltd. (French Horns, as well as
other brass instruments)
    14 Gerrard Street, W1.   Tel: 437 4892
Jacques Samuel Pianos Ltd. (Sales, tuning and repair)
    142 Edgware Board, W2.   Tel: 723 8818
Henri Selmer & Co. Ltd. (Sale and repair of instruments)
    114–116 Charing Cross Road, WC2.   Tel: 240 3386

Steinway & Sons (Pianos)
    1–2 St. George Street, Hanover Square, W1.   Tel: 629 6641
Mark Stevenson Harpsichord (Manufacture and repair of early
keyboard instruments)
    18 Gunter Grove, SW1.   Tel: 351 0799
Graham Webb (Music boxes, discs, cylinders, horns, lutes,
antique instruments)
    93 Portobello Road

Records: Retail Shops

A small group of record specialists. Those shops where records are sold
along with music, instruments, etc., are not mentioned here, but on p. 47.

Collectors Corner (Specializes in *bel canto*, historical recordings)
    63 Monmouth Street, WC2.   Tel: 836 5614
    62 New Oxford Street, WC1.   Tel: 580 6155
Collets Record Shop (Jazz and folk)
    70 New Oxford Street, WC1.   Tel: 636 3224
James H. Crawley (Rare operatic recordings from 1890.
Appointment only)
    246 Church Street, Edmonton, N9.   Tel: 807 7760
Discurio (Nostalgia)
    85 Shepherd Street, W1.   Tel: 493 6939
Dobell's Record Shops (Folk at number 75; jazz at number 77)
    75–77 Charing Cross Road, WC2. Tel: 437 5746 (folk); 437 4197 (jazz)
Gramophone Exchange Ltd. (Classical recordings including 78s)
    80 Wardour Street, W1.   Tel: 437 5313
Record Hunter (Specializes in artists appearing at the South Bank)
    27–29 York Road, Waterloo, SE1.   Tel: 928 8731
P. V. Winston (Rare recordings of operatic, lieder, and
instrumental music. Appointment only)
    32 The Uplands, Ruislip.   Tel: Ruislip 32415

Music Booksellers and Music Antiquarians

Herman Baron (Rare and unusual books and materials by
appointment only)
    136 Chatsworth Road, NW2.   Tel: 459 2035
Tony Bingham (Rare and unusual musical instruments,
musical iconography)
    At the Sign of the Serpent, 47 Poland Street, W1. Tel: 437 9576
Otto Haas (Albi Rosenthal, Prop. Rarities, autographs,
manuscripts by appointment only)
    49 Belsize Park Gardens, NW3.   Tel: 722 1488

May & May (Music and books on music in all languages;
catalogues, exports)

    5 Hotham Road, London SW15.   Tel: 788 9730

Travis & Emery (Music as well as books on music, song covers,
prints)

    16 Cecil Court, London WC2.   Tel: 240 2129

Wright Hepburn Gallery (Theater arts, featuring designs and
posters for opera productions)

    Motcomb Street, 10 Halkin Arcade, SW1.

Music Retail Shops

We have listed only a few of the most important, all-round retail music shops.
For a more exhaustive list, consult the London telephone directory.

Arcade Music Shop,	
13–14 Grand Arcade, Tally Ho Corner, N12.	Tel: 445 6369
Boosey & Hawkes Retail Ltd., 295 Regent Street, W1.	Tel: 580 2060
Chappell & Co. Ltd., 50 New Bond Street, W1.	Tel: 629 7600
Dawson Bros., 16 Fulham Street, SW6.	Tel: 736 6001
London Music Shop Ltd., 218 Gt. Portland St., W1.	Tel: 387 0851
Metro Music Stores, 14–16 Broadway Arcade, W6.	Tel: 748 2576
Modern Music Centre, 86 Turnham Green Terrace, W4.	Tel: 994 4895
Musica Rara, 2 Great Marlborough Street, W1.	Tel: 437 1576
Musicians Corner, 12 Heath Street, NW3.	Tel: 794 3297
Normans Eltham Music House, 32 Well Hall Road, SE9.	Tel: 850 1263
Paytons Music Stores Ltd.,	
112–114 Islington High Street, N1.	Tel: 226 5803
Francis, Day & Hunter Ltd.,	
138–140 Charing Cross Road, WC2.	Tel: 836 9351
Schott Ltd., 48 Great Marlborough Street, W1.	Tel: 437 1246
Stainer and Bell Ltd., 82 High Road, N2.	Tel: 444 9135
F. & R. Walsh Ltd., 217 Tottenham Court Road, W1.	Tel: 580 4179
E. Whiting & Co., 298 Clapham Road, SW9.	Tel: 622 2144
Willson & Newman, 42 Dingwell Road, Croydon.	Tel: 657 5817

Concert Ticket Agencies

Ticket agencies, also known as booking agencies, sell tickets for most major
London musical events: concerts at the Royal Festival Hall, opera at the Royal
Opera or the Coliseum. Tickets are available for the same advance period as
at the box offices of the respective theaters, but agencies have the advantage
of being centrally located. There is a small service charge on tickets at the
booking agencies.

A recent development of interest to the American tourist contemplating a trip to England is the service instituted by Keith Prowse in the United States. By calling a toll-free number (800) 223-9880 or 986-9688 in New York City, you can reserve tickets to Covent Garden, the Coliseum, and the major music festivals.

Here is a partial list of the major London ticket agencies for concert, opera and ballet, organized geographically for the reader's convenience:

W1

Chappell & Co. Ltd.,
  50 New Bond Street.   Tel: 629 7600/3665/1177/0513/1692
Edwards and Edwards, Palace Theatre, Shaftesbury Avenue.   Tel: 437 4695
Ibbs & Tillett, 124 Wigmore Street.   Tel: 935 8418
Keith Prowse & Co. Ltd., 50 New Bond Street.   Tel: 629 0414

W2

Lunn–Poly Holidays and Travel, 36 Edgware Road.   Tel: 262 3156

W3

Lunn–Poly Holidays and Travel, High Street.   Tel: 992 5804

WC1

Edwards and Edwards, 7 Southampton Row.   Tel: 242 4001
Keith Prowse & Co. Ltd., 24 Store Street.   Tel: 637 3131

WC2

Civil Service Stores, Strand.   Tel: 836 1212
Keith Prowse & Co. Ltd., 23 St. Martin's Court.   Tel: 836 1029
Premier Box Office Ltd., 190 Shaftesbury Avenue.   Tel: 240 2245

SE1

Lunn–Poly Holidays and Travel, 10 York Road.   Tel: 928 1968

SW1

Harrods Ltd., Knightsbridge.   Tel: 235 5000
Keith Prowse & Co. Ltd., Victoria Station.   Tel: 834 5495
Soho Booking Agency Ltd., 64 Victoria Street.   Tel: 828 8194

SW3

F. Talbot, 129 Fulham Road.   Tel: 589 7710

SW7

Cecil Roy Ltd., 74 Old Brompton Road.   Tel: 589 0121

SW11

Lunn–Poly Holidays and Travel,
   47 Northcote Road.   Tel: 228 4219/4386/4474

SW19

Cecil Roy Ltd., 5 The Pavement, Worple Road.   Tel: 946 0501/1336

SW20

Reynolds, Station Bldgs., Raynes Park.   Tel: 946 8501

NW1

Webster & Girling Ltd., 211 Baker Street.   Tel: 935 6666

NW3

Mansion House Travel and Theatre Agency Ltd.,
   211 Haverstock Hill.   Tel: 435 4451

EC2

Albemarle Booking Agency Ltd., 13 Liverpool Street.   Tel: 283 5314
Keith Prowse & Co. Ltd., 27f Throgmorton Street.   Tel: 606 6165
Lacon & Ollier Ltd., 1 Angel Court.   Tel: 606 8216
Soho Booking Agency Ltd., 76 Cheapside.   Tel: 236 6192

EC3

Keith Prowse & Co. Ltd., 50 Fenchurch Street.   Tel: 626 6828

EC4

Edwards and Edwards, 115 Cannon Street.   Tel: 623 4441

BIRMINGHAM (Warwickshire)   Tel. prefix: (021)

Birmingham with its radiating network of road and rail, dominates the
Midlands from the uplands of the Welsh borders to the sandy shores of
Lincolnshire. Rapidly becoming one of the most modern civic centers in
Europe, it is hard to recall, in the welter of stainless steel and thermal glass,
that Birmingham's musical tradition is firmly planted in the eighteenth century
and that Mendelssohn, Dvorak, Gounod, and Elgar all wrote commissioned
works for its triennial Festivals (see p. 130). Proud possessor of one of the great
symphony orchestras of Great Britain (and the first city orchestra to be

established), the CBSO, founded in 1920, provides a focal point for the musical life of this metropolis, further enriched by the active university schedules and an exceedingly modern, sophisticated official point of view.

Guides and Services

City of Birmingham Information Department
The Council House, Victoria Square.   Tel: 235 3411

What's On In Birmingham

Information Department, The Council House.
Published weekly and available free of charge at public libraries, hotels, and guest houses.

Opera Houses and Concert Halls

Alexandra Theater
John Bright Street and Station Street.   Tel: 643 5536
Season: In operation 26 weeks of the year.
Seating capacity: 1664
Visiting groups, such as the Sadler's Wells Opera Company (The National Opera), the Royal Ballet Company, the New London Ballet and the Welsh National Opera perform here regularly.

Town Hall
Congreve Street.   Tel: 235 3942
Season: throughout the year.
Box Office: open from 10:00 AM to 6:00 PM Monday to Saturday. Evening
concerts usually begin at 7:30 PM.   Tel: 236 2392
Seating capacity: 2000
Regular concerts by the City of Birmingham Symphony Orchestra, Promenade concerts in July and a variety of other musical events throughout the year. Organ recitals every Wednesday afternoon.
The Town Hall was built in 1834 and designed by architect Joseph Aloysius Hansom, inventor of the hansom cab. Modeled after the temple of Castor and Pollux in Rome, the structure was built as a result of the highly

successful triennial Music Festivals begun in 1768. The hall contains a fine organ by William Hill and has a healthy tradition of choral performances. Jenny Lind and Adelina Patti sang there and Mendelssohn conducted the first performance of his "Elijah" at the 1846 Festival.

The Barber Institute of Fine Arts
University of Birmingham, Edgbaston.

Primarily an art museum with a fine collection of European paintings and sculpture, the Barber Institute contains a good concert hall capable of seating 370 people. Recitals and chamber music concerts are held here. The University Musical Society holds midday concerts on Fridays during term. Both the Institute and the galleries are open to visitors.

Aston Hall
University of Aston in Birmingham, Gosta Green.   Tel: 359 3611
Seating capacity: 960

Used for opera performances by traveling companies, such as the Opera For All group (see p. 37).

City Museum and Art Gallery
Newhall St.

Chamber music concerts, solo recitals, etc.

Music may be heard in the following cathedrals and churches: Church of the Redeemer, The Cathedral Church of St. Philip, Cathedral of St. Chad, St. Paul's Church.

Libraries and Museums

Birmingham Public Libraries, Central Library [Ben. 8, Long 37]
Ratcliff Place.   Tel: 643 2948/5153/7670/7677
Hours: Monday to Friday, 9:00 AM to 8:00 PM. Saturday from 9:00 AM to 5:00 PM.
Collection: the library contains general musical literature. The Midland Institute within the library contains old manuscripts and program notes of the City of Birmingham Symphony Orchestra.

Birmingham School of Music Library [Long 38]
Paradise Circus   Tel: 235 4355
Hours: 10:00 AM to 6:00 PM. Admission to members only

Collection: in addition to a general working collection of reference works and
music material, the library holds part of the L. L. Key collection of musical
instruments.

City Museum and Art Gallery

Department of Science and Industry, Newhall Street.   Tel: 236 1022
Hours: Monday to Friday, 10:00 AM to 5:00 PM; Saturday 10:00 AM to 5:30
PM. Sunday 2:00 to 5:30 PM. Admission free.

Contains the Liddell collection of music boxes and a collection of mechanical musical instruments.

Birmingham University Music Library [Ben. 7, Long 39]

Barber Institute, P.O. Box 363, Edgbaston   Tel: 472 0622
Hours: Monday to Friday, 9:00 AM to 9:30 PM. Saturday 9:30 AM to 12:30 PM
during term. Monday to Friday, 9:00 AM to 5:00 PM during vacation.
Admission: for members only; others require special permission of the Librarian.
Collection: holdings include the Granville Bantock collection as well as standard
reference works and music materials, Purcell and Blow autographs, 4,400
books, c. 30,000 scores, 500 manuscripts, 80 periodicals, 1,000 records.

Conservatories and Schools

City of Birmingham Polytechnic: Birmingham School of Music

Paradise Circus.   Tel: 235 4356
Offers degree or degree-equivalent courses. Direct inquiries to Director
of Studies.

Barber Institute of Fine Arts (Music Department)

University of Birmingham.   Tel: 472 0622
University offering undergraduate and advanced degrees.

Musical Organizations

City of Birmingham Symphony Orchestra

60 Newhall Street.   Tel: 236 1555
Established in 1920 and made a permanent orchestra in 1944, the CBSO
is not a municipal orchestra in the strictest sense, but is administered by a

management committee which includes representatives of the City Council through which grants are administered. A season of concerts from October to March consists of a Thursday Series (Thursday evenings at 7:30 PM in the Town Hall; twenty-four concerts) and a Saturday Gala Pops Series (eight Saturday night concerts of a lighter and more popular nature). A gala Christmas Carol Concert with the Birmingham Choral Union is traditional. In addition there is a July season of Promenade Concerts. The CBSO tours all over the world, and performs, records, and broadcasts extensively. The artists who appear with this orchestra are of international repute.

City of Birmingham Choir
2 Cedar Drive, Streetly, Sutton Coldfield, Warks.   Tel: 353 4160

BBC Midland Light Orchestra
Broadcasting Centre, P.O. Box 168, Pebble Mill Road.

    Amateur performing organizations and concert promotional organizations exist in abundance in Birmingham. For information concerning their whereabouts and facilities, consult the City of Birmingham Information Department.

The Business of Music

George Clay Music Centre, 285–286 Broad Street.   Tel: 643 0593
Crane & Sons Ltd., 34–36 Colmore Circus, Priory Ringway.   Tel: 236 3734
Sydney Evans (Musical Instruments), 49 Berkley Street.   Tel: 643 0088
J. Hawtin (The Record Shop), 755 Alum Rock Road.   Tel: 327 2306
James Pass & Co. Ltd., 276 Corporation Street.   Tel: 236 1155
Thomas Smith (Violins) Ltd., 4 Bingley Hall Buildings,
        King Alfred's Place.   Tel: 643 7777

BRISTOL (Gloucestershire)   Tel. prefix (0272)

The city of Bristol, population nearly half a million, has been called variously and fancifully the City of Flowers, the City of Churches, the City of Adventure, and the City of Contrasts, not to mention Capital of the West, and the Birthplace of America. If all this seems rather an imposing burden to carry, let it be said at least that the thousand-year old port city of Bristol was the point from which John Cabot and his son sailed to the American continent in 1497; it was the home of William Penn, developer of Pennsylvania; and it is the hub of West Country industry and business today. As a busy cosmopolitan, contemporary city, it has a very active intellectual and musical life, but its chief and most specific distinction in the arts rests in the fact that it is the home of the Bristol Old Vic, one of the great European repertory companies, which is housed in the Theatre Royal, the oldest theater in the country.

Guides and Services

City Information Centre
Colston House (Next to Colston Hall), Colston Street.   Tel: 293891
Hours: Monday to Friday 9:00 AM to 5:00 PM; Saturday 9:00 AM to 12:30 PM.
   Information and advice on all aspects of Bristol and the services available in the city. Full schedule of all concert events, prices of tickets, etc.

The Official Visitors Guide to the City and County of Bristol
   Prepared under the direction of the City Public Relations officer, The Council House, College Green, Bristol 1. Tel: 26031. Available without charge at the City Information Centre or upon written request. Contains useful information and maps as well as factual and historical data about the city and county of Bristol. Arranged by geographical districts.

Events in Bristol and Cardiff
   Monthly publication which lists the Council meetings, concerts, exhibitions, lectures, meetings, recitals, services, and special events for both cities. Published cooperatively. Available on a subscription basis. The individual copy free of charge at the City Information Centre.

Bristol Civic News
   Monthly publication of more purely local events. Available from the City Public Relations Officer at the address above.
Note: Details of concerts are given in the local press: *The Bristol Evening Post* and the *Western Daily Press* as well as in the publications listed above.

Opera Houses and Concert Halls

Colston Hall
Colston Street.   Tel: 293891
Seating capacity: 2205   Box Office Tel: 291768
 Orchestral concerts, recitals, jazz and pop entertainments, wrestling. All year round.
 One of the finest concert halls in the country, it has been specially insulated against noises from the outside. There is a fine four-manual organ with a mobile console. The front of the auditorium, which is level, may be cleared for dancing.

The Little Theatre, Colston Hall
Colston Street.   Tel: 21182
Seating capacity: 370   Box Office Tel: 27421
 Located within the building which houses the larger Colston Hall, the Little Theatre is used primarily for theatrical performances. However it is also used for chamber music and solo recitals.

Bristol Hippodrome
St. Augustine's Parade.   Tel: 21091
Seating capacity: 1991
 Opera performances by visiting companies such as the Welsh Opera Company, the Sadler's Wells Company, and Opera for All. Variety shows, pantomimes, ballet also given here, as well as full-scale West End theatrical productions.

Victoria Rooms
Queens Road, Clifton.   Tel: 34460
Seating capacity: 750   Box Office Tel: 33857
 The Victoria Rooms, which resembles the exterior of a Greek temple, was begun in 1840 to answer the need for a large public building for concerts and entertainments in the city. It was opened in 1842 and has been in use ever since. Today it is used primarily for University-sponsored events, as well as chamber music recitals.

Bristol Art Centre
Frogmore Street, King's Square.   Tel: 48884
                                                       Box Office Tel: 45008
 A meeting place for all who are interested in the arts, with facilities for artistic and cultural activities. The aim of the Centre is to further activities

such as drama and films, music and ballet, poetry and painting. The facilities include a theater accommodating 130, rehearsal rooms, restaurant, coffee lounge, etc.

Concerts and recitals are also given in the University great hall, the University Reception Rooms, the Museum Lecture Theater, the Wills Memorial Building (Queens Road), and the City Art Gallery.

Church Concerts

Organ recitals and church music concerts may be heard during lunch hours and at evening hours throughout the year at the following (among others):

Lord Mayor's Chapel (St. Mark's)
College Green.

The only civic chapel in the Kingdom, St. Mark's was established in 1722. Open from 10:00 AM to 4:00 PM in winter and to 5:00 PM in summer (except Fridays), the Chapel is the scene of organ recitals as well as sacred music concerts.

St. Mary Redcliffe Church
Redcliffe Parade.

Called by Elizabeth I, "the fairest goodliest and most famous parish church in the Kingdom," the church was rebuilt in the fourteenth century by William Canynge the Elder and enriched a century later by William Canynge the Younger who, in 1467, gave up all his worldly goods to become a priest and who sang his first Mass at St. Mary Redcliffe. This event is commemorated every Whit-Sunday by the Rush Sunday service when the floor of the chancel is strewn with rushes, medieval fashion, and the Lord Mayor and Corporation attend the service in full civic dress. Organ recitals by the Redcliffe Bach Recital Trust are given here, as well as many other concerts of religious music.

Bristol Cathedral
Deanery Road.

In addition to the lunchtime concerts given in this erstwhile Augustinian monastery (founded in 1140), weekly evensong is given on Monday, Tuesday, Friday at 5:15 PM. and on Wednesday and Saturday at 4:00 PM. The visitor should not miss the Jesse Window and the misericords in the choir.

Libraries and Museums

Baptist College Library [Ben. 10]
Woodland Road. Tel: 20248
Special collection of Baptist church music in general theological library.

Blaise Castle House Folk Museum
Henbury (about four miles outside of Bristol). Tel: 625378
Hours: October to April: Open weekdays from 2:00 PM to 4:30 PM; Sundays
from 3:00 PM to 4:30 PM; May to September: weekdays from 2:00 PM to
5:30 PM; Sundays from 3:00 PM to 5:00 PM. Closed on Good Friday,
Christmas Day, and Boxing Day.
The Museum is housed in the beautiful Georgian mansion by Nash and
Paty. The various collections range in date from the fifteenth to nineteenth
centuries and include such varied objects as dolls, musical instruments, and
patchwork quilts. The entire Blaise hamlet is owned by the National Trust.

Bristol Public Libraries. The Central Library [Long 53]
College Green. Tel: 26121
Hours: Monday to Friday: Reference Room and Bristol Room from 9:30 AM
to 9:00 PM. Saturday to 6:00 PM.
Included in the reference collection of the Central Library is the Russell
Collection of Victorian songs and the Riseley and Harwood bequests (early
editions of Corelli, Geminiani, Handel, Mozart, and Haydn). Record library.

Bristol University, Wills Memorial Library [Ben. 11, Long 54]
Queens Road. Tel: 24161, ext. 742
Hours: Monday to Friday, 8:45 AM to 9:30 PM; Saturday, 8:45 AM to 1:00 PM.
Collection: in addition to a comprehensive collection of books and music, there
is a well-stocked library for students in the Department of Music itself.
There is a large record collection here, as well as the Otto Deutsch edition
of Schubert, signed copies of works by Holst, Vaughan Williams, Percy
Grainger, Stainer.

Music Instrument Museum
Mickelburgh Ltd., Stokes Croft. Tel: 41151
This instrument collection is owned by the firm of music dealers, Mickel-
burgh Ltd. The collection may be seen by appointment only.

Conservatories and Schools

University of Bristol, Department of Music
Royal Fort House.   Tel: 24161
    Much of the teaching within the department is carried out in small tutorial
groups and each undergraduate receives weekly supervision in composition,
history and keyboard work. No instrumental instruction is supplied by the
department, but students are encouraged to continue with their studies. There
is a summer chamber music course as well as a summer conducting course.
Membership in the performing groups affiliated with the University is open
to all department members without audition, except for the special choirs.

Musical Organizations

Bristol Sinfonia
16 Foye House, Bridge Road, Leigh Woods.   Tel: 311322

Telemann Opera
Rose Cottage, Wottan Road, Rangeworthy.   Tel: 045422 539

The Business of Music

Instrument Makers

J. M. Coulson, Esquire (Organ builder), 1 Didben Road, Downend.
A. E. Tinney, Esq. (Violin-maker), Cremona House, Perry Road.

Retail Shops

Bristol Music Centre, 10 West Street.
John Holmes Music and Organ Centre,
       221–223 Cheltenham Road.   Tel: 46136
W. H. Howard, 84 North Street, Downend, Fishponds.
Rayners Record Centre, 84 Park Street.   Tel: 23936
Whitcombe's Music Depot, 8–9, The Arcade.   Tel: 24690

CAMBRIDGE (Cambridgeshire)   Tel. prefix: (0223)

Over seven hundred years ago, early scholars made their way to Cambridge in search of knowledge. Today, twenty-three colleges on the banks of the Cam form a magnificent procession of self-governing corporate bodies, representing about every style of architecture that has been popular between the thirteenth century and the twentieth. The totality is wondrous—lofty stone walls lending the individual buildings an air of quiet exclusivity and peaceful contemplativeness. Music, performed, studied, and simply enjoyed, plays a dominant role in this community, but it is not the commercial, concert-hall, impresario-oriented music of the modern metropolis. Much as is the case in Oxford, it is a musical society which shaped and continues to influence the choice of musical events taking place in the community. In this case, it is the Cambridge University Musical Society which has been the single most important institution in the performance of music, apart from the college choirs, orchestras, and individual societies. CUMS was begun by a small group of dedicated amateurs in 1843 and was originally devoted almost exclusively to the performance of instrumental music. In time both the horizons and the range of activity of the organization broadened and today it remains the single most important performance and sponsoring society in Cambridge. The ranks were enlarged by the establishment of a counterpart to the Oxford Musical Union and affiliated to it, the Cambridge University Musical Club. Weekly meetings are still held for the playing of chamber music and an ensemble class is provided for members.

The appointment of Edward J. Dent to the Professorship of Music in 1926 greatly enhanced Cambridge's musical activities. Dent was very much interested in contemporary music and musical research and directed a remarkable series of performances ranging from Handel oratorios to a Vaughan Williams opera. You will notice a preponderance of music collections and library facilities in Cambridge and an almost corresponding absence of concert halls and opera houses. Concerts are held in the chapels, the halls, and the music rooms of individual colleges. A brief glance at a monthly calendar of events will confirm the impression that there is something of musical interest going on every night somewhere in the vicinity of Cambridge center. The University dominates the town and the University values dominate the musical life.

Guides and Services

Coming Events in the Cambridge Area

Published monthly with weekly supplements. Free of charge.

May be found at the Information Bureau, Wheeler Street, Cambridge. Tel: 58977, ext. 375. Information as to date, time, and place are very precise. No exact programs supplied.

Opera Houses and Concert Halls

Arts Theatre
Peas Hill. Tel: 55246
Seating capacity: 600 Box Office Tel: 52000

Part of the Cambridge Arts Theatre Trust founded by Lord Keynes in 1936, the Arts Theatre provides a varied program of drama, ballet, opera music, and cinema throughout the year. Both the Phoenix Opera Company and the touring company of Sadler's Wells perform here. In addition, there are presentations by the Cambridge University G & S Society and the Cambridge University Opera Society, to name but two performing organizations. There are also occasional music recitals.

The Guildhall Tel: 58977
Season: all year round.

Box Office: central library, Wheeler Street. Open Monday to Friday, 10:00 AM to 6:00 PM. Saturday from 10:00 AM to 5:00 PM. No standing room is allowed.

Seating capacity: 700

Used for concerts, dance recitals and as a conference and lecture hall as well.

The Guildhall does not belong to the Cambridge University complex and is available for hire by any group or individual who wishes to rent it. The majority of professional concert activities and visiting performing artists engagements are held here. Of the college facilities most often employed for musical purposes, we may mention:

King's College Chapel

The Chapel was the only part of this college completed during medieval times. The first stone was laid in 1446 and the Chapel was completed in 1515.

The organ in current use, a Harrison & Harrison, was modernized in the 1960s. Evensong is held Tuesdays to Saturdays at 5:30 PM.

St. John's College Chapel   Tel: 54932
The College was founded in 1511 by Lady Margaret Beaufort. The Chapel was designed by Sir Gilbert Scott. Evensong is held from Tuesday to Saturday at 6:30 PM.

Musical events are also scheduled at Emmanuel College Chapel, Corpus Christi Chapel, Selwyn College Diamond, Hall and Chapel, and others. There are many concerts held at The Senate House, designed in 1722 by James Gibbs (architect of St. Martin's-in-the-Fields), which is part of the University's administrative complex. In addition, noontime concerts are held at St. Edward's Church and in Gallery III of the Fitzwilliam Museum (see p. 63). Finally, mention must be made of the fact that Canterbridgians draw on a much wider area than the confines of their picturesque university town for their cultural activity: listed in the monthly calendar of events in the Cambridge area, one finds mention of a ballet season at the Theatre Royal in Norwich, an opera performance in Bury St. Edmunds, or a Handel oratorio at the Ely Cathedral. All are within driving distance of the University.

Libraries and Museums

Caius College Library   Tel: 53275
Collection includes sixteenth-century manuscripts.

Cambridge City Library
Wheeler Street.   Tel: 58977 and 53363
Hours: Monday to Friday, 10:00 AM to 6:00 PM. Saturday, 10:00 AM to 5:00 PM.
The music collection includes records and sheet music as well as a special collection of local concert programs.

Cambridge Union Society Library [Ben. 12]
Bridge Street.   Tel: 61521
Hours: term: 12:30 PM to 5:30 PM; Vacation: 1:30 PM to 4:30 PM.
Admission: members only.
Collection: music in general library, which belongs to this private debating
    society. Special music holdings include the Erskine Allan bequest of scores
    and the Fairfax Rhodes general music collection.

Cambridge University Library [Ben. 13, Long 78]

West Road.   Tel: 61441

Hours: Monday to Friday, all day; Saturday, morning only. Closed September 1
  to 15, six days at Easter, five at Christmas, and first two days of January,
  April, July.

Collection: included in the printed music collections are English lute tablatures,
  the F. T. Arnold library of thoroughbass practice, the Marion Scott library
  of Haydn material, autographs and prints of James Hook, and a complete
  depository collection of current literature.

Cambridge University Musical Club [Ben. 14]

University Music School, Downing Place.   Tel: 53322

  A private library for members only, exclusively musical. Chamber music
parts.

Cambridge University Music Society Library [Ben. 14]

University Music School, Downing Place.   Tel: 53322

  Collection includes approximately two hundred scores of early nineteenth-
century editions, scores, and parts.

Christ's College Library [Ben. 15]   Tel: 59601, ext. 40

Hours: Monday to Friday, 9:15 AM to 1:00 PM, 2:00 PM to 5:00 PM; Saturday (in
  full term only) from 9:15 AM to 1:00 PM. Closed for one week at Easter and
  at Christmas. For admission, apply to Librarian.

Collection: music contained in general library. Special collections include Orien-
  talia, Indian literature, Slavonic collection.

Clare College Library [Ben. 16, Long 70]

49 Grange Road.   Tel: 58681

Collection: the Cecil Sharp manuscript collection of folktunes and words from the
  English Folk Dance and Song Society and a good deal of eighteenth-
  century organ music. Open irregularly. Write for appointment.

Corpus Christi College, Parker Library [Ben. 17, Long 71]

Trumpington Street.   Tel: 59418

Hours: Monday to Friday, 9:30 AM to 12:30 PM and 2:00 PM to 4:00 PM; for
  research only, 9:30 AM to 12:30 PM, but the researcher is advised to make
  appointment well in advance. Closed for one week at Christmas, Easter,
  and some weeks in August–September.

Collection: general collection contains some music manuscripts and early printed
  treatises.

Fitzwilliam Museum [Ben. 18]

Trumpington Street.   Tel: 50023

Hours: open each day except Sunday from 10:00 AM to 1:00 PM and from 2:00 PM
to 5:00 PM. Closed first Wednesday of every month, Good Friday, Christmas, Boxing Day. For admission, application in writing in advance of visit
is necessary.

Collection: autograph manuscripts, especially of English and Italian composers.
The collection of autograph compositions by Handel are excelled only by
those in the Royal Music Library in the British Museum. Apart from
autograph music, there is the finest collection of English seventeenth-
century keyboard music extant. The contents of the *Fitzwilliam Virginal
Book*, as well as the *Lute Book of Edward, Lord Herbert of Cherbury* are to be
found here. There is also a small collection of printed music of the
seventeenth and eighteenth centuries, including opera scores by Lully, and
harpsichord music by D. Scarlatti, Soler, and others. There is a collection
of autograph letters by Haydn, Beethoven, Chopin, and Brahms. The
instrument collection includes a wide range of stringed, keyboard, and
wind instrument examples of a very high quality.

Associated only by name with Fitzwilliam College is this world-famous
museum which contains the chief works of art belonging to the University as a
whole. A great Corinthian portico on Trumpington Street identifies the
entrance to the Museum, founded by the Viscount Fitzwilliam of Merrion in
1816. The building was actually begun in 1837 and opened to the public in
1848. Its interior is a maze of marblework, statuary, mozaics, friezes, and rococo
endearments in the highest and most Victorian taste. The library includes the
collection of music, autographs, and instruments described above and is only a
small portion of the total museum complex. Concerts at midday, sponsored by
the Young Friends of the Fitzwilliam, are presented in Gallery III at regular
intervals.

King's College, Rowe Music Library [Ben. 20, Long 73]

Tel: 50411, ext. 232

Hours: Monday through Saturday. Closed for one week at Christmas and Easter
and for August bank holiday. For admission, apply to the Librarian.

Collection: includes the A. H. Mann collection, as well as the libraries of
Lawrence Harvard, Boris Ord, L. T. Rowe, and the papers of Edward J.
Dent.

Magdalene College, Pepys Library [Ben. 21, Long 74]   Tel: 61543

Hours: Monday to Friday from 11:30 AM to 12:30 PM, from 2:30 PM to 3:30 PM, in
term. For admission, apply to Librarian.

Collection: personal library of Samuel Pepys including a fourteenth-century
antiphonar and a sixteenth-century vocal manuscript.

Pembroke College Library [Ben. 22, Long 75]

1 Trumpington Street.   Tel: 52241, ext. 35

Hours: Monday to Saturday, 10:00 AM to 1:00 PM in term. Closed school
   vacations.

Collection: essentially a college library, including some general music reference
   books and some nineteenth-century chamber music, medieval part music,
   and some ancient books and manuscripts.

Pendlebury Library of Music [Ben. 23, Long 76]

University Music School, Downing Place.   Tel: 53322

Hours: Monday to Friday from 9:00 AM to 5:00 PM; Saturday from 9:00 AM
   to 1:00 PM. Closed school vacations. For access, apply to Curator.

Collection: essentially a departmental teaching and research library for the
   faculty of music with a few pre-1800 manuscripts. Includes the library
   of Richard Pendlebury (bequest in 1925–26), modern works from the
   Fitzwilliam Museum, part of the Boris Ord library, the Pickens bequest,
   and microfilms of contemporary music.

Peterhouse College Library [Ben. 24]

Trumpington Street.   Tel: 50256

Hours: Monday to Friday, 9:00 AM to 11:00 PM; Saturday 9:00 AM to 1:00 PM.

Collection: Music is housed in general library and includes sixteenth- and
   seventeenth-century English church music manuscripts, seventeenth-
   century organ manuscripts, and the church music collection of Dr. John
   Cosin.

St. John's College Library [Ben. 25]   Tel: 61821

Hours: Monday to Friday, 9:00 AM to 1:00 PM; 2:00 PM to 7:30 PM; Saturday
   9:00 AM to 1:00 PM during full term. Out of term: Monday to Friday,
   9:00 AM to 1:00 PM, 2:30 PM to 5:00 PM; Saturday from 9:00 AM to noon.

Collection: one hundred music titles in general library include manuscripts
   belonging to Samuel Butler, compositions by C. B. Rootham. The college
   chapel has separate library. For information, apply to the Organist of the
   chapel.

Trinity College Library [Ben. 26]   Tel: 58201

Hours: weekdays, 9:00 AM to 1:00 PM and 2:30 PM to 4:00 PM. Closed for two
   weeks at Christmas, ten days at Easter, last week in June and from August
   29 to September 22.

Collection: music included in general library consists of some medieval manuscripts, early books, and Shakespeariana, including the Copell collection.
      The Library was begun in 1676 to designs by Sir Christopher Wren. A
relatively plain classical building, the Library is raised to first-floor level above
a great ground floor open to the court through a round-arched arcade.

University Museum of Archaeology and Ethnology
Downing Street.   Tel: 59714/5
Hours: weekdays from 2:00 PM to 4:00 PM.
    A collection of instruments of mainly ethnological interest from Africa
and Oceania.

Conservatories and Schools

Cambridge University Music School
Downing Place.   Tel: 53322
    University offering undergraduate and advanced degrees in music.

Cambridgeshire College of Arts and Technology
Collier Road.   Tel: 63271
    College of further education offering full or part-time course of study.

Musical Organizations

As may be expected, Cambridge enjoys a university-oriented musical life. The
University acts as host and sponsor to a large number of musical organizations
and societies. These include performing groups, scholarly societies, as well as
concert sponsoring groups. The Cambridge University Musical Society, Purcell
Society, Opera Company, and Musical Club are but a few examples.

The Business of Music

Instrument Sale and Repair

Juliet Barker (Makes and repairs violins)
    19 Sedley Taylor Road.   Tel: 46065
Ian Harwood and John Isaacs (Lutes, theorbos, citterns,
bandoras, etc.)
    18 Barton Road, Ely.   Tel: (0353) 2221
Ken Stevens (Instrument sales & repairs)
    10 Guildhall Street.   Tel: 53159

Retail Shops

Cambridge Music Shop, 1 All Saints Passage.	Tel: 51786
Miller's Music Centre Ltd., 53–54 Sidney Street.	Tel: 54452
University Audio, 1–2 Peas Hill.	Tel: 54237

LIVERPOOL (Lancashire)   Tel. prefix (051)

Thriving seaport on the River Mersey, Liverpool's greatest claim to fame in
the contemporary music world is that it spawned the Beatles, the four young
men of Rock and Roll who have joined the ranks of the immortals and achieved
a high degree of respectability (albeit grudging) among musical intellectuals.
Music of a slightly heavier weight is supplied primarily by the resident
Liverpool Philharmonic and visiting companies and celebrities.

Guides and Services

What's On in Liverpool

City Information Office, 187 St. John's Precinct.
  Published every two weeks. Available at the City Information Office, at
newspaper stands, and at hotels. Activities which are covered extensively
include Theaters (Where, What's on, and When), Music (Where, Concert,
Composer, When), Folk, Jazz and Poetry, Special Interest Events, Sports and
Recreation, Parks, Lectures, Meetings, Exhibitions, and Sunday Church
Services. Private individuals pay a small charge to be included on the mailing
list for the publication.

Opera Houses and Concert Halls

St. George's Hall
Lime Street.   Tel: 709 3752
                              Box Office Tel. No.: 227 3911, ext. 129
Seating capacity: Small hall: 725. Large hall: 1600
  Used for chamber events and large-scale choral concerts.

Liverpool Stadium

Bixteth Street.   Tel: 236 1002
Seating capacity: 4060

Used primarily for sporting events, large-scale rock concerts and star attractions requiring an immense auditorium.

Royal Court Theatre

Roe Street.   Tel: 709 7980
Seating capacity: 1608   Box Office Tel: 709 5163/4

Built in 1938, this theater offers many visiting ballet and opera companies such as Sadler's Wells, Royal Ballet and Welsh National Opera, a stage upon which to present opera, ballet, and concerts throughout the year.

Philharmonic Hall

Hope Street.   Tel: 709 3789
Box Office hours: from 10:00 AM to the end of intermission of concert on per-
      formance days. From 10:00 AM to 12:30 PM on Saturdays when there is
      no concert. Closed on Sundays and bank holidays.
Seating capacity: 1771

Home of the Royal Liverpool Philharmonic and scene of orchestral concerts by visiting groups.

Empire Theatre

Lime Street.   Tel: 709 1555
Seating capacity: 2550

Used for visiting opera companies (like the Scottish Opera Company) and the presentation of large musical theatrical events such as visiting musical comedies, ballet, dance groups, etc.

Bluecoat Hall

School Lane.   Tel: 709 5297
Seating capacity: 399

The sponsoring organization, the Bluecoat Society of the Arts, acquired this hall—originally built in 1717 and a fine example of Queen Anne architecture—in 1927 to be used as a center for painters, sculptors, musicians, and the arts. The hall, in addition to being used for lectures and discussions, is a chamber music and recital hall.

Church Concerts

Churches and Cathedrals in which organ recitals, services, and concerts of religious music may be heard:

Liverpool Cathedral (Church of England)
St. James Mount.

Evensong is given regularly on Friday at 5:00 PM and Saturday at 3:00 PM. Organ recitals on the Grand Organ, completed in 1926, are given regularly.

Metropolitan Cathedral of Christ the King
Mt. Pleasant.

The newest cathedral in the British Isles, this Catholic establishment was consecrated in 1967 and maintains a high choral tradition.

St. Anne's Church
Overbury Street.

Excellent boys' choir which performs here regularly.

Libraries and Museums

Brown, Picton and Hornby Library [Ben. 51]
22 Church Alley.   Tel: 709 1799
Hours: Monday to Friday, 9:00 AM to 9:00 PM; Saturday from 9:00 AM to 5:00 PM.
Collection: separate music collection includes the library of J. A. Fuller Maitland (manuscripts of English church music) as well as a famous collection of letters, autographs, and signatures. The collection is particularly rich in materials on opera.

Liverpool City Libraries, Music Library [Long 250]
South Castle Street   Tel: 236 1238
Hours: Monday to Friday from 9:00 AM to 9:00 PM. Saturday from 9:00 AM to 5:00 PM.
Admission: unrestricted.
Collection: vocal and orchestral sets available on loan to non-resident societies and other libraries. Collection of 65,000 books and scores, 500 manuscripts, 10,000 records includes the Booth collection of Catholic liturgical music and the Earl of Sefton collection of early English editions. Autographs. Children's music library.

Liverpool University Library, Music Library [Ben. 52, Long 251]
12 Bedford Street South.   Tel: 709 6022
Hours: Monday to Friday from 9:00 AM to 5:00 PM.

Collection: includes a collection of Russian songs, houses part of the Fuller-Maitland collection. For permission, apply to Librarian.

Merseyside County Museum
William Brown Street   Tel: 207 0001
   Rushworth collection of early instruments.

Conservatories and Schools

Liverpool Matthay School of Music
25 Islington.   Tel: 207 0211
   Offers degree or degree-equivalent courses.

University of Liverpool, Department of Music
80–82 Bedford Street South, P.O. Box 147.   Tel: 709 6022
   Offers both undergraduate and graduate degrees. Catalog available by request to The Secretary.

Mabel Fletcher Technical College
Sandown Road.   Tel: 733 3314
   This is a college of further education providing full or part-time courses for those over 15 leading to diploma and occasionally degree standard.

Musical Organizations

Royal Liverpool Philharmonic Orchestra
Philharmonic Hall, Hope Street.   Tel: 709 2895/7
   Fully professional orchestra of 84 instrumentalists which gives a regular concert season from September to April and rounds out the year with tours, festivals, and recordings. This group has recently been in the vanguard of the move to break with the conventional division of concert programs. The effort, although not startlingly innovative, resulted in programs of a broader, wider-ranging nature. They generally introduce at least one or two first-performances a season.

Royal Liverpool Philharmonic Society
Philharmonic Hall.

Membership in the Society includes priority booking for concerts of the Royal Liverpool Philharmonic Orchestra, and the right to retain the same seating position. A copy of the annual Concert Syllabus and advance information about other concerts is part of the membership. The right to attend and vote at the Society's meetings is also a prerogative of members. This group cooperates with the Arts Council of Great Britain in seeking support and funds for the continuation of the Orchestra and its various series.

The Youth Music Centre
The Basement, Central Hall, Renshaw Street.

The Youth Music Centre is open five evenings a week for musicmaking for people under 25. Included are orchestral, jazz, and folk activities. Studios are available for other musical activities.

The Business of Music

Instruments Sale and Repair

Crane & Sons Ltd. (Instrument sales)
  85–91 Hanover Street.   Tel: 709 4714
Liverpool Piano and Electrical Services (Piano repair)
  15 Brunswick Road.   Tel: 263 4543
Thomas Wess (Builds and repairs harpsichords, clavichords, etc.)
  44 Bluecoat Chambers.   Tel: 677 3560

Retail Shops

Robert Crease, 14 Country Road.   Tel: 525 3238
Frank Hessy Ltd., 62 Stanley Street.   Tel: 236 1418
Rushworth & Dreaper Ltd., 42–46 Whitechapel.   Tel: 709 9071
James Smith & Son Music Sellers Ltd., Williamson Street.   Tel: 709 8401

MANCHESTER (Lancashire)   Tel. prefix: (061)

Manchester has long been the center of Britain's cotton industry. It is connected to the Mersey River by a ship canal which was constructed in 1894, thereby making it the third largest port in England. As the home of two important repertory companies and several of the finest theaters in the country, Manchester fares somewhat better in the dramatic than in the musical arts. However, the Hallé Orchestra guarantees the city's international respectability among the musical communities of the world, and the active university life provides stimulation for a good segment of the population.

Opera Houses and Concert Halls

Opera House
Quay Street.   Tel: 834 4777
Seating capacity: 2072   Box Office Tel. No: 834 1787/9
    Visiting opera companies such as the Glyndebourne and the D'Oyly Carte perform here. Also touring ballet groups and large theatrical-musical productions.

Palace Theater
Oxford Street.   Tel: 236 0405
Seating capacity: 2185   Box Office Tel: 236 0184
    Presents programs of opera, ballet, and concerts as well as drama by visiting companies.

Free Trade Hall
Peter Street.   Tel: 834 0943
Seating capacity: 2560
    Home of the Hallé Orchestra, the Free Trade Hall is also the place where many visiting orchestral groups perform. Rebuilt after it was bombed, it utilizes much of its original stonework of 1843 and 1856 and dates from 1951 in its present form. The hall is 123 feet long, 78 feet wide and 60 feet high—in short, rather large.

Northern College of Music
124 Oxford Street.   Tel: 273 6283
Seating capacity: Concert hall: 600
                       Opera theater: 626
                       Recital room: 150
    When this new college, formed by an amalgamation of the Northern School of Music and the Royal Manchester College of Music, moved to its present quarters, they included a concert hall, opera theater and recital room within the centrally-located building.

Libraries and Museums

Chetham's Library [Ben. 71, Long 98]
Hunt's Bank.   Tel: 834 7961
Hours: Monday to Friday, 9:30 AM to 5:00 PM; Saturday 9:30 AM to noon. Closed
    on religious holidays and from August 1 to 15.
    Contains the Halliwell-Philips collection of music. Founded in 1653, the
library contains printed books and manuscripts including a fine collection of
sixteenth to eighteenth-century works.

John Rylands University Library [Ben. 73]
Deansgate.   Tel: 273 3333
Hours: Monday to Friday, 10:00 AM to 6:00 PM; Saturday 10:00 AM to 2:00
    PM. Closed legal holidays and the Saturday preceding them. Also Spring
    bank holiday and the three days preceding it.
    The collection totals half a million books with music forming only a small
part of the total. Founded by the widow of a wealthy businessman and opened
in 1900, the library occupies a neo-Gothic building designed by Basil Champ-
neys. Its collection of early printed books and manuscripts is world-famous.
There is a considerable music collection of liturgical manuscripts from the
ninth to the fifteenth centuries and the printed music collection ranges from
the fifteenth to the twentieth centuries.

Northern College of Music Library
124 Oxford Road.   Tel: 273 6283
Hours: Monday to Friday from 10:00 AM to 5:00 PM. Closed from mid-July
    to mid-September.
    Aside from the usual materials of music, the collection, which represents
the merging of the Royal Manchester College of Music library with the library
of the Northern School of Music, has some Grieg manuscripts. It also houses
part of the Henry Watson collection of musical instruments: specifically, the
string, keyboard, and wind portions.

Arthur D. Walker Orchestral Score Library [Long 430]
51 Acres Road.   Tel: 881 5119
    A privately-owned library, mainly of orchestral scores, available through
the National Central Library at the discretion of the owner. Over 4,400 scores
including first edition of the Bruckner Mass, autographed works, letters,
presentation copies. Early editions of Haydn and Marcello.

Henry Watson Music Library, Manchester Public Libraries [Ben. 72, Long 269]
St. Peter's Square.   Tel: 236 7401

Hours: Monday to Saturday from 9:00 AM to 9:00 PM.
Admission: unrestricted.
Collection: 12,000 books, 358,000 scores, 450 manuscripts, includes the Aylesford
(Newman Flower) collection of Handel manuscripts and some 2,200 early
printed and manuscript items from before 1801, from the original collection of Dr. Watson, deposited here in 1899. Collections of orchestral and
vocal sets available to any society, church, or library on subscription. A
record library opened mid-1971. Music instrument collection (strings,
keyboard, and wind instruments) including Handel's portable harpsichord
on display in the Library.

University of Manchester, Faculty of Music Library [Ben. 74, Long 270]
Oxford Road. Tel: 273 3333
Hours: Monday to Friday, 9:00 AM to 9:30 PM (during vacation, 9:00 AM to
5:30 PM); Saturday from 9:00 AM to 1:00 PM. Closed on legal holidays.
The music department of the University has a collection with the same
facilities, which is open from 9:30 AM to 5:15 PM daily.
Admission: restricted to members and others on demonstration of need and
credentials.
Collection: 2,000 books, 910 scores and 17 periodicals. Additional material,
particularly scores, records, and tapes in faculty of music library adding
up to a total of 8,000 volumes.

Conservatories and Schools

University of Manchester, Faculty of Music
Oxford Road. Tel: 273 3333
One of the major advanced degree-giving institutions with a separate
faculty of music.

Royal Northern College of Music
124 Oxford Road. Tel: 273 6283
This name represents the amalgamation, in September 1972, of the Royal
Manchester College of Music and the Northern School of Music. Gives both
a performing and a teaching degree. New quarters include an Opera Theater,
Concert Hall, and Recital Hall (see p. 71).

Manchester School of Music
16 Albert Square. Tel: 834 4654
This institution offers a degree-equivalent course of study.

Chetham's Hospital School of Music
Long Millgate.   Tel: 834 7509

Manchester High School of Art [LEA]
Southall Street.   Tel: 834 7417 and 834 9015

Musical Organizations

BBC Northern Symphony Orchestra
P.O. Box 27, Broadcasting House, Piccadilly.   Tel: 236 8444
     Seventy-member, full-fledged professional symphony orchestra. The BBC
Northern Singers frequently perform with this group.

British Scriabin Society
6 Lexton Avenue.   Tel: 740 9866

Hallé Orchestra
30 Cross Street.   Tel: 834 8363
     One of the finest professional orchestras in the world, which achieved
international recognition under the direction of Charles Hallé and Sir John
Barbirolli. The ninety-four musicians are joined by the Hallé Choir in performances of major oratorio works.

Manchester Chamber Music Concerts Society
153 Grove Lane, Cheadle Hulme, Ches.   Tel: 439 8492

North West Arts Association
44 Sackville Street.   Tel: 236 9958
     Regional arts association sponsored by the Arts Council of Great Britain
in cooperation with local organizations.

Society for Research in the Psychology of Music and Music Education
Dept. of Education, Manchester University.

Wagner Society (Manchester)
12 Atholl Road, Bramhill, Stockport, Ches.

The Business of Music

Instrument Sale and Repair

Barretts of Manchester Ltd. (Instrument sale)
    72–74 Oxford Street.   Tel: 236 0052/4843
Crane & Sons Ltd. (Instrument sale)
    11–13 Whitworth Street West.   Tel: 236 6994
Thomas Reynolds Senior & Son Ltd. (Instrument repair—brass
and woodwinds)
    120a Great Clowes Street, Lalford 7, Lancs.   Tel: 834 5530
Tonal Technics Ltd. (Various instrument repair)
    Manchester Road, Denton, Lancs.   Tel: 336 4477/8

Retail Shops

Forsyth Bros Ltd., 126–128 Deansgate.   Tel: 834 3281
Highams Harmony House, 7 Shudehill.   Tel: 834 9432
Music Exchange Ltd., 124 Portland Street.   Tel: 236 1766
Rare Records Ltd., 36 John Dalton Street.   Tel: 832 7344
David E. Vernon, Kings House, Kings Street West.   Tel: 832 5719

NEWCASTLE-UPON-TYNE (Northumberland)

Tel. prefix: (0632)

This important shipbuilding port was once known as Pons Aelii and surrounded by a Roman wall, a fragment of which is still visible on the south
side of Denton bank. The name Newcastle is derived from the Norman castle
built in 1080 by Robert, eldest son of William the Conqueror. The original
building was replaced between 1172 and 1177 by the castle which still stands.
A thriving, commercial city, in constant counterpoint with its ancient monuments of cathedral and castle keep, Newcastle-upon-Tyne has recently begun
to develop a most unusual and provocative musical profile. Programs tend
to be aggressively unconventional (witness a "scandalous" performance by
Cornelius Cardew at the Civic Centre where, at the composer's instructions,
Cardew did "behave as vulgarly as possible") at most and pleasantly off-beat
at least. There is a concerted effort being made to enliven the music life of
this Northern city, and to a great degree, it is succeeding.

Guides and Services

Arts North
Great House, Collingwood Street.   Tel: 29861
> Published monthly by the *Northern Echo* on behalf of *Northern Arts*.
> In newspaper format, articles as well as detailed listings of events, times, and places with comments on special items. Illustrated.

Opera Houses and Concert Halls

City Hall
Northumberland Road.   Tel: 20007
Seating capacity: 2,226
> Home of the Northern Sinfonia Orchestra and the house where all the visiting symphony orchestras—CBSO, Leningrad Philharmonic, Hallé, etc.—perform.

Guildhall
Sandhill   Tel: 21037
> Used primarily for folk concerts, lectures, discussion groups, small recitals.

Laing Art Gallery
Higham Place.   Tel: 27734
> The Laing Art Gallery and Museum, in addition to an excellent collection of oil paintings of the British School from the eighteenth century on, uses its small auditorium for a lunchtime concert series, and for solo and duo recitals in the evenings.

People's Theatre
Stephenson Road.   Tel: 655191
Seating capacity: 900   Box Office Tel: 655020
> Used for visiting dance groups, drama, song recitals of a popular sort, etc.

Theatre Royal
Grey Street.   Tel: 22061
Seating capacity: 1,687
> All opera performed by visiting companies is given here, as well as repertory drama presentations and visiting theater groups.

University Theater
Barras Bridge.   Tel: 27184
Seating capacity: 449   Box Office Tel: 23421
    Theater, chamber opera, and some concert events.

Church Concerts

Concerts of organ music, choral music and liturgical music in all combinations
may be heard frequently at: The Cathedral Church of St. Nicholas, St. John's
Church, St. John's Church Hall, Saint James's Church (by the St. James's
Group very often), and at St. Thomas's Church.

Libraries and Museums

Central Library
Clark Music Library.   Tel: 610691
Hours: Monday to Friday from 9:00 AM to 9:00 PM. Saturday from 9:00 AM
    to 5:00 PM.
    The collections include concert and festival programs dating back to the
nineteenth century, as well as liturgical music, folk ballads, etc. There are also
books and printed music of a local Northumbrian character dating back to
the early 1800s.

Conservatories and Schools

University of Newcastle-upon-Tyne, Department of Music
Armstrong Building.   Tel: 28511
    Offers both undergraduate and graduate degrees.

Newcastle-upon-Tyne Polytechnic, Department of Music
Ellison Building, Ellison Place.

Newcastle College of Further Education, School of Music
Bath Lane.   Tel: 22752
    Provides full or part-time courses for students over 15 years of age.

Spanish Guitar Centre
Norwood House, West Avenue, Gosforth.   Tel: 855046

Musical Organizations

Northern Arts Council
31 New Bridge Street.   Tel: 610446
 Regional arts association sponsored by the Arts Council of Great Britain.

Northern Opera Ltd.
Opera Centre, Lynwood Terrace.   Tel: 39543
 Presents a regular season of opera in Newcastle and environs.

Northern Sinfonia Orchestra
28 Osborne Road.   Tel: 811366/7, 81500
 Fully professional orchestra housed in the Newcastle City Hall, when not
on tour. The Northern Sinfonia Concert Society, which supports the activities
of the Orchestra, works in association with the Arts Council.

Youth and Music Tyneside
28 Osborne Road.
 Affiliate of Youth and Music (see p. 44), this organization functions in
Newcastle-upon-Tyne and environs to encourage youth participation in music
activities.

The Business of Music

Instrument Sale and Repair

Baliol Musical Instruments Ltd. (String instruments)
 35 Percy Street.
Kitchens of Newcastle (Band instruments, guitars, drums,
organs. Instruction)
 Higham House, New Bridge Street.

Music Retail Shops

Jeavons Musical Enterprises Ltd.,
 33–35 Percy Street.   Tel: 20895, 28714, 21430
Saville Bros. Ltd., 5–7 Keppel Street, South Shields,
and 19 Holmeside, Dunserland.
 Specialists in recordings of all kinds, music, instruments, etc.

Record Centre, 3–4 Grainger Market.

    In addition to recordings, this is a ticket agency for concert events.

J. C. Windows Ltd., 1–7 Central Arcade.

    From trombones to triangles, from sheet music to recordings.

NORWICH (Norfolk)   Tel. prefix (0603)

From its humble beginnings as a Saxon settlement over a thousand years ago, Norwich has grown and thrived through the centuries and is today the capital city of Norfolk as well as the market center for all of East Anglia. Dominated by the Cathedral, whose elegant fifteenth-century spire soars 315 feet into the sky, and by its castle with its splendid Norman keep, the city retains a pleasantly eclectic and historical look, a look which is maintained with care by the local authorities. Boasting thirty-two pre-Reformation churches, Georgian Assembly Rooms, and a contemporary town hall, Norwich also lays claim to over three hundred pubs—one for every day in the year, one is told. The musical history of the town compares very favorably with that of other English provincial cities, going back to the cathedral organists and schools of choristers affiliated with the above-mentioned Cathedral since its establishment in mid-twelfth century. The Norwich Waits were originally night watchmen and were also minstrels who performed at the medieval Guild of St. George processions and at other festivities from the thirteenth century on. In 1475 they were commanded by King Edward IV to accompany him to France, and they played for Queen Elizabeth I on her visit to Norwich in 1578. They continued into the eighteenth century, keeping alive the traditional instruments such as the shawm, cornett, recorder, and sackbutt, as well as the more usual stringed instruments. Among Norwich's more famous sons are the composer John Jenkins (1592–1678), buried at Kimberley Church near Norwich, and William Crotch (1775–1848), organist, infant prodigy, first Principal of the Royal Academy of Music (born in Norwich). The music life of the city today is active and rich, being in no way distinguishable from other provincial cities by anything other than the well-developed interests of her citizenry and the healthy respect and affection they maintain for their own traditions.

Guides and Services

Norwich Publicity Association
24 Exchange Street.   Tel: 20697

Eastern Daily Press

The important local paper, carries announcements and reviews of all musical events in the area on a regular basis.

Concert Halls

Assembly House
Theatre Street.   Tel: 26402

Box Office Tel: 27526

Originally built in 1754, Assembly House is Norwich's best example of Georgian architecture. It was reopened in 1950 to be used as a social and educational center and regular musical events are held there.

Lecture Theatre
University Plain, University of East Anglia.   Tel: 56161
Seating capacity: 500

Most of the events of the University Concert Series are held here. It is also the location of a series of Lunchtime Concerts given by members of the faculty of the School of Fine Arts and Music (see p. 83) and the Students' Music Society.

St. Andrew's Hall   Tel: 28477
Seating capacity: Main hall: 850

Blackfriars Hall: 400

Formerly the church of the Dominican friars, St. Andrew's Hall has served as the principal concert hall of the town for two centuries. Most of the events of the triennial Festival of Music and the Arts (see p. 141) are also held here.

Theatre Royal
Theatre Street.   Tel: 23562
Season: from September through May. Closed during June.
Box office: open daily from 10:00 AM to 8:00 PM, Monday to Saturday.

Tel: 23205/6

Seating capacity: 1275

Used for touring presentations, both theatrical and musical, concerts, ballet, etc.

Church Concerts

Churches in which concerts are held or music is regularly performed:

The Cathedral
In addition to concerts of sacred music, both instrumental and choral, which are held in the Cathedral and which are announced in the local press, there are regular evensong services held daily at 5:15 PM, Monday to Friday.

Church of St. Peter Mancroft
Concerts are held regularly at what is considered by the majority to be the most impressive of Norwich's many churches. Begun in 1430, and conse-crated in 1455, there is a richly decorated west tower and a lead spire with flying buttresses dating from the end of the nineteenth century. The interior is a hall without a chancel arch. The organ gallery dates to 1707.

Church of St. George Colegate
Another regular venue for concerts of a sacred nature, this church dates back to the fifteenth and sixteenth centuries. It boasts an excellent 1802 organ which was inaugurated with a performance of Handel's *Messiah.*

Libraries and Museums

Castle Museum   Tel: 22233
Collection: keyboard, wind, and string instruments.

Colman and Rye Libraries of Local History
Norwich Central Library.   Tel: 22233
Collection includes music scores, biographies, histories, local hymnody, full sets of concert programs of all past festival seasons (begun in 1824). Materials on Norfolk organs, church bells, notes, and illustrations on Norwich and Norfolk history.

Norfolk and Norwich Record Office
The Office houses manuscript material belonging to the Norwich Central Library, including the important series of notebooks on East Anglian musical history by Dr. A. H. Mann and the Crotch collection.

The Norwich Cathedral, Library

The outstanding library of the Norfolk area in the realm of sacred music. Includes sets of printed music from Thomas Tompkins and William Boyce on general musical works which reflect the local taste and performance practices at different periods.

St. Peter Hungate Museum

Princess Street.   Tel: 22233

Hours: Open daily from 10:00 AM to 5:00 PM.

Collection of stringed, keyboard, and wind instruments used previously in church performances in Norwich.

Formerly a parish church originating in the fifteenth century, the majority of the exhibits are English and mainly East Anglian but there are also many illuminated manuscripts dating from the thirteenth to the sixteenth centuries and service books and theological works. Outstanding among these is the Wycliffe Bible of 1380.

Strangers' Hall Museum

Charing Cross.   Tel: 22233

Hours: Open daily from 10:00 AM to 5:00 PM.

Collection of stringed, keyboard, and wind instruments, especially examples of the harp-lute, eighteenth-century tambourines, etc.

The house, which has fourteenth-century origins, was given in 1922 to the city of Norwich together with the owner's collection of furniture and domestic equipment. Rooms are furnished in the style of different periods from early Tudor to late Victorian. The musical instruments are placed in the context in which they might have been found at the time of their original use.

University of East Anglia Library [Long 134]

University Plain.   Tel: 97154

Hours: Term, Monday to Friday, 9:00 AM to 10:00 PM; Saturday 9:00 AM to 5:00 PM; Sunday 2:00 PM to 7:00 PM; vacation, Monday to Friday, 9:00 AM to 6:00 PM.

Collection: Vaughan Williams and Holst autograph items. Complete reference section for the use of the music students, a complete file of periodicals, and a collection of 2,000 gramophone records which are available for loan.

Conservatories and Schools

School of Fine Arts and Music, University of East Anglia
Earlhan Hall, University Village.   Tel: 56161
　　Very active and diversified program in music toward undergraduate or advanced degree.

Summer School in British Music
Wensum Lodge.
Dates: September, one week.
　　For further information apply to the Honorable Secretary, Cheriton, Bramble Reed, Lane, Matfield, Tonbridge, Kent.

The Business of Music

Instrument Sale and Repair

A. W. Cooke & Son (Music instrument shop)
　　19 St. Benedicts.   Tel: 25970
R. P. Garrod (Violin Repair)
　　The Rookery, Hingham Road, Little Melton, Norfolk. Tel: 060540 389

Retail Music Shops

William Elkin Music Services, Deacon House, Brundall.
　　Mail order generalized music service offering professional discounts on music and books on music.
Willson & Ramshaw, 10–12 Bridewell Alley.   Tel: 22464
W. E. Willson Music Ltd., 24 White Lion Street.   Tel: 26414

NOTTINGHAM (Nottinghamshire)   Tel. prefix (0602)

The county city of Nottinghamshire has endured trouble and turbulence, feud and strife, since it was settled by the Anglo-Saxons in the sixth century and given the unfortunate name of Snotingaham. During the ninth century it was raided by the Danes, who seized it and made it one of their "burghs" or boroughs. Important because of its position on the river Trent, it changed occupiers many times until the eleventh century when William the Conqueror ordered a stone castle built which served as Norman headquarters during the continuous feud that followed—a feud which gained literary prominence via Robin Hood and his men of nearby Sherwood Forest. The castle was destined to bring success and joy to no one: it was John Lackland's headquarters when he tried to usurp the throne of his brother, Richard I; it was the meeting place for the judges who condemned Richard II in 1387; Richard III used it as headquarters before the battle of Bosworth Field; in 1642, Charles I set up his standard in Nottingham and broke with Parliament. Subsequently, the castle was destroyed in 1651 under Oliver Cromwell's orders. (The Nottingham Castle Museum was opened in 1878 on the site of the old castle.) The eighteenth century brought industrialization to Nottingham, and with it serious Luddite disorders and Chartist demonstrations which culminated in the violence at the Goose Fair of 1831. Happily, however, the Reform Bill of 1832 restored order and by the end of the nineteenth century, relative stability and reasonable prosperity had finally come to Nottingham, now one of the industrial centers of England, and famous for the manufacture of lace.

None of the aforementioned can begin to explain the surprisingly active and imaginative musical life that abounds in Nottingham today. In her musical history, only the name of John Blow (1648–1708) shines with any particular brilliance and he spent most of his productive life in London, not in the suburb of Nottingham where he was born. Yet a glance at the programs, the facilities, the resources, and the organizations listed below will confound the reader who looks for a logical explanation behind the festival programs, concert life, university-sponsored events, amateur activity, and bustling music businesses in this town of half a million, 121 miles northwest of London.

Guides and Services

Music in Nottingham, A Diary of Musical Events

Published annually by the City of Nottingham Music Committee. Contains monthly listings of all concert events, lectures, and classes on music appreciation.

Concert Halls

Albert Hall
Derby Road. Tel: 43921
Seating capacity: 1657

Major concert hall of Nottingham for symphonic concerts by visiting groups as well as the local English Sinfonia Orchestra (see p. 87). Also used for large pop concerts, competitive festivals, and full-scale oratorio performances by large, massed groups.

Co-Operative Arts Theatre
George Street. Tel: 46096

Visiting groups from London perform here, as well as local groups presenting Gilbert & Sullivan and full-scale opera performances.

Great Hall, The University of Nottingham
Nottingham Park. Tel: 56101

The various performing organizations based at the University perform in this hall also used for academic and non-musical purposes.

The Music Studio
Beeston Lane.

Hall used for chamber music, recitals, and generally off-the-beaten-track musical events. Part of the University performance compound which also includes the Assembly Rooms and the Great Hall.

Theatre Royal
Theatre Quadrant. Tel: 42328/9
Seating capacity: 1481

The oldest of Nottingham's theaters was opened in 1865 and is used primarily for theater, opera, and ballet.

Churches in which recitals are given, as well as music services, include: The Church of St. Mary, the Cathedral of St. Barnabas, Kingswood Church, St. Cyprian's, St. Giles', St. Nicholas', St. John's, St. Francis', the Derby Road Methodist Church, among others.

Libraries and Museums

Nottingham Public Libraries, Central Library [Long 307]
South Sherwood Street.   Tel: 43591
Hours: Monday to Friday, 9:00 AM to 8:00 PM. Saturday 9:00 AM to 4:00 PM.
    Small collection of literature on music, nearly 3,000 musical scores; over 1,000 phonograph records.

Nottinghamshire County Library [Long 308]
County Hall, West Bridgford.   Tel: 863366
Hours: Monday to Friday, 11:00 AM to 5:30 PM. Saturday closes at noon.
    Nearly 15,000 items of music, including choral and orchestral materials which are borrowed by 165 affiliated groups.

Schools

Nottingham University, Department of Music
Lenton Grove, Beeston Lane, University Park.   Tel: 56101
    Undergraduate and graduate degrees in music. Specializes in Baroque and Renaissance Music.

Clarendon College of Further Education, Music Department
Pelham Avenue.   Tel: 62201

Spanish Guitar Centre (Midlands Area)
64 Clarendon Street.   Tel: 48325

University of Nottingham, Department of Extra-Mural Studies
Adult Education Centre, 14–22 Shakespeare Street.
    Music courses offered every evening. A very ambitious and commendable program.

Summer Courses

Recorder in Education Summer School
Mary Ward College of Education, Keyworth, Nottingham.
Date: one week, end of July to beginning of August, annually (founded in 1949).
    Brochures obtainable from The Secretary, Miss Ida Mabbett, 23 Old Farm Road, Birchington, Kent.

Musical Organizations

English Sinfonia

72 St. James's Street.   Tel: 43653

Professional orchestra of about forty players with a policy of having a composer-in-association each season who conducts performances of his own works as well as other contemporary works.

The Business of Music

Instruments Sale and Repair

Jack Brentnall (Repair of all stringed instruments)
   2 Goldsmith Street.   Tel: 47166
Clement Pianos Ltd. (Pianos, also tickets for musical events)
   19–23 Derby Road.   Tel: 47912
Ken Neil Music Centre (All musical instruments)
   87 Mansfield Road.   Tel: 46911

Music Retail Shops

Henry Farmer, The Music House & Co. Ltd., 57 Long Row.   Tel: 45761
The Music Inn, 30–32 Alfreton Road   Tel: 74403
Nequests Music House, Central Market.   Tel: 46313

OXFORD (Oxfordshire)   Tel. prefix: (0865)

The town of Oxford is three centuries older than the university which bears its name. According to popular legend, the city was founded in approximately 726, but there are no documents extant dated earlier than 912. By the end of the eleventh century, the town had become a place of some commercial importance and a castle was built by the Normans to oversee the fast-developing territory. Of the original castle, only the "motte" (moat) and St. George's tower still stand. Simon de Montfort led a rebellious Parliament against King Henry III in 1238 from Oxford. The first school of the present-day University was University College, established in 1249. The other colleges soon followed:

Balliol (1263), Merton (1264), St. Edmund Hall (ca. 1270), Exeter (1314), Oriel (1326), Queen's (1340). By the mid-fourteenth century, Oxford University was a full-fledged rival of Paris and the other Continental universities. The growth of the University was continuous and more colleges appeared: New College (1379), Lincoln (1427), All Souls (1438), and Magdalen (1458). The sixteenth century saw the establishment of Brasenose (1509), Corpus Christi (1516), Christ Church (begun by Wolsey in 1525, and concluded by Henry VIII in 1546), St. John's (1555), Trinity (1555), Jesus (1571). Wadham, which contains the music faculty, was founded in 1612, followed by Pembroke in 1624. Worcester College dates back to 1714, Keble to 1870 and Hertford to 1874. There are five women's colleges, all late arrivals understandably: Lady Margaret Hall (1878), Somerville (1879), St. Hugh's (1886), St. Hilda's (1893), and St. Anne's (1952).

Oxford's musical life may be chronicled as far back as 1656, when weekly "music meetings" took place in the house of William Ellis, organist of St. John's College. These meetings were generally well-attended by enthusiastic groups of amateurs. In 1733, Handel paid a visit to Oxford and gave five concerts in the theater. Haydn was given an honorary degree in 1791, bearing increased witness to the high esteem in which music was held in this academically-oriented community. The nineteenth century saw the formation of three important performing societies, which, in one form or another, have dominated and determined Oxford musical life since: the Oxford Choral Society (founded in 1819 by William Crotch), The Philharmonic Society (established in 1865 by Sir John Stainer), and the Oxford Bach Choir, which was begun in 1896. Then, as now, membership in all Oxford musical performance societies was open to the University and town alike. During the latter part of the nineteenth century, separate musical societies representing individual colleges were formed and met regularly for practice to give at least one concert a year in competition with one another. Some of these societies have persisted to this day and still contribute greatly to the richness and variety of Oxford's musical life.

Opera activities, aside from the annual visits of touring companies, are firmly based in another Oxonian institution: the Oxford University Opera Club (sometimes known as Oxford Opera and other times as the Oxford University Opera Society) was founded in 1926 as a result of the historic performance of Monteverdi's *Orfeo,* which had been reconstructed and resurrected by J. A. Westrup (the almost legendary Sir Jack). The success of this production led to regular annual presentations of neglected classics and exotica long before such esoteric activities were common practice, as they are today.

As may be expected, the number of offbeat (and onbeat) musical events which dot the Oxford calendar are far in excess of what would be considered average for a community of its size. Oxford's music tradition is stronger than Cambridge's, so this activity is not merely a reflection of academic tradition per se. Sacred music services and concerts are to be heard in every college chapel, the elaborateness of the ceremony varying with the individual school. Although Oxford is close enough to London to allow for a moderate amount of exurban dependency, the Oxonians have maintained through the years a musical life of a very high and independent caliber.

Guides and Services

Oxford Information Centre
St. Aldate's.   Tel: 48707

What's On in Oxford

10 Kingston Road.   Tel: 5444
    Available from newsstands. Appears every two weeks and weekly in high summer. Describes the major forthcoming events in Oxford itself and in places within easy driving distance to the city.

Opera Houses and Concert Halls

New Theatre
George Street.   Tel: 43041
Seating capacity: 1710   Box Office Tel: 44544/5
    Used for visiting opera company performances as well as theatrical repertory groups and large-scale symphonic concerts promoted by concert managements.

Oxford Playhouse Theatre
Beaumont Street.   Tel: 47134
Seating capacity: 700   Box Office Tel: 47133
    Used for staged musical productions (chamber operas, etc.) as well as for dramatic performances. One of the theaters used during the Oxford segment of the English Bach Festival for staged musical performances.

Town Hall
St. Aldgates.   Tel: 49811
Seating capacity: Main Hall: 1114
                    Assembly Hall: 350
    Used for concerts, oratorios, orchestral-choral performances all year.

The above-mentioned concert halls are not directly affiliated with any college of the University. The following are but a few of the college-affiliated halls commonly used for musical performances. Actually, all of the college chapels are the scene of concerts, recitals, rehearsals—in short, musical activity—at some time during the year. We are going to mention only the most prominent of the halls, chapels, or libraries in which music is heard.

Christ Church Hall
Christ Church College.

The College was founded in 1525 by Cardinal Wolsey, and is recognizable by the great octagonal tower designed by Christopher Wren (built in 1682), containing Great Tom, a 7-ton bell which is rung each evening at 9:05 PM. The Hall is probably the most often-used concert hall of any of the university halls in Oxford and is the scene of chamber music concerts all year round.

Holywell Music Room
Faculty of Music, 32 Holywell.

The oldest room in Europe built solely for the performance of music, the Holywell Music Room has been in continuous use since 1748, except for a brief period in 1900–1901. The room adjoins and belongs to the Faculty of Music and is used not only for chamber concerts and solo recitals, but is also available for rehearsals and performances of a number of Oxford music societies. An extension to the Faculty, containing several practice rooms and linking the Music Room with the School of Music, was opened in 1952. The Music Room is used extensively for the Oxford segment of the English Bach Festival during the summer months.

New College Chapel
New College.

New College was founded by William of Wykeham, Bishop of Winchester in 1367–1404. The Chapel may be found to the left of the first quadrangle, along with the kitchen, and across from the Library. The bell tower and the cloister attached to the Chapel date from 1400. The Chapel is used for liturgical dramas, as well as concerts, recitals, and musical services.

Sheldonian Theatre
Broad Street.
Seating capacity: 1500

Open daily from 10:00 AM–1:00 PM and from 2:00 PM to 5:00 PM.

The Sheldonian Theatre was designed by Christopher Wren in 1664-9, as a University theater and to house the University press. It is roughly semi-circular and is based on the principle of Roman theater design. The roof is a complicated arrangement of beams and trusses supporting a flat ceiling which was painted by Robert Streater with an allegory of "Truth descending on the Arts and Sciences," and a network of ropes to suggest the canvas awning of a Roman amphitheater open to the sky. It was originally used for official University ceremonies and is still sometimes reserved for such occasions, but it is now used primarily for large performances of oratorios requiring massed forces of singers and instrumentalists.

Church Concerts

Christ Church Cathedral
Christ Church.

In addition to regular evensong performances on Mondays, Tuesdays, Thursdays, Fridays, and Saturdays at 6:00 PM, there are frequent performances of oratorios, organ recitals, and choral concerts in the Cathedral. Originally a magnificent example of Norman architecture, later additions include a thirteenth-century spire. The church was formerly an Augustinian priory built during the twelfth century to house the remains of St. Frideswide, a Saxon lady who died in 735. What remains of her shrine is now the presbytery. Cardinal Wolsey, who founded Christ Church College, of which this is part, demolished the western end in the process of building the College. The organ-case is from the seventeenth century as is the pulpit. The Cathedral was restored in the 1870s by Sir Gilbert Scott.

Magdalen College Chapel
Magdalen College.

Evensong on Mondays, Wednesdays, Thursdays, Fridays, and Saturdays at 6:15 PM. The Chapel, which was completed in 1474–5 is T-shaped in plan with good proportions and graceful arches.

Libraries and Museums

Ashmolean Museum
Beaumont Street.   Tel: 57522
Hours: Daily from 10:00 AM to 4:00 PM. Sunday from 2:00 PM to 4:00 PM.
Collection: the Hill collection of musical instruments.

The oldest public museum in Britain, named after Elias Ashmole, antiquary and astrologer, the Ashmolean is housed in the same building as the Taylor Institution. Designed by C. R. Cockerell in 1841 and paid for by the architect Sir Robert Taylor, the museum is famous for its collection of master paintings and drawings. In addition to the Hill collection, there are collections of bronzes, sculptures, tapestries, miniatures, and coins.

Bate Collection of Historical Wind Instruments
Faculty of Music, 32 Holywell.   Tel: 47069
Hours: Monday and Thursday from 2:00 PM to 4:00 PM. Closed during University vacations. No special credentials necessary for admission.
Collection: four hundred woodwind and brass instruments from the late seventeenth century on.

Bodleian Library [Ben. 75, Long 314]
Oxford University.   Tel: 44675
Hours: Monday to Friday during term from 9:00 AM to 10:00 PM; out of term from 9:00 AM to 7:00 PM; Saturdays during term and out of term from 9:00 AM to 1:00 PM. Annual holidays Good Friday to Easter Monday, the first week of September, and from December 24 to December 31.
Special credentials: letter of recommendation advisable if the facilities are to be used for study. Exhibitions are open to the general public.
Description of collection: tenth to twentieth-century manuscripts, including the Wight bequest, the Bourne collection, the William Heather library, and the William Forest library. The general collection emphasizes English music.

One of the largest libraries in the world, with something over three million books, the Bodleian was originally built in 1488 to house the three hundred manuscripts belonging to Duke Humfrey, youngest brother of Henry V. The Library was donated to Oxford University. During the Reformation, it was virtually stripped of its books, and in 1598 Sir Thomas Bodley decided to devote the rest of his life to refitting and restoring the Library. The Radcliffe Camera, a circular building with a great cupola, which now serves as a reading room, was added in 1866 as a result of a bequest by Dr. John Radcliffe, founder of the Radcliffe Science Library. In 1940, the new Bodleian building was completed with the help of a considerable contribution from the Rockefeller Foundation. The three buildings are connected by tunnels and book-conveyer links. Only Duke Humfrey's Library is open without restrictions to the public.

Christ Church Library [Ben. 77, Long 316]
Christ Church College.   Tel: 43957
Hours: Open to the public Monday to Friday, 2:00 PM to 4:30 PM during July and September only. The music collection is not open to the public at any time. It may be used only by bona fide researchers with proper credentials. The entire library is closed during August and at Christmas and Easter.

The music collection, nearly all bequeathed by Henry Aldrich, who was Dean of Christ Church until his death in 1710, amounts to approximately 8,000 items of early English and foreign composers, including an important collection of printed editions of the English madrigalists.

Pitt Rivers Museum
University Department of Ethnology and Prehistory, Parks Road.

Tel: 54979

Hours: Daily from 2:00 PM to 4:00 PM.

General collection of musical instruments of ethnological interest. The entire collection was the gift of General Pitt Rivers to the University in 1883 on the condition that a special building be constructed to house it.

University Faculty of Music Library [Ben. 84, Long 317]
32 Holywell.   Tel: 47069

Hours: Monday to Friday, 9:30 AM to 1:00 PM; 2:00 PM to 5:30 PM and Saturday morning 10:00 AM to 1:00 PM. Closed for two weeks at Christmas and Easter and for one month in the summer.

Exclusively musical collection rich in medieval and Byzantine holdings. Editions of early English music and theoretical treatises. Special collections include the Ellis collection of scores, the Terry Bach collection, Heron-Allen collection of works dealing with the violin, and the libraries of J. H. Mee and Ernest Walker.

University Music Club and Union Library [Ben. 85]
33 Holywell.

Hours: Wednesday and Friday, 2:00 PM to 3:30 PM in term. Closed during University vacations. For admission, apply to the Librarian.

Large lending library of chamber music and books on music.

Of the individual colleges making up Oxford University, many, while not possessing separate music collections do boast some interesting musical holdings. They include Brasenose College, Lincoln College, Magdalen College, New College, Oriel College, Queen's College, and St. John's College.

Schools

Oxford University, Faculty of Music
32 Holywell.   Tel: 47069

Although music degrees have been offered at Oxford for centuries, the formalization of the examination was only initiated in 1862 and the faculty of music became an independent entity in 1944. The Chair of Music was founded in 1627 by William Heather. Both Bachelor of Music and advanced degrees in research are offered.

Oxford Polytechnic, Music Department

Headington.   Tel: 64777

College of further education providing full or part-time courses.

Musical Organizations

Almost each college at Oxford boasts a music society which promotes concert series, sponsors choral societies, chamber groups, orchestras, and opera clubs, invites visiting artists to perform under its auspices, etc. In principle the membership of these societies is limited to college student bodies and faculties. In addition, there are many Oxford-wide groups organized for the performance of music. They range from Bach choirs to orchestras and opera clubs and contribute incalculably to the richness of Oxford musical life.

The Business of Music

Instrument Sale and Repair

Robert Goble & Son, Ltd. (Harpsichords)
Great Stones, Kiln Lane, Headington.   Tel: 61685
David Rubio (Baroque stringed instruments)
Ridge House, Duns Tew, Oxford.   Tel: 08694 698

Retail Shops

Russell Acott Ltd. (Music, records, instruments)
124 High Street.   Tel: 41195/6
Blackwell's Music Shop, 38 Holywell Street.   Tel: 49111
Probably the outstanding mail-order house for books on music and music in Great Britain. Retail shop selling books, music, and recordings of all labels.
Pickett & Sons Ltd., 258–260 Cowley Road.   Tel: 43494/5
C. Taphouse & Son Ltd. (Music, records, instruments, books, ticket agency)
3 Magdalen Street.   Tel: 44655/7

READING (Berkshire)   Tel. prefix: (0734)

Reading lies at the point in the Berkshire Downs and the Chiltern Hills where the Thames becomes a major river. Like many other strategically located towns, it was the target for Danish raids between 871 and 1006 and rose to importance along with the rise of the Normans. Henry I founded the Cluniac abbey in 1121 and was buried there in 1136. Thomas à Becket consecrated the Abbey Church in the presence of Henry II. The abbey was dissolved in 1539 when the last abbot was hanged before his own door. Henry VIII granted the town its first charter in 1542. The industrial importance of the town declined steadily until the beginning of the nineteenth century when the Kennet and Avon Canal was opened, followed shortly thereafter by the arrival of the railway.

Reading's claim to musical fame hangs on a rather thin thread: in the thirteenth century the oldest known canon, "Sumer is icumen in" is *said* to have been written down by a monk, possibly named John of Fornsete, at Reading Abbey. In that entire statement the only thing we can be absolutely certain of is that there is a canon called "Sumer is icumen in" and that it is probably the oldest canon ever written down. It is also fairly certain that a record of this canon was found at Reading Abbey dated about 1225. In any case, the manuscripts are now all carefully preserved in the British Museum in London, a gift from the Reading Abbey!

Today music is a most important element in the cultural life of Reading. A monthly publication supplies a calendar of activities in and around the city; a program of lunchtime concerts, and a university concert series form the basis of an active and interesting schedule. There are also many musicmaking societies, a distinctive feature of English provincial life.

Guides and Services

List of Events In and Around Reading

Reading Public Libraries. Published monthly. Gratis. Lists events, times, and places but no details of programs or ticket prices.

Opera Houses and Concert Halls

University Great Hall
Whiteknights. Tel: 85123
Seating capacity: 400

Located in one of the two buildings which the music department occupies at the University of Reading (see p. 97), the Great Hall is the main venue for musical events in Reading. Besides the regular University Concert Series consisting of chamber music, opera, solo recitals, and orchestral concerts, the Great Hall is used by visiting artists and local musicmaking societies giving public performances.

Town Hall
Blagrave Street. Tel: 55911

The Town Hall is the alternate site for Reading concerts. Together with the University Great Hall, the two places comprise the major locations for local concerts. All other events taking place in Reading itself would be likely to be of an exceptional nature. The lunchtime concerts, which are usually held at 1:10 PM and sponsored by the Reading Public Libraries, are held here.

Reading Museum and Art Gallery
Blagrave Street. Tel: 55911

Occasional concerts sponsored by the National Trust and featuring chamber music performed by local artists are given in the Reading Museum and Art Gallery, which contains a comprehensive collection of Roman antiquities from the area.

Reading shares its music life with several of its immediate neighbors such as Dorchester, Maidenhead, Oxford, Guildford, Windsor, and Henley-on-Thames. The tiny (capacity 277) but perfect little Kenton Theatre in Henley is the scene of many concerts and recitals attended by the citizens of Reading; the same may be said for the somewhat larger (capacity 656) Royal Theatre in Windsor, due east of Reading toward London. The Yvonne Arnaud Theatre in Guildford, southeast of Reading, is regularly visited by the Reading dweller, but primarily for theater, while the various theaters of Oxford (see p. 89), which is to the northwest, are also attended by their neighbors for musical events. This very easy interchange greatly enriches the musical life of those interested people who live too far out of London for easy access but not far enough to necessitate the construction of a totally independant cultural existence.

Libraries and Museums

Central Public Library [Long 341]

Blagrave Street.   Tel: 55911

Hours: Monday, Tuesday, Thursday, Friday 9:30 AM to 7:00 PM; Wednesday
9:30 AM to 1:00 PM. Saturday 9:30 AM to 5:30 PM.

Large music section in a general library from which music, books, and
scores may be borrowed. Very extensive and popular record library also
available on loan for cardholders.

Reading University Music Library [Ben. 87, Long 342]

35 Upper Redlands Road.   Tel: 83584

Hours: Not open to the general public at all. Open to members of the University.
Others with special interest in music may be admitted upon the discretion
of and application to the Librarian. During University term, Monday to
Friday, 9:00 AM to 6:45 PM. During vacation, Monday to Friday, 9:00
AM to 1:00 PM; 2:00 PM to 5:00 PM. Saturdays, term, and vacation, except
before public holidays 9:00 AM to 12:30 PM. Annual holidays one week
at Christmas, one week at Easter, one week at stocktaking (June) and
all public holidays.

Collection in the music library includes about 10,000 items, most of which
are standard reference works and performance materials.

Written Archives, British Broadcasting Company

Caversham Park.

Archival records of the BBC. Entrance by special written permission only.

Schools

Reading University, Department of Music

35 Upper Redlands Road.   Tel: 83583

The first classes in music were held in the University Extension College
in 1893 under the direction of a Mr. J. C. Tirbutt, whose name is still honored
by the annual prize in his memory. In 1897, a school of music was formed,
directed by Sir Walter Parratt, and in 1908 the well-known Sir Hugh Allen
became director of that school, a post he held until 1918 when he became
Director of the Royal College of Music, and Professor of Music at Oxford.
In 1930, music was added to the list of subjects which could be taken toward

a B.A. degree. In 1950, a Chair of Music was established. Music education and the training of music teachers comprises an important part of the department.

County School of Music
St. Nicholas Hall, Guildford, Surrey.   Tel: 0483 4335

Musical Organizations

Reading boasts an unusually high number of both amateur and professional performing groups. Many are University-based, for the department of music has a very active performance program. Ranging from a Palestrina choir to a pipe band, the musical activities available to the resident of Reading are of a catholicity which must be regarded with admiration and astonishment.

The Business of Music

Barnes & Avis Ltd. (Music, records, instruments)
   138–141 Friar Street.   Tel: 55361
Norman Hackett Ltd. (Music and musical instruments)
   5 Bristol and West Arcade.   Tel: 54773
Hickie & Hickie Ltd. (Music, records, instruments)
   153 Friar Street.   Tel: 55771
Modern Music Centre (Berks) Ltd.
   78 Oxford Road.   Tel: 581320
Rumbelow Ltd.
   138 Friar Street.   Tel: 55361
Leon Smallbone (Repair of string instruments and bows)
   84 Shaftesbury Road.   Tel: 582964

Cities Briefly Noted:
BOLTON (Lancashire)

Tel. prefix: (0204)

Guides and Services

Bolton Civic Entertainments

Published annually. Gratis.

Contains the programs and schedules of all the musical events and lectures which will be taking place in Bolton in the season ahead.

A small diary entitled *Summer Programme* lists the band concerts, children's events and civic dances which take place during the summer months.

Concert Halls

Albert Hall
Town Hall.   Tel: 22311
Seating capacity: 1000

This hall is used for all concerts requiring the use of an organ.

Central Library, Lecture Theatre
Civic Centre.   Tel: 22311
Seating capacity: 283. Small lecture hall: 80

Most of the chamber concerts and recitals are given in the lecture theater. Tickets are on sale at the Entertainments Office, The Town Hall. Hours: 9:30 AM to 5:15 PM, Monday to Friday. If there are any available, tickets are also sold at the door for each event.

Victoria Hall
Knowsley Street.   Tel: 22569

The location of all large symphonic concerts presented by visiting groups such as the Hallé and the Royal Liverpool orchestras.

Libraries

Bolton Public Libraries [Long 43]
Central Library, Civic Center.   Tel: 22311, 23543
Hours: Monday, Tuesday, Thursday, Friday 9:30 AM to 7:30 PM; Wednesdays
     9:30 AM to 1:00 PM; Saturday 9:30 AM to 5:30 PM.
     Large collection of books on music and music scores. Record library
opened early in 1971.

Schools

The Bolton School of Music
Manchester Road.

The Business of Music

Booth's Music, 17 Churchgate.   Tel: 22908
Harker & Howarth Music, Ltd. (Music, instruments, recordings, tickets)
     28–32 Churchgate, and Goodwin Street.   Tel: 26623/4
Woods Pianos and Organs Ltd., 15–17 Manchester Road.   Tel: 27271/2

KINGSTON-UPON-HULL ("HULL") (Yorkshire)

Opera Houses and Concert Halls

City Hall
Victoria Square.   Tel: 20123/28732
Box Office: tickets go on sale exactly two weeks prior to any event and may
     be obtained at Gough & Davy Ltd., Savile Street.   Tel: 26525

Seating capacity: 1981

Principal concert hall of Kingston-upon-Hull for visiting orchestras such as the English Sinfonia Orchestra, the Northern Sinfonia Orchestra, the Hallé Orchestra, etc. Both the Hull Choral Union and the Hull Philharmonic Society sponsor and perform there. Publishes an annual concert diary, *Concerts in the City Hall.*

The Middleton Hall, Gulbenkian Centre, University of Hull
Cottingham Road. Tel: 43611, ext. 7234
Seating capacity: 514

Concerts sponsored by the department of music, University of Hull, are given here.

Tickets for all such events are available from the University (music department, reception or the Student's Union) and from Gough & Davy Ltd. (see above).

Active center of academic musical life, presenting musical programs in a very wide range of genres. An annual booklet called *Music in the University* is published in which the entire season's concert schedule is given.

New Theatre
Kingston Square. Tel: 20244
Seating capacity: 1179 Box Office Tel: 20463

Visiting opera groups perform in this theater in March and April. Ballet given here as well. Mainly a dramatic theater, however.

Arts Centre
Spring Street. Tel: 20925

Small recitals and special chamber events are held in this small auditorium.

Libraries

Hull City Libraries [Long 207]
Albion Street. Tel: 36680
Hours: Monday to Friday, 9:00 AM to 8:00 PM; Saturday 9:00 AM to 5:30 PM.
Collection: 4,000 books on music, 12,069 scores, 13 periodicals, and 10,000 records. Music lectures and concerts are arranged by the Library.

Hull University, Brynmor Jones Library [Long 208]   Tel: 52530
Hours: Monday to Friday, 9:00 AM to 10:00 PM (5:30 PM on vacation); Saturday
  9:00 AM to 1:00 PM. Record Lending Library 2:00 PM to 5:00 PM in term
  only.
Collection: about 1300 books, 5,000 scores, 25 periodicals. Facilities available
  for private listening to recorded music.

Schools

Department of Music, University of Hull
Cottingham Road.   Tel: 408960
  Offers undergraduate and advanced degrees in music.

The Business of Music

J. Cleveland (Music, records, instruments)
  409 Hessle Road.
J. P. Cornell (Music, records, instruments)
  21 Spring Bank   Tel: 215335
Gough & Davy Ltd. (Music, instruments, concert tickets)
  13–15 Savile Street.   Tel: 26525/6
Paragon Music Stores (Musical instruments)
  60 Paragon Street.   Tel: 213331

LEEDS (Yorkshire)   Tel. prefix: (0532)

Opera Houses and Concert Halls

Civic Theatre
Cookridge Street.   Tel: 26343
Seating capacity: 1500
  Major concert hall for the Leeds Triennial Festival as well as major concert
events all year round.

Grand Theatre and Opera House
New Briggate.   Tel: 26014
Seating capacity: 1554   Box Office Tel: 20891
    Used primarily for visiting opera companies, ballet and repertory groups.

Leeds Institute Gallery
Cookridge Street.   Tel: 22064

Main Hall, The Library
Municipal Building.   Tel: 31301

Music Centre
Cookridge Street.   Tel: 22069

Libraries and Museums

Abbey House Museum
Abbey Road.
Hours: Open April to September, weekdays, 10:00 AM to 6:00 PM. Sundays,
    2:00 PM to 6:00 PM. October to March, weekdays, 10:00 AM to 5:00 PM.
    Folk museum originally the great gatehouse of Kirkstall Abbey, founded
in 1152 by Cistercian monks. The museum contains costumes, dolls, toys,
musical instruments, and three completely reconstructed streets, removed from
the Leeds area and rebuilt within the museum.

Brotherton Collection, Brotherton Library [Ben. 47]
University of Leeds.   Tel: 31751
Hours: Monday to Friday, 9:00 AM to 5:00 PM; Saturday mornings only. Closed
    Christmas week, Easter weekend, bank holidays and Tuesdays following
    bank holidays.
Collection: approximately 4,000 volumes of music literature and 10,000 scores,
    including the Mendelssohn–Moscheles correspondence, the Novello–
    Cowden Clarke collection, and the Charles Didbin manuscripts. Primarily
    for the use of students reading at the University.

Leeds City Libraries, Central Library, Music Department [Ben. 48]
Municipal Building, Calverley Street.   Tel: 26619 and 31301, ext. 421
Hours: Monday to Friday 9:00 AM to 8:00 PM; Saturday 9:00 AM to 5:00 PM.
Collection: included in the collection are 7,000 books, 26,000 scores, and 12,500
    recordings, in addition to the Taphouse bequest of eighteenth and nine-
    teenth-century scores and music literature. Record recitals given regularly,
    and mid-day and Saturday concerts as well.

Schools and Conservatories

University of Leeds, Department of Music
14 Cranmer Terrace.   Tel: 31751
> One of the most adventurous university music departments offering both undergraduate and graduate degrees.

College of Music, City of Leeds
Cookridge Street.   Tel: 22069
> Formerly the Leeds Music Centre, the College of Music offers full-time foundation and external diploma courses. In addition, they now have equivalent courses in jazz and light music. Prospectus may be requested from the Director.

Yorkshire College of Music and Drama
19 Shire Oak Road.

The Business of Music

L. P. Balmforth and Son (Instruments)
    31–33 Merrion Street.   Tel: 27583
Banks Music House (Music and instruments)
    25 Country Arcade.   Tel: 25727
Classical Record Shop
    95 Albion Street.   Tel: 22059
James T. Cuppock Ltd. (Repair of stringed instruments)
    Highfield House, Royds Lane.   Tel: 634652/3
R. S. Kitchen Ltd. (Music, recordings, instruments)
    22 King Edward Street.   Tel: 34071

SHEFFIELD (Yorkshire)   Tel. prefix: (0742)

Services

Civic Information Service
Central Library, Surrey Street.   Tel: 78771
Hours: Monday to Friday, 9:00 AM to 5:30 PM; Saturday, 9:00 AM to 5:00
PM.

Opera Houses and Concert Halls

The City Hall
Barker's Pool.   Tel: 22885
Concert Box Office: Leopold Street.   Tel: 27074
    The City Hall complex, opened in 1932 and designed for concerts, meetings, and dances, contains six halls.
    Oval Hall: seating capacity 2,695. Used for symphony concerts, visiting musical companies, and organizational meetings. The concerts take place principally on alternate Friday evenings at 7:30 PM and Saturdays at 7:00 PM from September to May.
    Memorial Hall: seating capacity 522. Used for chamber and solo recitals.

Library Theatre
Surrey Street.   Tel: 78771

Merlin Theatre
2 Meadow Bank Road.   Tel: 51638
    New theater used by the Sheffield Grand Opera for the presentation of its annual season of opera performances, as well as evenings of instrumental music and ballet.

Church Concerts

Music is also heard regularly in the Cathedral Church of St. Peter and St. Paul, founded in the twelfth century and rebuilt in the fifteenth. Of special interest is the sixteenth-century Shrewsbury Chapel and the Chapter House.

Libraries

Sheffield City Library [Long 375]
Central Library, Surrey Street.   Tel: 78771/7
Hours: Monday to Friday, 10:00 AM to 8:00 PM; Saturday, 10:00 AM to 5:00
    PM.
Collection: the music collection, which is not separate from the rest of the
    Library, consists of some 6,000 items including nearly 1,000 miniature
    scores. There is also a growing record collection and recorded recitals are
    regularly held.

Sheffield University Library [Long 376]
Western Bank.   Tel: 78555
Hours: Monday to Friday, 9:00 AM to 9:00 PM (open only until 5:00 PM during
    Christmas and long vacations); Saturday, 9:00 AM to 1:00 PM.
Collection: general music reference collection incorporated into the All-Univer-
    sity Library. Available to students of the University. All others by special
    permission only.

Schools

University of Sheffield, Department of Music
Faculty of Arts, Western Bank.   Tel: 78555
    Offers undergraduate and advanced degrees in music. Emphasis on com-
position.

Stannington College of Further Education
Myers Grove Lane.   Tel: 340691
    Provides full or part-time courses which can lead to a standard degree.

The Business of Music

Bradley's Music (Instruments, music, records, books, etc.)
    50 Fargatem and 103–105 West Street.   Tel: 77416
Crane & Sons Ltd. (Musical instruments, sale and repair)
    125 The Moor.   Tel: 24831

Len Stewart (Music and musical instruments)
    274 London Road.   Tel: 581801
J. M. Taylor (Piano tuning and repair)
    43 Granby Street.   Tel: 386394
Wilson Peck Ltd. (Music, instruments, records, ticket sales)
    64–70 Leopold Street and 2–8 Barkers Pool.   Tel: 24123

YORK (Yorkshire)   Tel. prefix: (0904)

Concert Halls

Arts Centre
St. John's, Micklegate.   Tel: 27129

Central Hall
The University, Heslington.   Tel: 59861

Guildhall
Coney Street, St. Leonard's Place.   Tel: 59881
    Built between 1447 and 1453 as the civic hall of York, the Guildhall was partially destroyed in an air raid in 1942, but has been carefully restored.

Lyons Concert Hall
The University, Heslington.   Tel: 59861

Tempest Anderson Hall
Yorkshire Museum, Museum Gardens.   Tel: 29745

Theatre Royal
St. Leonard's Place.   Tel: 58162
Seating capacity: 950   Box Office Tel: 23568
    Recently completely renovated, this eighteenth-century theater offers a wide variety of opera, ballet, and concert events.

Church Concerts

York Cathedral (*York Minster*)
1 Minster Court.   Tel: 53875
    Evensong may be heard on Monday, Tuesday, Thursday, Friday, and
Saturday at 4:00 PM. In addition, concerts of religious music are held in the
Minster regularly. There is a modern Walker organ as well as a small Lincoln
chamber organ.

Libraries and Museums

Castle Museum, The Music Gallery   Tel: 53611
Hours: Daily 9:30 AM to 7:30 PM. Sundays, 9:30 AM to 2:00 PM.
    In the Music Gallery of the Castle Museum, which is one of the leading
folk museums of the country, are such minstrel instruments as the serpent,
bassoon, and ophicleide; a virginal of 1651, a harpsichord of 1789, and a
Johannes Player spinet, as well as harps and wind instruments. There is a
music shop in the reconstructed street of the museum.

J. B. Morell Library [Long 465]
The University, Heslington.   Tel: 59861
Hours: Monday to Friday from 9:00 AM to 5:00 PM in the summer; Monday
    to Saturday from 9:00 AM to 10:00 PM in the winter. Annual closing: one
    week at Christmas and one at Easter.
Collection: utilitarian collection of reference works primarily for university
    students.

York City Libraries [Long 463]
Central Library, Museum Street.   Tel: 55631
Hours: Monday, Tuesday, Friday from 9:30 AM to 8:00 PM. Wednesdays, 9:30
    AM to 1:00 PM. Saturday from 9:30 AM to 5:00 PM. Thursday 9:30 AM to
    5:30 PM.
Collection: among the 4,000 books and scores and 2,600 recordings, there is a
    complete Arnold edition of Handel.

York Minster Library [Ben. 100, Long 464]
Dean's Park.   Tel: 25308
Hours: Monday to Friday, 10:00 AM to 5:00 PM. Closed public holidays.
    Collection predominantly historical and literary, contains some seven-
teenth-century anthems, eighteenth-century Handel material and Walmsley
autographs.

Schools

University of York, Department of Music
Heslington.   Tel: 59861
    Offers undergraduate and advanced degrees in music.
    The Music Teachers' Association (106 Gloucester Place, London W1H 3DB) sponsors a week of school music and piano concentration at York University each August for applicants over the age of 16.

The Business of Music

Banks & Sons Music Ltd. (Music, instruments, records)
    Stonegate.   Tel: 58836
Gough & Davy Ltd. (Records and musical instruments)
    10 Clifford Street.
Nicholas Keen (harpsichords)
    6 Eastfield Crescent.
Music Service (music and musical instruments)
    1 Driffield Terrace.   Tel: 25179
York Piano Service (Recordings and musical instruments)
    8 Tower Street.   Tel: 55536

ENGLAND, GENERAL

Opera Houses and Concert Halls

The brief list which follows mentions only those concert halls or opera houses which are of special interest to the reader, usually for extra-musical reasons. As noted elsewhere, almost every town worthy of that political appellation has one theater (and usually many more) which is used for the presentation of concerts and recitals by local and visiting performers. The fact that the White Rock Pavilion in Hastings seats 1,300 and is operative from September to

March is not sufficiently different from the indisputable fact that the Assembly Hall in neighboring Worthing seats only 1,004 and has excellent acoustics, to warrant a specific mention much less a lengthy exposition. The bare facts concerning thousands of concert halls in hundreds of cities, towns, and villages of Great Britain may be found in abundance in *The Music Yearbook.* Those cited here have something other than their existence to recommend them.

Abingdon (Berkshire)

Unicorn Theatre
Abingdon.   Tel: Abingdon 1432
Seating capacity: 100
     This little theater was constructed in 1953 in the Elizabethan style and tucked into what was formerly the granary of Abingdon Abbey. Originally founded in 675, there are few visible remains of the old ecclesiastical structures. What remains—the medieval Chequer, a square stone building with an unusual chimney, and the Long Gallery, a fifteenth-century guesthouse—lends the tiny "Elizabethan" theater a nostalgia and charm that are quite delightful. The Unicorn Opera Group, founded in 1959 under the direction of Frances and Alan Kitching, performs Handel operas scaled to the small theater.

Aldeburgh (Suffolk)

The Maltings (*see Aldeburgh Festival of Music and Arts, pp. 127–128*)

Bath (Somerset)

Assembly Rooms.   Tel: (0225) 28411, ext. 326
Seating capacity: Ballroom, 529. Tearoom, 300.
     This magnificent suite of rooms was designed by John Wood in 1771 and for many years was the center of the city's social life. The rooms were restored by the National Trust, with decor by Oliver Messel, and reopened in 1963. The suite consists of the ballroom (in which musical events take place) and a tearoom as well as a multitude of smaller, finely appointed rooms. A Museum of Costume has been added recently.

Guildhall   Tel: (0225) 28411, ext. 326
Seating capacity: 300
     The Guildhall is the work of Thomas Baldwin, the City Architect who in 1775 redesigned the old seventeenth-century building. Baldwin's work comprises the central portion of the present building, to which wings were added in 1893. The room which is used for concerts, the Banqueting Room, is one of the noblest rooms in the West Country. Richly decorated in green, cream, and gold, it is a perfect example of the Adam style. It is 80 feet long,

40 feet wide, and 31 feet high. The room contains some fine portraits of famous people connected with the city's history, and three glass chandeliers dating from 1778.

Holburne of Menstrie Museum
Pulteney Street, Sydney Place.   Tel: (0225) 3669
Chamber recitals are given in this museum which now houses a fine collection of paintings, silver, porcelain, and pottery. It was designed in 1795 as a pavilion in the Sydney Gardens, by C. Harcourt Masters.

Pump Room
                                                                 Tel: (0225) 28808
                                           Box Office Tel: (0225) 28411, ext. 326
Seating capacity: 300; concert room, 290
The Pump Room has been the center of the city's life for 250 years and it is still the focal point of assembly for conversation, concerts, and other forms of entertainment. Originally constructed in 1706 over the ruins of the ancient Roman Baths twenty feet below, it was not until the end of the nineteenth century that an intensive effort was made to excavate the area. In the years following, the Roman Baths around which the Pump Room is built were discovered. The ancient and unique hot springs still remain active.

Bexhill-on-Sea (Sussex)

De La Warr Pavilion
Marina.   Tel: Bexhill 2023
Seating capacity: 1300   Box Office Tel: Bexhill 2062
Owned and operated by the Bexhill-on-Sea Corporation, the De La Warr Pavilion is the pride of this resort town. Unique in design and the first of its kind in the country, the Pavilion is a completely modern building complex which combines sun lounges, a restaurant overlooking the sea, lecture hall, conference rooms, and a cafe with a concert hall which offers its large audience an unimpeded view of the stage. A repertory company performs all year in this theater, which is also the place where leading musical figures give performances. Sunday evenings there are orchestral concerts, and annual festivals of music feature symphony, chamber music, ballet, and light music as regular fare.

Bletchley (Buckinghamshire)

The Claydon Concerts, Claydon House
Sixty miles from London, 25 miles from Oxford, in the heart of the country, Claydon House is the home of Mr. and Mrs. Ralph Verney. There are no hotels in the immediate vicinity of Claydon House, a handsome eight-

eenth-century mansion noted for its rich interior decor as well as for its close association with Florence Nightingale. There is also no public transport and you must drive to London or Oxford after the concerts.

There are six concerts a year on Sunday evenings between June and October. The programs are primarily chamber music and solo recitals. It is always essential to book tickets well in advance. Supper is available for a limited number of patrons. All arrangements must be made through the management in London: Basil Douglas, 8 St. George's Terrace. Tel: (01) 722 7142

Brighton (Sussex)

Dome
Royal Pavilion Estate.   Tel: (0273) 682046
Seating capacity: 2102   Box Office Tel: (0273) 682127

Music Room
Royal Pavilion Estate.   Tel: (0273) 63005
Seating capacity: 300
In 1786, George, Prince of Wales leased a small house in Brighton which Henry Holland reconstructed as a classical building complete with a central rotunda and a dome. After he became Regent in 1811, George had the house rebuilt; John Nash transformed it into something very like an Indian mogul's palace by adding a great onion-shaped dome, tent-like roofs to the pavilions, numerous pinnacles, and several strategically located minarets. The Pavilion was closed in 1845 and reopened after the Second World War by Queen Elizabeth II. The Dome Room and the Music Room are sumptuously decorated and appointed, with painted walls and elaborate chandeliers. They are both used extensively for major musical events of the Brighton season.

Bury St. Edmunds (Suffolk)

Theatre Royal
Westgate Street.   Tel: (0284) 5127
Seating capacity: 333   Box Office Tel: (0284) 5469
Built in 1819 by William Wilkins and recently restored, the Theatre Royal is the only provincial Regency theater now in use. Theatrical performances as well as concerts, chamber operas, and chamber ballets are presented here.

Derby (Derbyshire)

Guildhall Assembly Rooms
7 Market Place.   Tel: (0332) 31111, ext. 393

The hall, used for small concerts and recitals and closed only in July and August, is housed within a lovely Georgian building. It has been completely refurbished inside and boasts one of the best Bechstein grand pianos in England.

Museum and Art Gallery
Strand.

A room in the museum devoted to the works of Joseph Wright of Derby (1734–97) is used for recitals of music on old instruments played by candlelight.

King's Lynn (Norfolk)

Guildhall of St. George
King Street.   Tel: (0553) 4725
Seating capacity: 359   Box Office Tel: (0553) 3578

The Guildhall of St. George is the largest and oldest example in England of a medieval merchant guild's house. Built in the early fifteenth century, it was restored and adapted as a theater in 1951.

Lewes (Sussex)

Glyndebourne Opera House (see p. 135)

Paignton (Devon)

Oldway Mansion.   Tel: (0803) 26244
Seating capacity: 350

Built circa 1900 in neo-classical style by Paris Singer to designs inspired by Versailles. Now used for recitals and chamber concerts.

Richmond (Yorkshire)

Georgian Theatre
Friars Wynd.   Tel: Richmond (Yorks) 3021
Seating capacity: 238

A small theater built by Samuel Butler in 1788, there were no stage presentations in it from 1848 to 1943 when a production was staged as part of the 850th anniversary of the Borough of Richmond. In 1960–62, the theater was restored and reopened.

Rotherham (Yorkshire)

Civic Theatre
Doncaster Gate.   Tel: (0709) 77150

Box Office: weekdays from 11:00 AM to 8:00 PM (9:00 AM to 6:00 PM when there is no evening performance).

Seating capacity: 387

Known as the "Showplace of Yorkshire," the Theater is well-equipped indeed for concerts, opera, and ballet, as well as drama and variety. It was opened on March 7, 1960 by Sir Lewis Casson. Originally an old priory, the interior was completely reconstructed into a very modern auditorium with a foyer and coffee lounge as well as a bar, and up-to-date front and backstage facilities, making it today one of the best-equipped civic houses in Britain.

Winchester (Hampshire)

Guildhall   Tel: (0962) 68166

Seating capacity: Large Hall, 736; Banqueting Hall, 220; Sessions Hall, 150.

A Gothic-Revival building dating from 1873 and containing numerous paintings from the sixteenth century on.

Libraries and Museums

Practical considerations of space and length make it impossible to enumerate the hundreds of libraries, public and private, scattered throughout England, in which music collections of interest and distinction repose. Fortunately, at least three sources now exist from which most of this information may be gleaned. None of the three is complete, however, and the interested reader will have to collate what is available and await the publication of yet a fourth volume in which it will all be laid out before him. We have made mention, in the pages following, of a few unique collections which will be of great interest to the musical bibliophile visiting England. We have also sought to direct the musical traveler to instrument collections of distinction and interest lying somewhat off the beaten track.

Bentley (Hampshire)

Gerald Coke Collection [Ben. 6, Long 103]

Jenkyn Place.   Tel: 04204 3118

Collection is housed in the owner's residence and is open weekdays and weekends except for a vacation period in August and September. For admission, apply to Mr. Coke in writing. The collection is usually available to anyone engaged in bona fide research. It includes a formidable Handel Collection consisting of scores, books, contemporary manuscripts, iconography, and objects relating to the composer, and incorporates the library of the scholar W. C. Smith.

Bethersden (Kent)

The Colt Clavier Collection
Bethersden, near Ashford.   Tel: 023382 456
Hours: Open only by appointment applied for well in advance and in writing.
Admission fee: five pounds sterling!

One of the largest and most comprehensive collections of piano in working order in the world, with well over one hundred keyboard instruments, including harpsichords, pianos, clavichords, spinets, barrel organs, and claviharpes. Due to some unpleasant encounters with importunate visitors, Mr. Colt wishes to emphasize that this private, unsubsidized collection may be viewed only at the discretion of the owner (hence the inappropriately large entrance fee). Written application does not guarantee admission. The collection is in a remote village and there is no public transportation available. It would be advisable, upon making a request to view the collection, to enclose something by way of credentials. The collection, inaccessible and private though it may be, is well worth the effort to see it.

Bradford (Yorkshire)

Bolling Hall
Bolling Hall Road.   Tel: 0274 23057
Hours: Open daily from 10:00 AM to 5:00 PM

The ancestral home of Edith Bolling, wife of President Woodrow Wilson, the old manor house dates back to the fifteenth century. Now a museum, it contains, besides furniture, books, and paintings, a collection of eighteenth century musical instruments.

Brighton (Sussex)

Brighton Museum
Church Street.
Hours: Monday to Friday, 10:00 AM to 6:00 PM. Sunday, open from 2:00 to 4:00 PM.

Included among the collections of Old Masters and the Willett collection of English pottery is a well-arranged display of 170 early musical instruments, including harpsichords, claviers, and recorders.

Broadheath (*Worcestershire*)

Elgar Museum

Hours: Daily from 1:30 to 6:30 PM. Sunday from 2:00 to 5:00 PM. Closed
Wednesday.

Sir Edward Elgar (1857–1934) was born in this red-brick cottage in June
of 1857. After early lessons on the organ, violin, and bassoon, he succeeded
his father as organist of St. George's Roman Catholic Church. His birthplace
was turned into a museum which houses a collection of his personal belongings,
including a manuscript of his Second Symphony, his violin case and bow, and
metronome. The grave of Sir Edward and his wife may be found in the churchyard of St. Wulstan's in Little Malvern.

Canterbury (*Kent*)

Canterbury Cathedral Library

The Precincts.   Tel: 0227 63510
Hours: Tuesday to Thursday from 11:00 AM to 4:30 PM by appointment only.
Closed late August to early September.

The Library, located in the upper part of the water tower (rebuilt in the
fifteenth century), contains medieval manuscripts and early printed choral
music. It is private and application for admission is necessary.

Carlisle (*Cumberland*)

Tullie House, Carlisle Museum and Art Gallery

Castle Street.   Tel: 0228 34781
Collection of string and wind instruments, outstanding among which is
an Amati violin dated 1574.

Chester (*Chestershire*)

Grosvenor Museum

Grosvenor Street.   Tel: 0244 21616
Hours: Open weekdays from 10:00 AM to 5:00 PM; Sunday, from 2:30 to 5:30 PM.

The Museum's archeological exhibits are mainly from the Roman legion-
ary fortress of Deva and include important inscribed stones. The Museum also
has a unique set of Bressan recorders.

Hailsham (*Sussex*)

Michelham Priory

Upper Dicker.   Tel: 03216 224

Hours: Monday to Friday, 10:00 AM to 2:00 PM; Sunday, 2:00 to 5:00 PM.

This eleventh-century priory, now a museum, houses the Mummery collection of Musical Instruments.

Haslemere (*Surrey*)

Dolmetsch Collection of Early Musical Instruments
Jesses, Grayswood Road.

Undoubtedly one of the best collections of early English musical instruments in the country, the house is on view to the public by appointment only. However, during the Haslemere Festival in July, there are regular visiting hours from Monday to Friday from 10:00 AM to 5:00 PM.

Hereford (*Herefordshire*)

Hereford Cathedral Library [Ben. 46]   Tel: 0432 3537
Hours: Weekdays 10:30 AM to 12:30 PM; 2:00 PM to 4:00 PM from Easter to
September.

The famous chained library, the largest of its kind in the world, with nearly 1,500 handwritten and printed books. Each has a chain attached to the front edge of one cover and to a rod on the bookcase. Only by turning the key to free the rods can books be removed or added. The music collection includes the Roger North autographs and eighteenth- and nineteenth-century church music; also glees, songs, and piano music belonging to Fanny Kemble.

Huddersfield (*Yorkshire*)

Tolson Memorial Museum
Ravensknowle Park, Wakefield Road.   Tel: 0484 30591
Collection of wind instruments.

Ingatestone (*Essex*)

Ingatestone Hall
Hours: open Tuesday to Saturday, 10:00 AM to 12:30 PM; 2:00 to 4:30 PM.

Built circa 1540 for Sir William Petre, the permanent display in the Long Gallery includes a rare sixteenth-century virginal (William Byrd was a frequent visitor to the house), as well as a large archive of Essex historical prints, paintings, and furniture.

Ipswich (*Suffolk*)

Christchurch Mansion
Christchurch Park.   Tel: 0473 53246

String, keyboard, and wind instruments distributed throughout the period rooms of the museum.

Maidstone (Kent)

Chillington Manor House (Museum and Art Gallery)
St. Faith's Street.   Tel: 0622 54497
Hours: Weekdays, April to September, 10:00 AM to 6:00 PM. October to March, 10:00 AM to 5:00 PM.

An early Elizabethan building to which has been added an art gallery, county rooms, and the Bearsted Wing. Among the exhibits displayed are a collection of string, keyboard, and wind instruments. Prominently featured are Handel's portable harpsichord and Lady Hamilton's songbook.

Newport (Isle of Wight)

Carrisbrook Castle Museum
Hours: open daily from 10:00 AM to 5:00 PM. Sunday from 2:00 to 5:00 PM.

Founded on the site of a Roman fort, the castle served as the prison for Charles I from 1647 to 1648. Now a museum, the collection includes archeological items, local antiquities, and the oldest functioning organ in Britain, dated 1602.

Rossendale (Lancashire)

Rawtenstall Public Libraries
Central Library.   Tel: 0706 24553
Hours: Monday to Friday, 10:00 AM to 8:00 PM; Saturday, 10:00 AM to 5:00 PM.

Collection of musical instruments and volumes of music used by an eighteenth to nineteenth-century Rossendale society, "The Deighn Layrocks" (The Larks of the Dean). Part of a general library.

St. Albans (Hertfordshire)

St. Albans Organ Museum
Camp Road.   Tel: St. Albans 51557

Contains a vast collection of large and small organs, built by foreign as well as English builders. Also included in the collection are symphoniums, polyphons, musical boxes, and other unusual keyboard instruments.

Snowshill Manor (Gloucestershire)

Snowshill Manor
Near Broadway, Worcestershire.   Tel: Broadway 2410

Hours: Easter to October, Saturday, Sunday, and bank holidays. May to October, Wednesday and Thursday from 11:00 AM to 1:00 PM and 2:00 PM to 6:00 PM.

A typical sixteenth-century Cotswold house, it contains an unusual collection of musical instruments, clocks and toys; 15,000 items in all.

Stratford-upon-Avon (Warwickshire)

Shakespeare Centre Library [Ben. 92]
Henley Street.
Hours: Monday to Friday 10:00 AM to 1:00 PM and 2:00 PM to 5:00 PM. July and August from 9:30 AM to 12:30 PM and Saturday from 9:30 AM to 12:30 PM. Closed bank holidays. Write ahead to arrange for reader's ticket.

Music in the collection connected with Shakespeare, also the manuscripts of Vaughan Williams.

Tenbury Wells (Worcestershire)

St. Michael's College Library [Ben. 93]
Hours: Open in term only. Apply to Librarian.

This boys' prep school was endowed by a choral foundation with a great antiquarian music collection. Rich in early English music, early eighteenth-century French opera, manuscripts and printed books from the Ouseley collection.

Warwick (Warwickshire)

Doll Museum (Oken's House)
Housed in an Elizabethan dwelling is an interesting collection of all kinds of dolls: china, wood, metal, fabric, and wax, as well as mechanical and musical dolls.

Wigan (Lancashire)

Wigan Museum and Art Gallery
Station Road.   Tel: 0942 41387/9
Hours: Monday to Friday, 9:30 AM to 8:00 PM; Saturday, 9:30 AM to 5:00 PM.

In addition to the collection of music in the Wigan Public Libraries, a special gallery section houses the William Rimmer collection of antique musical instruments.

Worcester Cathedral Music Library   Tel: 0905 28854
Exclusively musical collection which may be seen only by appointment.

Apply to the Cathedral organist. Contains medieval antiphonaries, Tomkins' *Musica Deo Sacra* and Barnard's *First Book of Selected Church Musick* (1641).

Conservatories and Schools

We will mention very briefly those universities with faculties of music or degree-giving departments, as well as a very few of the special schools of music (both summer and regular) which may be of interest to the foreigner. We will not even flirt with the concept of completeness, but will refer the reader for that to the extensive chapter on Education in Arthur Jacob's exhaustive *Music Yearbook*. We also advise the visitor interested in investigating the educational possibilities of Great Britain for the non-resident, to get in touch with the Department of Education and Science, Elizabeth House, York Road, London SE1 7PH for information and registration forms.

Brighton (Sussex)

University of Sussex
Stanmer House, Falmer. Tel: 0273 66755
    Offers a B.A. in music.

Bromley (Kent)

Southern Music Training Centre
Thanet Lodge, 16 Holyrood Road. Tel: 01 460 8600

Colchester (Essex)

North-East Essex Technical College, Department of Music
Sheepen Road. Tel: 0206 70271
    Grants a B.Mus. degree.

Durham (Durham)

University of Durham, Faculty of Music
Music School, Palace Green. Tel: 0385 3489
    Grants undergraduate B.A. and B.Mus. as well as advanced teaching and research degrees. Prospectus available from the Registrar and Secretary, University of Durham, Old Shire Hall, Durham.

Exeter (*Devonshire*)

University of Exeter
Knightley, Streatham Drive   Tel: 0392 77911
    Offers both undergraduate and graduate degrees in music. Courses offered in conjunction with the cathedral school.

Guildford (*Surrey*)

University of Surrey, Faculty of Music
Stag Hill.   Tel: 0483 71281
    Grants B.Mus. as well as advanced research degrees. Special courses offered in recording techniques.

Huddersfield (*Yorkshire*)

Huddersfield School of Music
The Polytechnic, Queensgate.   Tel: 0484 30501
    Grants B.A. in music.

Lancaster (*Lancashire*)

University of Lancaster, Department of Music
Music Rooms, University, Bailrigg.   Tel: 0524 65201
    Music is available in the second and third years of degree taking only. Special offerings in chamber music and ensemble playing.

Leicester (*Leicestershire*)

University of Leicester, Faculty of Music
University Road.   Tel: 0533 50000
    Degrees offered include the B.A., B.Sc., M.A., and Ph.D, the latter two in research.

Shrewsbury (*Shropshire*)

Royal Normal College and Academy of Music for the Blind
Albrighton Hall, Broad Oak,   Tel: 09396 537
and Rowton Castle.   Tel: 074378 202
    In addition to traditional studies, professional training is offered in piano technology, tuning, and repair.

Southampton (Hampshire)

University of Southampton, Department of Music
Highfield.   Tel: 0703 59122
      Degrees granted include B.A. (with honors in music), the dual B.A., the
M.Phil., Ph.D., M.A., and B.Mus. in composition.

Stoke D'Abernon (Surrey)

Yehudi Menuhin School
Cobham Road.   Tel: 266 4739
      For stringed instrument and piano students from age 8 to 18. Foreign
students are accepted.

Summer Courses

There are a great many summer courses in music given in England each year.
Some of them spring up around an occasion or a particular festival; some are
peripatetic and change locale each year. For further information on the widest
variety of courses, organized by the British Federation of Music Festivals and
the Music Teacher's Association, contact The Summer School Organizer,
British Federation of Music Festivals, 106 Gloucester Place, London W1H 3DB
(Telephone: 01-935 6371). The small selection of summer courses listed below
are arranged alphabetically according to the county in which they take place.

Berkshire

Bradfield College
Bradfield, Berkshire.
      Junior Orchestral Summer Course. Sponsored by the Ernest Read Music
Association (ERMA), 143 King Henry's Road, London NW3. Tel:
(01) 722 3020
      For children from 12 to 17.
      One week in August annually.
      For further information apply to 39 Cassiobury Park Avenue, Watford,
Hertfordshire.

Devon

The Summer School of Music Ltd.
Dartington Hall, Totnes.   Tel: 08046 2721
      Four weeks, late July to late August, annually.

The summer school combines festival, school, and holiday. Concerts, lectures, and classes designed so that the visitor may book for one week or more.

For further information: The Registrar, Summer School of Music, 48 Ridgway, London SW19.

Dorset

Canford Summer School of Music.
Canford Magna, Wimborne.
> Sponsored by Belwin-Mills Music Ltd.
> Two weeks in August.
> For further information, apply to the Admissions Officer, 230 Purley Way, Croydon CR9 4QD.

Gloucestershire

Viola da Gamba Summer School.
Cheltenham.
St. Paul's College, Cheltenham.
> One week in August.
> Information: Viola da Gamba Summer School, 'Little Critchmere,' Sholtermill, Haslemere, Surrey.

Lute Society Summer School.
St. Paul's College, Cheltenham.
> One week in August. For players and interested non-players.
> For information contact the Lute Society, 71 Priory Road, Kew Gardens, Richmond, Surrey. Tel: (01) 940 7086.

Kent

Summer School of Music.
Benenden School, Cranbrook.
> Eight days at the end of July or the beginning of August.
> For students over 18 years of age.
> For information apply to the Masters House, The Old College, Maidstone.

Surrey

Dolmetch Recorder School.
Wey Centre, Haslemere.   Tel: 0428 3619
> One week in August.

Brochures and enrollment forms may be obtained from the Secretary, Morley Copse, Morley Common, Haslemere, Surrey.

Sussex

Roedean School.
Brighton.
> Sponsored by the Ernest Read Music Association (ERMA).
> For adults over 17.
> One week in August. Symphony orchestra, string and wind ensembles.
> For information, apply to ERMA, 143 King Henry's Road, London NW3.

University of Sussex, Summer School of Music.
Music Office, Stanmer House, Brighton.
> Ten days, end of July, beginning of August.
> Brochure available upon request of The Secretary, address above.

Yorkshire

Music at Ilkley.
Ilkley.
> One week in July. Strings and winds, early English music, and recorders.
> For further information: Airedale and Wharfedale College of Further Education, Ashtofts, Mt. Oxford Road, Guiseley, Leeds.

Orff-Schulwerk Courses.
Lady Mabel College, near Rotherham.
> For further information, contact Orff-Schulwerk Courses, 31 Roedean Crescent, London SW15.

The Business of Music

For the convenience of the visitor to England who is in hot pursuit of a musical *rara avis,* we are here presenting a highly selective list of off-the-beaten-track instrument manufacturers and repairers, rare book dealers, and music antiquarians. For ease of finding, they will be listed by their specialties.

Instruments

BAGPIPES

George Alexander, 11a High Street, Shanklin.   Tel: 098386 3867
Miller Browne & Co. Ltd., New Ford, Waltham Cross,
        Hertfordshire.   Tel: Waltham Cross 29912

BASSOONS

V. Elliott, 3 Maxted Park, Harrow, Middlesex.   Tel: (01) 422 5984

BOWS

C. W. Jacklin, 25 Avondale Drive, Loughton, Essex.   Tel: (01) 508 3759
Garner W. Wilson, 36 Vinery Road,
        Bury St. Edmunds, Suffolk.   Tel: 0284 4207

BRASS INSTRUMENTS

Besson & Co. Ltd, Besson House, Burnt Oak Broadway,
        Edgware, Middlesex.   Tel: (01) 952 7711
British Band Instrument Co. Ltd., Sonorous Works,
        Deansbrook Road, Edgware, Middlesex.   Tel: (01) 952 7711

CITTERNS (See HISTORICAL INSTRUMENTS)

CONCERTINAS

C. Wheatstone & Co. Ltd., Sonorous Works, Deansbrook Road,
        Edgware, Middlesex.   Tel: (01) 952 7711

CORNETTI (See HISTORICAL INSTRUMENTS)

DRUMS

A. F. Matthews Ltd., 40 Northwick Avenue, Kenton,
        Middlesex.   Tel: (01) 907 4805
B. L. Page & Co., 18–19 Wood Street, Doncaster,
        Yorkshire.   Tel: 0302 69707

ELECTRONIC INSTRUMENTS

Wurlitzer Ltd., St. Anne's House, Parsonage Green, Wilmslow,
        Cheshire.   Tel: 09964 23046

FIDELS (See HISTORICAL INSTRUMENTS)

HARPS

Keith Theobold, Albany Cottage, Church Street, Tisbury,
        Salisbury, Wilts.   Tel: 074787 595

HARPSICHORDS

John Feldberg, 24 Pembroke Road, Sevenoaks, Kent.   Tel: 0732 51460
William Foster, 67 Ashurst Road, Tadworth, Surrey.   Tel: Tadworth 2772

Michael Johnson, Blandford Barn, Fontmell Magna,
Shaftesbury, Dorset.   Tel: 074781 248
John Paul Co., Parkway, Waldron near Heathfield,
Sussex.   Tel: 04352 2525
Dennis Woolley, 54 High Street, Haslemere, Surrey.   Tel: 0428 2696

HISTORICAL INSTRUMENTS
Arnold Dolmetsch Ltd., (early keyboard instruments)
Kings Road, Haslemere, Surrey.   Tel: 0428 51432
Christopher Monk (Cornetti, Serpents, Lysardens)
Stock Farm House, Churt, Farnham, Surrey.   Tel: 042873 5991
Ian Harwood and John Isaacs (Theorbos, citterns, bandores)
18 Barton Road, Ely.   Tel: 0353 2221
Robert Haddaway (lutes, viols)
Gayton, Norfolk.   Tel: 055384 384

OBOES AND OBOE REEDS
Anthony Aspden, 17 Battlefield Road, St. Albans,
Hertfordshire.   Tel: St. Albans 53510
J. S. Faulkes, 110 Carlton Avenue West, North Wembley,
Middlesex   Tel: (01) 904 7806

ORGANS: ELECTRIC
Bentley Organ Co., Ltd., Woodchester, Stroud,
Gloucestershire.   Tel: 045387 3243
Livingston Organs Ltd., The Abbey Mill, Abbey Mill Lane,
St. Albans, Herts.   Tel: St. Albans 64653/4

ORGANS: PIPE
Cedric Arnold, Williamson & Hyatt Ltd., The Organ Works,
Thaxted, Essex.   Tel: 037183 338
Brian H. Bunting, 24 Bury Road, Epping, Essex.   Tel: Epping 3249
Harrison and Harrison Ltd., Hawthorne Terrace, Durham   Tel: 0385 3155

ORGANS: PORTATIVE, POSITIVE, CHAMBER
John Nicholson and Peter Slater. Camden House, Sissinghurst, Kent.

PIANOS
Bentley Piano Co. Ltd., Woodchester, Stroud,
Gloucestershire.   Tel: 045387 3243
W. G. Eavestaff & Sons Ltd., 28 Spencer Street, St. Albans,
Hertfordshire   Tel: St. Albans 64518
Alfred Knight Ltd., Langston Road, Debden Estate,
Loughton, Essex.   Tel: (01) 508 3826/8

RECORDERS (See HISTORICAL INSTRUMENTS)

STRINGED INSTRUMENTS

Maurice K. Bouette, Manor House, South Clifton, Newark,
    Nottinghamshire.   Tel: 052277 276
Gilbert Garrett, Mytten House, Mytten Mews, Broad Street,
    Cuckfield, Sussex.   Tel: 0444 56162
George King, 42 High Street, Halberton, near Tiberton,
    Devon.   Tel: 0884 820 460
Alfred Langonet, 8 Little Crescent, Rottingdean, Sussex.   Tel: 0273 34178
Dolland and Norman Daines, 2 Church Street,
    Bath, Somerset.   Tel: 0225 21 452
Dennis G. Smith, 51 The Street, Ashtead, Surrey.   Tel: Ashtead 72300

BOOKSELLERS AND ANTIQUARIANS

Deval & Muir, Taylors, Bishop's Stortford,
    Hertfordshire.   Tel: 027973 312
Raymond Elgar, 31 Charles Road West, St. Leonard-on-Sea,
    Sussex.   Tel: Hastings 5405
First Edition Bookshop Ltd., c/o Middleton, Hawkins & Co.,
    82 Eden Street, Kingston-upon-Thames, Surrey.   Tel: (01) 546 4441
Sheila Gwilliam, 3 London Street, Walcott, Bath.
Holleyman & Treacher, Ltd., 21a Duke Street, Brighton.   Tel: 0273 28007
Richard Macnutt Ltd., 29 Mt. Sion, Tunbridge Wells, Kent,
    (Appt. only)   Tel: 0892 25049
Kenneth Mummery Ltd., 9 St. Winifreds Road, Bournemouth,
    Hampshire.   Tel: 0202 25170
Old Bookshop, 52 North Street, Worthing, Sussex.   Tel: 0903 20266
Second Fiddle, 27 North Street, Romford, Essex.
Wilsons, Henlion House, Cliff Road, Hythe, Kent.

Festivals

Aldeburgh (Suffolk)

Aldeburgh Festival of Music and the Arts
Festival Office, High Street Aldeburgh, Suffolk   Tel: 072885 2935
Dates: annual, three weeks in June, in addition to which there is an early edition
    called *Spring at the Maltings,* see below, and a week of opera in late summer.
    The facilities of the Aldeburgh Festival are used sporadically throughout
    the year for special events.
Performance Locations: The Maltings, Snape, Saxmundham (capacity 840).

Blythburgh Church, Blythburgh (capacity 700).

Jubilee Hall, Aldeburgh (capacity 300).

Orford Church, Orford (capacity 475).

Also used for specific occasions are the Aldeburgh Cinema and the parish church.

Box Office: open for mail bookings at the address above from March 15 to May 1. After May 3, the box office hours are: 10:00 AM to 1:00 PM and 2:15 PM to 6:00 PM daily; Saturday morning only. An advance program offering subscription advantages and priority booking can be sent by airmail to people living outside of England, by prior arrangement. They will go out two weeks earlier than the regular booking form. Requests for this priority booking form should be sent to the Festival Office during January.

Transportation: the trip by car from London can take three to four hours on a busy day. The train journey to Saxmundham from Liverpool Station in London takes two hours, the remaining seven miles covered by bus or taxi.

Accommodations: a list of housing facilities may be obtained from the Festival office.

Regularly scheduled on a daily basis are opera, art exhibitions, Festival services, concerts, recitals, lectures. The English Opera Group is the performing organization for theatrical presentations. Besides the director-founders, Britten and Pears, the names of Rostropovitch, Richter, and Dietrich Fischer-Dieskau are often associated with this festival.

Benjamin Britten and Peter Pears, who started this festival in 1948 with fellow musicians, writers, and artists, have turned the fishing village of Aldeburgh on the North Sea into an international center for music and musical theater. The grey skies and pebbly beaches which characterize this part of the country may not be to everyone's liking, nor, indeed may the Festival, which is very personalized and very special. The usual international circuit of concert artists have no place here. The programs are off the beaten track and quite raffiné. A choir concert called "Schütz and Stravinsky," may be followed by a recital by the English Consort of Viols or another event called "Wine and Music from Burgundy" (featuring both). There will surely be a rare opera beautifully staged and there may well be a lecture-demonstration on making percussion instruments. Although it is not essential, a car is useful for the visitor spending his first Festival holiday at Aldeburgh.

Spring at the Maltings

Festival Office, Aldeburgh, Suffolk IP15 5AX.

Weekend concerts in March and April. (There is also a late summer opera schedule.) The Maltings was recently rebuilt after being destroyed by fire and is a fine house with excellent acoustics. The restaurant and bar are open to ticketholders only during the intervals and following each performance.

Ashford (Kent)

Stour Music (*International Festival of Music and Art in East Kent*)

Barton Cottage, The Street, Kennington.   Tel: Ashford 23838

Dates: one week in June

Box Office: for direct mail order or ticket information, address Miss E. M. Skinner, 33 Sussex Avenue, Ashford, Kent. Tel: Ashford 21127. For information concerning patronage of Stour Music, address The Honorable Treasurer Ian Reid, 20 Bridge Street, Wye.

Concerts and recitals of seventeenth- and eighteenth-century music revolving around the person of Alfred Deller. Some of the events are offered with dinner, some with after-concert wine and cheese. The locations are the Wye Church, the Chapter House at Canterbury, the Boughton Aluph Church, and Olantigh at Wye. There are exhibitions of paintings and drawings held in conjunction with the musical events.

Bath (Somerset)

Bath Festival

Linley House, 1 Pierrepont Place.   Tel: 0225 22531

Dates: ten days from the end of May into early June.

Locations: the principal locations for performances are the Bath Abbey, the Assembly Rooms, the Guildhall, Bath University, Holy Trinity Church at Bradford-on-Avon, Wells Cathedral, Colston Hall in Bristol, Holburne Museum. Free buses are provided from Bath to all concerts taking place outside of Bath, but tickets for the buses must be obtained together with the concert tickets.

Box Office: 1 Northgate Street, Bath. Tel: Bath 63362 (after May 10th). Open daily from 10:00 AM to 5:30 PM except Sunday. Priority booking by mail from March 17; mail orders other than priority are filled as of April 5; personal and telephone reservations from May 10.

Accredited Ticket Agencies: Keith Prowse & Co. Ltd., 90 New Bond Street, London W1. Tel: 493 6000

Transportation: direct line trains for Bath, Reading, and Bristol from Paddington Station in London. By special arrangement there are late trains which return to London after concerts during the Festival. The trip takes two hours.

Symphonic concerts, solo recitals, chamber music, exhibitions, plays, lectures, and opera. There are anywhere from one to six events scheduled daily during the Festival period. They are sometimes held simultaneously, but there are things occurring as early as 9:15 in the morning up to the regular 8:00 PM concert time.

Bath is an incredibly beautiful spa town with incomparable Georgian architecture and blissful climate. The Bath Festival is of an international character and presents major performers from all over the world. The wide variety of locations in which the wide variety of events are presented gives the Festival-goer the opportunity to do considerable sight-seeing along with his music-hearing.

Bexhill-on-Sea (Sussex)

Bexhill-on-Sea Summer Festival of Arts
Bexhill Corporation, De La Warr Pavilion.   Tel: Bexhill-on-Sea 2023
Dates: held during May and September.

The Festival features evening concerts, morning lectures, wine and cheese tastings, afternoon coach rides to historical castles, supper parties, and dancing, interwoven with concerts featuring such organizations as the Hallé Orchestra.

Birmingham (Warwickshire)

Birmingham Triennial Musical Festival
City of Birmingham Estates Department, Bush House,
65 Broad Street.   Tel: (021) 235 3352
Dates: ten days in late September, early October. Next Festival 1977.
Performance Locations: Birmingham Town Hall, Congreve Street (021) 236 2392
    Aston Hall, Gosta Green   (021) 359 3611
    Museum and Art Gallery, St. Chad's Cathedral; and the
    Arts and Science Centre, Margaret Street   (021) 236 3591
Box Office: Town Hall and the usual agencies. Subscription rates are available.

Orchestral concerts by major symphonic groups, chamber music, and solo recitals. Lectures and discussions on music and related topics.

In June 1768, a musical festival was organized with the object of raising funds to build a general hospital in Birmingham. The Festival took place at a theater in King Street and in St. Philip's Church and featured important works by Handel, the composer who was so popular at the time.

Bolton (Lancashire)

The Bolton Festival of Music
Room 12, Civic Center, The Crescent.   Tel: 0204 22311, ext. 466
Dates: one month, from mid-September to mid-October in odd-numbered years.
Performance Locations: the Central Library Lecture Hall (capacity 283)
    Albert Hall, Town Hall, (capacity 600)
    Victoria Hall, Knowsley Street, and the Bolton Parish Church.

Box Office: there is no central box office. For orchestral concerts, tickets are obtainable at Harker & Howarth, 28–32 Churchgate, Bolton. (Closed Wednesdays.) (Tel: 26623). If tickets are still available at concert time, they can be purchased at the door. Otherwise, tickets may be obtained from the Entertainments Office, Town Hall, Monday to Friday from 9:30 AM to 5:15 PM.

Chamber music recitals, featuring one major chamber group in a series of concerts, popular music, solo performances, lecture recitals, and orchestral concerts by the Hallé Orchestra, the Royal Liverpool Philharmonic Orchestra, as well as midday recitals from 12:45 PM to 1:30 PM, admission free.

Brighton (Sussex)

Brighton Festival
Brighton Corporation, Royal York Buildings.   Tel: 0273 29801
Dates: two weeks in May.

A large professional international festival featuring symphony orchestras, ballet and opera companies, as well as international soloists from all over the world. The concerts take place in various theaters and halls such as the Dome, the Royal Pavilion Music Room and the Theater Royal. Each Festival has a unifying theme around which related exhibitions, discussions, and similar events are organized. Highly commercial; should be booked well in advance by writing to the address above or through leading ticket agencies in London.

Bristol (Gloucestershire)

Thornbury Arts Festival
The Aucklands, Gloucester Road.   Tel: 04544 3864
Dates: one week in May annually.

Formerly a mixture of professional and amateur competitive events, the Festival has expanded in recent years to include performances by international musicians and performing groups, such as the London Opera Group and the Welsh National Opera Company.

Bromsgrove (Worcestershire)

Bromsgrove Festival
28 Victoria Road.   Tel: 07393 73749
Dates: from mid-April into May.

More than two weeks of music, drama, and art exhibits. Concerts and recitals by international musicians; presentation of new works. A different country is chosen as the theme each year.

Cambridge (*Cambridgeshire*)

Cambridge Festival
3 Parsons Court.   Tel: 0223 58977
Dates: last week in July and the first week in August.

A variety of concerts, recitals with fringe events in pop, folk, jazz held on weekends. Attractive location, at the very least, since concerts are given in places like the Ely Cathedral and the chapels, halls, and cloisters of the Colleges.

Canterbury (*Kent*)

King's Week Festival
King's School, 25 The Precinct.   Tel: 077 62963
Dates: annually in July and August.
Place: The Marlowe Theater, St. Margaret's Street (capacity 652).

Program includes opera, ballet, and orchestral concerts, as well as solo events.

Cheltenham (*Gloucestershire*)

Cheltenham Festival
Town Hall.   Tel: 0242 21621
Dates: first ten days in July each year.
Performance Locations: Town Hall, Oriel Road (capacity 1100), St. Matthew's Church, Pittville Pump Room (capacity 350), Shaftesbury Hall, and Tewkesbury Abbey.
Box Office: Town Hall box office open every day except Sunday from 10:00 AM to 6:00 PM.
Housing: all inquiries should be addressed to the Information Bureau, Municipal Offices, Cheltenham.

There may be as many as five events scheduled for the same day, but they do not overlap. There are recitals at 11:00 AM, and there are very often visits with a composer, whose works have been featured at the 8:00 PM concert, as late as 11:00 PM. The Festival has been described as contemporary British music without tears, but this cannot describe the range and variety of the presentations, from a madrigal concert to a Beethoven recital, and from a symphony orchestra performance to an electronic music session. There are debates, discussions, tours, exhibitions, sporting events, dancing, etc.

In addition to the established policy of giving prominence to music by living British composers, the Festival examines contemporary trends in other countries. In addition, it provides an opportunity to look more closely at the work of a composer in depth or to review the works of a period that has become démodé. The particular orientation of the Festival includes looking back before Bach and forward to the Aleatory Age. The town is quiet and pleasant and the ten days of the Festival are well filled.

Chester (*Cheshire*)

Chester Festival
Town Hall.   Tel: 0244 40144
Dates: triennial Festival will next take place for ten days early in July, 1976.
      Centering about the Chester Mystery Plays, the triennial Festival also features chamber music recitals, organ recitals, and symphonic programs. A series of films of operas are also included, as well as fringe events such as parades, garden parties, and historic exhibitions. The ancient walled city of Chester offers a unique location for these events.

Chichester (*Sussex*)

Southern Cathedrals Festival
The Festival Secretary, The Festival Office, The Cloisters.
Mailing address: 2 St. Richard's Walk, Chichester (1977); or Festival Secretary,
      6 The Close, Winchester, Hampshire (1978); or Festival Secretary, 5 The
      Close, Salisbury, Wiltshire (1976)
Box Offices: in all cases the box office and the Festival Secretary address given
      above are identical. In addition, it is important to note that priority
      bookings may be obtained from that Secretary through the month of May.
      General bookings begin on June 1 in all three locations.
      The Southern Cathedrals Festival, which rotates between Chichester, Winchester, and Salisbury, is held for four days in late July. Dating from 1961, in its present form, the Festival features the best of the English cathedral repertoire with an emphasis on works demanding large resources. In addition to the magnificence of the individual cathedrals, the Festival offers the visitor innumerable fringe events involving the libraries, important local halls, exhibitions on related subjects, and tours of local gardens, and sites of historic interest.

Dorchester (*Oxford*)

Dorchester Abbey Festival
Festival Office, The Manor House, Manor Farm Road   Tel: 086732 593
Dates: one week in early October.
      Presentation of pageant-operas and chamber music in the extraordinary Abbey.

Durham (*Durham*)

Durham Music Festival
9 Neville's Cross Villas.   Tel: 0385 2274
Dates: annually from October to end of November.

Concerts, opera, art exhibitions and recitals held in the great Hall of Durham Castle.

Contemporary British composers' works are emphasized with one major orchestra participating each year.

Edington (*Wiltshire*)

Edington Priory Festival of Church Music
Tudor Cottage, Edington near Westbury.   Tel: 038083 453
Dates: one week to ten days, late in August or early September.

Choral and instrumental (i.e., organ) music of a sacred nature.

There is no admission charge for any of the concerts held in Edington Priory, but there is a collection taken for expenses. The church holds approximately 400.

Gloucester (*Gloucestershire*)

Three Choirs Festival
Mailing address: 8 College Green, Gloucester (1977);
        or Festival Secretary, 25 Castle Street, Hereford (1976);
        or 5 Edgar Street, Worcester (in 1978).
Box Office: before July 11, priority postal bookings may be arranged by writing
        to the appropriate festival office listed above. After that date, a ticket office
        will be opened at the appropriate location.

The Three Choirs Festival, which rotates between Gloucester, Worcester, and Hereford, is held from the Sunday service to the following Friday evening late in August. Dating from about 1715, when it was called the Musick Meeting, the Festival is now the oldest surviving music festival in Great Britain. In addition to the presentation of choral music in superb settings, the Festival further serves the cause of contemporary music in that living composers are regularly commissioned to write for it. In each of the three cathedral towns, related events are organized along with the regular performances which traditionally begin with Sunday matin service. There are morning rehearsals, chamber concerts, afternoon concerts and lectures, and evening events on a grand scale. All three choirs perform and also sing evensong at 5:15 PM each day.

Glyndebourne (Sussex)

Glyndebourne Festival Opera

Glyndebourne, Lewes, Sussex.   Tel: 0273 81231

Dates: late May to early August.

Box Office: main Box Office is at Glyndebourne, Lewes, Sussex. Tel: Ringmer 411. Box Office hours: until May 21, weekdays from 10:00 AM to 5:00 PM, Saturdays from 10:00 AM to noon. After May 22, on days of performance, the box office is open from 10:00 AM to 8:00 PM. When there is no performance, from 10:00 AM to 5:00 PM. Booking by mail only from April 1. Telephone applications from April 30.

Note: It is very difficult to obtain tickets for this festival and it is strongly recommended that arrangements be made as far in advance as possible.

London Branch Office of Box Office: Ibbs & Tillett, 122/124 Wigmore Street (Tel: [01] 935–1010). The hours of service are Monday to Friday, 10:00 AM to 5:00 PM and Saturday 10:00 AM to noon.

Transportation: two full hours of driving time are required for the fifty-four miles from London. There are trains which leave Victoria Station and make special flag stops at Glynde Station. The train trip takes just over one hour.

Customary Dress: evening dress is strongly recommended.

Every year since its founding in 1934, at least four, and sometimes five, operas are performed in repertory. The performances are held on Sunday, Wednesday, Thursday, Friday, and Saturday from late May until the beginning of August. The starting time for each opera varies according to the length of the work, but it always begins in the late afternoon, between 4:30 and 5:55. A dinner break is traditional during the Long Interval. Seating capacity of the house is 769. No standing room.

The Glyndebourne Festival Opera was founded in 1934 as a private venture and labor of love by the late John Christie and his wife, the opera singer Audrey Mildmay. They built an opera house on the grounds of their Sussex manor house in which they could give opera performances of a standard that was unknown at that time in England. The project received instantaneous recognition and attracted many of the world's finest artists as well as consistently full houses. The manor house is still a family home, occupied by the founder's son, George Christie and his family. Mr. Christie is the chairman of Glyndebourne Productions Ltd., the company which administers the Festival. They have founded a touring company and preparations are being carried along which will allow the excellent company to remain together for more than the summer season, by providing them with performances in other places.

Glyndebourne remains the prestige opera festival of Europe, and a social event. The production level is kept very high; the works chosen are invariably of great interest. Some of the operas which have been presented in recent years include Cavalli's *La Calisto,* Nicholas Maw's *The Rising of the Moon,* a contemporary operatic comedy, Tschaikovsky's *Pique Dame* and Monteverdi's *Il Ritorno d'Ulisse in Patria.*

Guildford (Surrey)

The Guildford Festival
University of Surrey Union, Guildford Surrey   Tel: Guildford 65017/131
Dates: first ten days in March.
Performance Locations: the Cathedral (capacity 1500), the Civic Hall (capacity 1040), as well as the University Hall, Christ Church on Waterden Road, the Congregational Church, St. Mary's Church, the Yvonne Arnaud Theatre (capacity 568), and Lecture Theatre D at the University.
Box Office: booking form with full schedule, prices, and seating plan is available. Tickets can be reserved by telephone for a maximum of three days. Box office open from Monday to Friday from 10:00 AM to 4:00 PM. Tel: 70679. Tickets also available at the University Bookshop, University of Surrey, or the Central Library, North Street, Guildford. If there are any tickets left, they will be put on sale one hour before a concert begins at the concert hall.
  Choral and orchestral concerts, recitals, contemporary music, folk, jazz, theater, symposia, poetry readings, films, exhibitions.
  The Guildford Festival, founded in 1969, has as its goal the provision of something for everyone. Hence the wide range of performance types and performing groups, from the Royal Philharmonic Orchestra to Gilbert Biberian's Omega Players (a ten-guitar ensemble playing contemporary works).

Harrogate (Yorkshire)

Harrogate Festival of Arts and Sciences
Royal Baths.   Tel: 0423 68387
Dates: the first two weeks in August.
Performance Locations: Royal Hall, Ripon Road (capacity 1312), as well as in many of the local churches and the Assembly Rooms at the Royal Baths (each seats 300). There is an opera house and theater on Oxford Street, which seats 800, and a festival theater is planned for ballet and drama.
Box Office: Festival box office at the Royal Baths opens on June 7 for priority booking. General booking opens on June 21. Box office open Monday to Saturday from 11:00 AM to 6:00 PM.
Authorized agents: American Express International, 6 Haymarket, London SW1, and its worldwide branches.
Housing: write to The Information Bureau, Parliament Street, Harrogate, for a list of hotels and boarding houses.   Tel: (0423) 65912.

Concerts, plays, ballet, exhibitions, talks, discussions, poetry readings, etc.

The basic aim of the Harrogate Festival, now established as one of Britain's leading annual festivals, is to bridge the arts and sciences via the social sciences. Included in the comprehensive program is a selection of chamber, orchestral and chamber music concerts, literary events and poetry readings, as well as discussion groups and seminars. New and experimental works are featured, and subjects of concern to society at large are examined. Harrogate itself is a very lightly modernized Victorian spa town and the atmosphere and architecture are quite delightful. The position of the town within Yorkshire makes it an ideal jumping off place from which to visit the Cistercian Abbeys.

Hereford (Herefordshire)

Three Choirs Festival (see Gloucester)

Haslemere (Surrey)

Haslemere Festival

Jesses, Grayswood Road, Haslemere, Surrey   Tel: 0428 3818
Dates: two weeks in mid- to late July.
Box Office: Haslemere Hall, Haslemere, Surrey.   Tel: 90428 2161
Hours: 9:00 AM to 12:30 PM Monday to Saturday before July 3. After July 3, from 9:00 AM to 4:00 PM. Booking opens to the members of the Dolmetsch Foundation on February 21 and to the general public on March 6.
London Ticket Agent: Chappell's Box Office, 50 New Bond Street, London W1.
          Tel: 629 7600
Transportation: fast trains leave Waterloo Station in London at fifty minutes past the hour. The trip takes fifty-five minutes. The Hall is seven minutes' walk from the station.

Concerts and recitals of early instrumental and vocal music, on instruments and in styles as authentic to their period as possible under the direction of the Dolmetsch family.

Hintlesham (Suffolk)

Hintlesham Festival

Hintlesham Hall.   Hintlesham 268
Dates: from late July to late August on weekends.

A regular feature of this festival is the group Opera Rara, who do indeed perform rarely heard operas by well-known composers. In addition, there are programs of Elizabethan music, piano recitals, and programs devoted to offbeat music.

King's Lynn (Norfolk)

King's Lynn Festival
Guildhall of St. George, King Street.   Tel: 0553 4725
Dates: the last week in July.
 Founded in 1951, the King's Lynn Festival serves up good solid festival fare in a charming setting. The programs include symphony concerts, recitals, poetry readings, drama, lectures, films, and exhibitions of painting and sculpture. The Corn Exchange, which seats 1,000, and the St. George Guildhall (capacity 373), as well as one of the beautiful churches and historic buildings in the town, are used for the week of performances.

Leeds

Leeds Musical Festival
40 Park Lane.   Tel: 0532 22153
Dates: biennial festival held for one week in May, even-numbered years.
 Choral and orchestral concerts held in the Civic Theatre (seating capacity 1500).

London

Camden Festival
Libraries and Arts Department, St. Pancras Library,
100 Euston Road, NW1.   Tel: (01) 278 4444
Dates: one month in Spring.
Performance Location: the events take place throughout London's northern precincts, but the opera performances are held for the most part in the Collegiate Theatre, Gordon Street, London WC1 (capacity 500–600).
Box Office: Town Hall, Euston Road, NW1.
Hours: Monday to Friday, 10:00 AM to 6:00 PM; Saturday from 10:00 AM to noon.
 Performances of all kinds, concerts, recitals, chamber music, solo, choral, dance; poetry readings, exhibitions, lectures, but most especially, rarities from the operatic archives, and the choicest repertory in all of Great Britain. (For example, in 1972, they put on Rachmaninov's *Aleko,* Massenet's *La Navarraise,* Smetana's *The Secret,* Delius's *Koanga,* and Donizetti's *The Prima Donna's Mother is a Drag.*)

English Bach Festival (*see Oxford*)

Festival of the City of London
City Festival Management, Harold Holt Inc.,
122 Wigmore Street, W1.   Tel: (01) 935 2331

Dates: biennial; two weeks in mid-July in even-numbered years.
Performance Location: the Festival takes place within the "Square Mile" in the center of London embracing St. Paul's Cathedral, Tower of London, the Mansion House, and the historic city halls. Chamber concerts are held in the livery halls, and the various guild halls are used for solo recitals. The Carl Flesch International Violin Competition takes place during the Festival and the winner will appear with Yehudi Menuhin in a concert.
Box Office: Harold Holt Ltd., 122 Wigmore Street, London W1. Phone as above.

Henry Wood Promenade Concerts

Royal Albert Hall, SW7   Tel: (01) 589 8212
BBC Publicity Department, 12 Cavendish Place, W1.   Tel: (01) 580 4468
Dates: mid-July to mid-September.
Box Office: from mid-June until two weeks before the Proms begin, tickets will be sold by mail order only. Envelopes should be marked "Proms" in lefthand corner and sent directly to Royal Albert Hall. From two weeks before the opening concert, postal, telephone, or personal applications at the box office or through ticket agents. Telephone bookings accepted between 10:00 AM and 6:00 PM only. Standing room places are available at the door.
Note: Tradition has it that the last night is the great gala at the Proms. Therefore the last night tickets, other than season subscriptions, are allocated by ballot or the luck of the draw. The atmosphere on this occasion is worth making an effort to get one of these rare tickets.

Symphony concerts, chamber music, opera, solo recitals—a total of over fifty major performance events, all of them broadcast by the BBC—some of them televised—and characterized by a great historical range and a free composition of the individual concerts. Seating capacity 7,300; standing 2,500.

The Promenade Concerts began in 1896 and in the ensuing years have not only changed their character completely, but have become a major force on the British music scene. Originally conceived as a light-music series for the summer season, the Proms programs leaned heavily on overtures and war-horses of the more programmatic kind. The emphasis was on the nineteenth century and the purpose was as much social as it was musical. Gradually, the change in audience attitudes and in program patterning allowed the series greater liberty. Today, medieval Florentine music is paired with Elliott Carter's Double Concerto, followed tomorrow by Tim Souster and Terry Riley, like as not. *Pierrot Lunaire* may be rubbing elbows with the *Diabelli Variations* or some Byrd motets. The number of performing organizations annually involved with the Proms is only slightly less breathtaking than the number of soloists and conductors and the extraordinary breadth of their backgrounds and origins.

With very few exceptions, all concerts begin at 7:30 PM and are, again with very few exceptions, usually sold out.

Dress is exceedingly informal.

In addition to the Camden and City of London Festivals already described, there are borough festivals annually, biennially, and triennially throughout the city. From Barking to Westminster, from Haringey to Kensington and Chelsea, festivals of differing lengths, contents, and degrees of regularity are organized and presented within the individual boroughs. For up-to-date information concerning the latest developments in these activities, apply to The Greater London Arts Association, 27 Southampton Street.

South Bank Summer Music (*see Royal Festival Hall, p. 14*)

Ludlow (Shropshire)

Ludlow Festival Society

4 Vernolds Common, Craven Arms.   Tel: Onibury 212
Dates: last week of June through first week in July.
Performance Location: Ludlow Castle (seating capacity 1100), as well as other
    venues which seat between 400 and 500. No standing room.
Box Office: Festival Box Office, Castle Gates, Ludlow Castle. Tel: Ludlow 2150
Hours: daily from 10:00 AM to 4:00 PM except Sunday.

Performances include one Shakespeare play annually, orchestral concerts, and puppet theater, as well as recitals, chamber music, and ballet.

Newcastle-upon-Tyne (Northumberland)

Newcastle Festival

7 Saville Place.   Tel: 0632 28520
Dates: one month from mid-September to mid-October.
Performance Locations: range all over the city in as wide an arc as the swath cut by
    the events themselves, but the principal locations are the City Hall, the
    Theatre Royal, the University Theatre, the Gulbenkian Theatre, and the
    People's Theatre.
Box Office: mail orders may be made in advance to the Central Box Office, City
    Hall, Northumberland Road, Newcastle 1. Booking opens one month
    before the Festival begins, but printed booking forms with advance notice
    of the programs are available in the late spring.
        Personal booking is made at the theater in which the event is taking
        place:
        Theatre Royal Box Office, Grey Street, Newcastle 1.
                                                    Tel: 22061
        University Theatre Box Office, Barras Bridge, Newcastle 1.
                                                    Tel: 23421
        People's Theatre Box Office, Stephenson Road, Newcastle 6.
                                                    Tel: 655020

Also: Record Centre, 3 Grainger Market, Newcastle 1. Tel: 24410
J. G. Windows Ltd., Grainger Arcade, Newcastle 1. Tel: 21356
Central Box Office (see above).

Widest possible range of events: classical concerts featuring English and foreign symphony orchestras of major stature; opera by the Glyndebourne touring company and the Scottish Opera company; drama by several established and experimental groups; pop, folk, band, and choral concerts; jazz concerts; dance recitals; poetry readings by Northern poets; and lunchtime recitals. Choral works at the Cathedral, lectures, and art exhibitions.

This has been characterized as a "with it" festival in a lively, interesting town and decidedly worth a trip into the Northern Marches.

Norwich (*Norfolk*)

Norfolk and Norwich Triennial Festival of Music and the Arts
Deacon House, Brundall. Tel: 0603 713385
Dates: ten days in mid-October. Next Festival 1976.
Location of Performance: St. Andrews Hall (capacity 1063), the Norwich Cathedral, Maddermarket Theatre (capacity 323).
Box Office: Festival Office, 24 Exchange Street, Norwich 60G. Mail order booking opens on the first of July. Direct booking from August 1 at: George Wortley Ltd., 2 Charing Cross, Norwich.

Symphonic concerts, choral and orchestral concerts, recitals, opera, organ recitals, discussion seminars between composers and students, drama, art exhibitions, and special late-night events.

If only for the glorious cathedral in which some of the performances are given and for the medieval churches with which the town is peppered, this festival would be worth visiting. Originating in 1824, these triennial festivals are the mainstay of Norwich musical life. (For some interesting insights into nineteenth-century county artistic life, we refer you to the *Annals of the Norfolk and Norwich Triennial Musical Festivals 1824–1893* by R. H. Legge and W. E. Hansell, 1896.)

Nottingham (*Nottinghamshire*)

Nottingham Festival
54 Milton Street. Tel: 0602 40661
Dates: two weeks in mid-July.

A festival with a difference, providing entertainment on a huge scale for all tastes. Events include symphony orchestras, jazz bands, folk and pop music, dance, D'Oyly Carte opera, poetry readings, and, above all, drama at one of Europe's foremost theaters, the Nottingham Playhouse. In addition, there is an international horse show, Morris dancing, medieval banquets, and a massive firework concert and pageantry to conclude the festivities on the Trent Embankment.

Oxford (and London)

English Bach Festival
15 South Eaton Place, London SW1.   Tel: (01) 730 5925

Dates: approximately three weeks in April and May.

First half of Festival held in the following locations in Oxford: Blenheim Palace, Christ Church Hall, Holywell Music Room, Town Hall, New College Chapel, Weston Manor, Sheldonian Theatre, and Christ Church Cathedral.

Second half of Festival held in the following locations in London: Royal Albert Hall, Queen Elizabeth Hall, St. Paul's Cathedral, Royal Festival Hall, Purcell Room, Westminster Cathedral, St. John's, Smith Square, the Round House, German Institute, St. Margaret's, Westminster, and the Brompton Oratory.

Box Office: for Oxford concerts: Charles Taphouse Ltd., 3 Magdalen Street. For London Concerts: English Bach Festival Box Office, 155 Charing Cross Road, London WC2, Tel: (01) 434 1171. Except for: Royal Albert Hall Box Office, London SW7, Tel: (01) 589 8212 and Royal Festival Hall Box Office, London SE1, Tel: (01) 928 3191. General booking opens first week in March for the Oxford concerts and the third week in March for the London concerts. Complete schedule available for the coming season from the English Bach Festival Trust at the beginning of each year.

Concerts and recitals featuring the music of Bach and his contemporaries and predecessors as well as rare nineteenth-century and contemporary music.

The English Bach Festival celebrated its tenth anniversary in 1973. Dividing its activities between Oxford and the beautiful historical halls of the various colleges, and London with its incredibly active musical life and informed audiences, it has become in rather short order one of the most important occasions on the European musical calendar.

Each year the programs are planned around specific themes relating to composers, anniversaries, or specific countries. A point is made of performing rarely-heard works as well as contemporary and commissioned ones. In each year's schedule, one may find unusual events (such as an opening concert at a castle, in costume), timely ones (such as a memorial concert on the anniversary of Stravinsky's death), and elaborate productions (such as a dressed premiere of Xenakis' *Oresteia*).

Reading (Berkshire)

Reading Festival of the Arts
Students, Union, Reading University, Whiteknights Park.   Tel: 0734 5591

Dates: last two weeks in June.
Performance Locations: Abbey Ruins, Town Hall, Small Town Hall, St. Laurence Church, University Great Hall, and the Progress Theatre. Seating capacities range from 100 to 1100.
  Concerts, plays, art exhibitions, photographic exhibitions, poetry readings.

St. Albans (Hertfordshire)

International Organ Festival, St. Albans
The Abbey. Tel: St. Albans 64738 or 51810
Dates: one week at the end of June to the beginning of July, biennially. Next festival 1975. The Abbey can accommodate 1500, not necessarily within sight of the performers.
Box Office: postal bookings open in mid-April. Telephone inquiries may be made between 10:00 AM and noon daily. After June 14, the office is open daily from 10:00 AM to 6:00 PM.
  Organ recitals, two competitions with public elimination sessions, lecture and demonstration recitals, and instrument exhibits. Master classes.

Salisbury (Wiltshire)

Southern Cathedrals Festival (see Chichester)

Southend-on-Sea (Essex)

Southend-on-Sea Festival of Music and the Arts
Cliffs Pavilion, Station Road, Westcliff-on-Sea. Tel: 0702 47382
Dates: two weeks at the end of September, beginning of October; triennial. Next festival 1976.
Performance Locations: College Theatre, and Cliffs Pavilion.
Box Office: Cliffs Pavilion Box Office, open daily from 10:00 AM to 8:00 PM. Sunday from 10:00 AM to 6:00 PM.
  Musical comedy, drama, oratorio, folk dance, song and music, orchestral symphony concert.

Wangford (Suffolk)

Wangford Festival
Festival Office, Wangford, Beccles. Tel: 050278 235
Dates: second or third weekend in July.
Box Office: Festival office, Wangford, or Barclay's Bank, Halesworth, Suffolk.
Tel: Halesworth 2218
  Concerts, art exhibitions, and drama with an emphasis on young British

composers. Performances are held in churches and various halls in the area. Standing room available if necessary.

Winchester (Hampshire)

Southern Cathedrals Festival (see Chichester)

Windsor (Berkshire)

Windsor Festival

140 Peascod Street.   Tel: Windsor 68835

Dates: two weeks at the end of September to the beginning of October.

Performance Locations: State Apartments of Windsor Castle by permission of Her Majesty the Queen. Also in St. George's Chapel and in the theater, halls, and chapel of nearby Eton College.

Box Office: Ian Hunter, Harold Holt Ltd., 122 Wigmore Street, London
Tel: (01) 935 2331

Concerts, orchestral, solo, and chamber recitals. Menuhin Festival Orchestra.

Woburn Green (Buckinghamshire)

Woburn Festival

Fern Villa, Princess Road, Bourne End.   Tel: 06285 24547

Dates: two weeks during September.

Performance Locations: Red Lion Clubhouse, Woburn Parish Church, Hedsor Court, Bourne End Community Centre, Burleighfield House, Cliveden House (Taplow), and the Wilton Park Theatre (Beaconsfield). Seating capacity average: 400.

Box Office: Woburn Festival Box Office, Woburn Green, High Wycombe, Bucks. Tel: 06285 25775. General booking begins mid-August. Patron booking, August 1. The box office opens for personal applications on August 22. It is open Monday through Saturday from 10:00 AM to 7:00 PM.

Operas, plays, concerts, exhibitions, recitals, readings, and related social events.

Worcester (Worcestershire)

Three Choirs Festival (see Gloucester)

Competitions

Throughout Great Britain there are annual competitive festivals held in towns and villages from Aberdeen in the north of Scotland to Carrickfergus on the east coast of Ireland; from Cardigan in the west of Wales to Truro in deepest Cornwall. They are colorful, festive, and bursting with tradition and local talent. The competitive element is the spur urging the native amateurs to greater and greater achievements. County championships, medals, and even prizes of twenty or thirty pounds are regularly vied over. Music advisors and adjudicators are brought from different parts of the country—trophy collectors are discouraged and the motto is "Pacing each other on the road to excellence." The visitor finding himself in Bromsgrove in July would do well to listen to the woodwind competition at the Catshill Music Festival. And the traveler fortunate enough to be in Leeds in April will long remember the Yorkshire-Over-Sixties Choir Festival—a unique experience! For an exhaustive and very definitive list of these local competitions, contact the British Federation of Music Festivals (originally called the British Association of Competitive Music Festivals), 106 Gloucester Place, London W1H 3DB. Tel: (01) 935 6371. They publish an annual calender with full particulars for participants as well as spectators.

The competitions we will list here are of a different stripe. They are all of international standing and aim at a very high level of professionalism, and they all offer prestigious rewards. We have included only those which are well-established and place no restrictions on applicants based on national origin. Where precise information was not available, we have tried to provide an exact address where that information may be obtained.

Leeds

Leeds International Pianoforte Competition
Triennial: 1978, 1981, etc. in September.
Age Limit: 30 years old.
Awards: prizes totaling 2,500 pounds sterling plus numerous concert engagements.
Deadline: May 1 of year of competition.
For information apply to: Edmund Williamson, Administrator, University of Leeds, Leeds LS2 9JT.   Tel: 0532 31751

London

Carl Flesch International Competition
Violin and Viola.

Biennial. Competitions take place in July of even-numbered years.

Age Limit: 32 years old.

Awards: first prize £1,000, Carl Flesch Medal, engagements. Five additional prizes ranging from £600 to £50.

Deadline: May

Apply to: The Competition Office, Guildhall School of Music and Drama, John Carpenter Street, London EC4.   Tel: (01) 353 7774

Clements Memorial Chamber Music Competition

Work for any combination of three to six instruments, lasting between fifteen and thirty minutes.

Biennial. Competitions take place in October of odd-numbered years.

For information apply to: F. V. Hawkins, St. Margaret's, Broomfield Avenue, London.   Tel: (01) 886 7009

Emily Anderson Prize for Violin Playing

Held biennially in June of odd-numbered years. Sponsored by the Royal Philharmonic Society.

Age limits: over 18 and under 30 years of age.

Award: approximately £500.

Apply to: The Royal Philharmonic Society, 29 Exhibition Road, London SW7.
                                Tel: (01) 584 5751

Light Music Society Competition for New Orchestral Works

Work for light orchestra, maximum nine minutes.

Annual.

Deadline: December 31.

Apply to: 10 Heddon Street, Regent Street, London W1.

Maggie Teyte Prize

Female singers.

Biennial. Held in September, even-numbered years.

Age limit: 30 years old.

For information apply to: 75 Woodland Rise, London N10.

Menuhin Prize for Young Composers

Triennial: 1976, 1979, etc.

For information apply to: Marylebone Library, Marylebone Road.
                                Tel: (01) 723 1764

Stella Murray Memorial Prize

Held annually in May.

Age limit: 25 years old for instrumentalists; 30 years old for singers.

For information apply to: Miss A. Strange, Royal Over-Seas League, Park Place, St. James's Street, London SW1.　　　　　　　Tel: (01) 493 5051

Radcliffe Music Award
Work for string quartet and voice.
Held irregularly.
Age limit of composer: 40 years old.
Apply to: Mrs. B. Whatmore, 11 Coulson Street, London SW3.

Manchester

BBC Piano Competition
Triennial: 1977, 1980, etc.
Age limit: 30 years old.
For information apply to: P.O. Box 27, Manchester M60 1SJ. Tel: (061) 236 8444.

Stroud (Gloucester)

Stroud Festival International Composers Competition and Stroud Festival Antiphon Competition
Annual competition. Each year for a different group or combination or for a different prescribed text.
Age limit of composer: 40 years old.
Deadline: Entries close end of April. Judging takes place end of October.
For information concerning awards, combinations, time limits, etc., apply to: Stroud Festival Antiphon Competition, St. Mary's Hill, Woodchester, Stroud, or Stroud Festival International Composers Competition, Lenton, Houndscroft Lane, Houndscroft, Stroud.

St. Albans (Hertfordshire)

International Organ Festival Interpretation Competition and International Organ Festival Improvisation Competition
Biennial competition held in conjunction with the International Organ Festival (see p. 143). Held in odd-numbered years, end of June, beginning of July.
Age limit of competitors: Interpretation Competition, 31 years old. Improvisation Competition, 36 years old.
Awards: Interpretation: first prize: £100 and broadcast recital; second prize; £50 and broadcast recital.
Improvisation: first prize: £75; second prize: £40.
Deadline for application: limited to 22 applicants. Deadline end of March. There

is a registration fee: £4.00 for Interpretation; £2.00 for Improvisation.
Competitors remain anonymous throughout the competitions. Six judges.
Public elimination sessions. The finals are played on the great Harrison
organ in the abbey church. Selection of applicants by April 10.

Address: Artistic Director, International Organ Festival Society, 31 Abbey Mill
Lane, St. Albans.

Periodicals

By actual count, there are at the present time one hundred and fifty-one music
periodicals being published on a regular basis in England alone. Of course,
many of these are of a highly specialized nature (*Piano Tuners' Quarterly* [in
Braille]) not likely to be of great interest even to the most dedicated amateur,
but many are fine magazines with international circulation (*The Gramophone,
The Musical Times,* etc). On the pages following, we have listed the outstanding
music periodicals of interest to the music lover. We give the reader as much
information as is necessary to secure the periodical by mail, since easy newstand
access, even in London, is not widespread. As a general rule, you will find
music magazines for sale at the major stationers and in the foyer of the main
concert halls throughout the country.

About the House (publication of the Friends of Covent Garden)
Royal Opera House, Covent Garden, London WC2.
quarterly
> Gives news of the activities of the opera and ballet companies at home
> and on tour.

The Angel
79 Ashacre Lane, Offington, Worthing, Sussex.   Tel: 0903 60927
twice yearly
> Church music for choir schools.

Audio
Fleetway House, Farringdon Street, London EC4.   Tel: (01) 634 4344
monthly

Blues and Soul Music Review
Contempo International Ltd., 42 Hanway Street,
London W1.   Tel: (01) 636 2283
bi-weekly

Bells and Bellringing
19 Lonewood Way, Hadlow, Tonbridge, Kent.
quarterly

Braille Music Magazine (in Braille)
Royal National Institute for the Blind, 224–228 Great Portland Street,
London W1.   Tel: (01) 387 5251
monthly

Brio (Publication of the International Association of
Music Libraries, UK branch)
The Music Room, National Library of Scotland, Edinburgh.
twice yearly

British Catalogue of Music
Council of British National Bibliography Ltd., 7–9 Rathbone Street,
London W1.   Tel: (01) 580 3681
twice yearly and annually

Chelys (Journal of the Viola da Gamba Society)
123 Russell Lane, Whethsone, London N20.
annual

Church Music (publication of the Church Music Association)
15 Denbigh Road, London W1.   Tel: (01) 727 6387
six times a year

Composer (publication of the Composers Guild of Great Britain)
10 Stratford Place, London W11.   Tel: (01) 499 8567
quarterly

The Consort (publication of the Dolmetsch Foundation)
Fonthill, Hurtmore, Godalming, Surrey.
annual

Crescendo International
Crescendo Publications Ltd., 122 Wardour Street,
London W1.   Tel: (01) 437 8892
monthly
        Jazz, etc.

Delius Society Newsletter
45 Redhill Drive, Edgward, Middlesex.

Early Music (publication of Oxford University Press)
37 Dover Street, London W1.   Tel: (01) 629 8494
quarterly

English Church Music (publication of the Royal School of Church Music)
Addington Palace, Croydon.   Tel: (01) 654 7676
annual

English Dance and Song (publication of the English Folk Dance and Song Society)
2 Regent's Park Road, London NW1.   Tel: (01) 485 2206
quarterly
     A *Folk Directory,* published by the same society, appears annually.

Galpin Society Journal (publication of the Galpin Society)
Phillimore & Co., Ltd., Shopwyke Hall, Chichester, Sussex.
annual

The Gramophone
General Gramophone Publications Ltd., 177–9 Kenton Road,
Harrow, Middlesex.   Tel: (01) 907 2010
monthly
     Respectable and reliable record magazine. Reviews and evaluations.

Hallé Magazine (Magazine for the Music Lover)
Editorial Committee, Hallé Club, 30 Cross Street,
Manchester.   Tel: (061) 834 8363
annual

Hi-Fi News and Record Review
Link House Publications Ltd., Link House, Dingwall Avenue,
Croydon.   Tel: (01) 686 2599
monthly

Jazz Times (publication of the British Jazz Society)
10 Southfield Gardens, Twickenham, Middlesex. Tel: (01) 892 0133
monthly

Jazz Journal
Jazz Journal Ltd., 27 Soho Square, London W1. Tel: (01) 437 1222
monthly

The Lute Society Journal
The Hermitage, Barton Square, Ely, Cambridgeshire.
annual

Living Music
44 Berners Street, London W1.   Tel: (01) 580 7811
quarterly

Making Music (publication of the Rural Music Schools Association)
Little Benslow Hills, Hitchin, Herts.   Tel: (0426) 3446
three times a year

Melody Maker
IPC Specialist and Professional Press Ltd., 161–166 Fleet Street,
London EC4.   Tel: (01) 353 5011
weekly.
    Contains information pertaining to clubs, entertainers, jazz musicians, etc.
    Publishes an annual *Year Book*.

Music and Letters (publication of the Oxford University Press)
44 Conduit Street, London W1.   Tel: (01) 450 8080
quarterly
    Important and serious scholarly publication.

Music and Musicians
Hansom Books, Artillery Mansions, 74 Victoria Street,
London SW1.   Tel: (01)799 4452
monthly
    Concerned with the current world of serious music and its performance.
    Features a highly detailed music guide for the month of the issue.

Music Review
104 Hills Road, Cambridge.   Tel: (0223) 51571
quarterly
    Scholarly publication.

Music Yearbook
Bowker Publishing Ltd.
annual
    Cloth-bound compendium, first published in 1972 for the year 1972–73.
    Sponsored by the National Music Council of Great Britain, a survey and
    evaluation of the preceding year in music is offered in the form of a series

of articles. In addition, comprehensive directories cover every aspect of musical activity in the United Kingdom. Invaluable reference tool.

Musical Events
13 Heath Drive, Hamstead, London NW3.   Tel: (01) 435 1315
monthly
> A concert-goers guide book with a complete diary of events in the music world, record reviews, and music-book reviews.

Musical Opinion
87 Willington Street, Luton, Beds.   Tel: 0582 30963
monthly
> Articles, news, reviews of books and music, reports and criticism of concerts and recitals. Regular columns, coming events and feature articles. Concerns itself a good deal with organ music and the problems of organists.

The Musical Times (published by Novello & Co. Ltd.)
37 Soho Square, London W1.   Tel: (01) 437 1222
monthly
> A very lively as well as learned publication ranging in content from book reviews, record reviews, radio and television news, church and organ music news, to a highly detailed and invaluable London Music Diary for the month of the issue. Includes serious discussions on technical, philosophical, and aesthetic subjects written by highly qualified experts.

Opera
6 Woodland Rise, London N10.   Tel: (01) 883 4415
monthly plus one extra issue each year
> One of the best opera magazines in the world. Surveys the activities in opera houses throughout the world as well as in England.

Proceedings of the Royal Musical Association
Blackwell's Music Shop, 39 Holywell Street, Oxford.   Tel: 0865 49111
annual
> This is the journal of the British musicological society.

Record Collector (A magazine for collectors of recorded vocal art)
Hanover Publications, 61 Berners Street, London W1.   Tel: (01) 637 0507
monthly

Records and Recording
Hansom Books, Artillery Mansions, 75 Victoria Street,
London SW1.   Tel: (01) 799 4452
monthly

Recorded Sound (publication of the British Institute of
Recorded Sound)
29 Exhibition Road, London SW7.   Tel: (01) 589 6603/4
quarterly
> Serious publication which concerns itself with sound archive activities in
> Britain and throughout the world.

Rolling Stone
Straight Arrow Publishers Ltd., 28 Newman Street,
London W1.   Tel: (01) 580 6045
twice a month
> Rock-and-roll publication which has become very popular in the United
> States.

Strad (monthly journal for professionals and amateurs of all
stringed instruments played with a bow)
Lavender Publications, 27 Soho Street, London W1.   Tel: (01) 437 1222
monthly

Tempo (A quarterly review of modern music)
Boosey and Hawkes, 295 Regent Street, London W1.   Tel: (01) 580 2060
quarterly
> Serious discussions on contemporary music of all kinds and contemporary
> music activity throughout the world.

Scotland

GLASGOW (Lanarkshire)

Glasgow, the largest city in Scotland, would appear to be a place which sprang into existence with the industrial revolution. For the most part, the city has the brash, bustling, and straightforward look of a community whose development has been largely shaped by practical necessity recently amended by scientific planning and contemporary urban trends. Glasgow was, however, founded in the sixth century by the missionary St. Mungo, who became its patron and the namesake of its fine twelfth-century Gothic cathedral. The University, which dominates the city from atop Gilmorehill, was established in 1451 by Bishop William Turnbull. In the sixteenth century, Glasgow was described as "a flourishing cathedral city reminiscent of the beautiful fabrics and florid fields of England," and in 1727, Daniel Defoe spoke of it as one of the cleanest and most beautiful cities in Great Britain. It was not until the late eighteenth century, when the dredging and widening of the River Clyde improved the city's navigation and gave the shipbuilding trade an enormous impetus, that Glasgow began to grow, quickly expanding beyond the old town limits. Today this industrial giant straddling the Clyde is a thriving urban center. Its parks are superb, its educational facilities excellent, and its libraries and museums first-rate. Glasgow has a musical life which is of a very high caliber. Its local institutions, described below, are of international quality, and its performance facilities, although hardly sumptuous, are more than adequate. There is no official music season in Glasgow; the concert life continues throughout the year and the Glaswegians are proud to the point of chauvinism of their Scottish musical traditions.

Guides and Services

Clyde Tourist Association
Information Centre, George Square.   Tel: 221 9600

Opera Houses and Concert Halls

The Athenaeum Theatre
The Royal Scottish Academy of Music and Drama
St. George's Place.   Tel: 332 5294
Seating capacity: 500
    The Athenaeum Theatre is part of the main Academy building. It is used
for the presentation of dramatic and operatic performances given by students
of the Academy. Several operas are given a series of performances each session.
Admission to these performances is by invitation only, obtainable from the
Academy without charge. The Theatre was extensively modernized and ren-
ovated in 1967.

Bute Hall (see University of Glasgow)

City Hall
Candleriggs, 205 Hope Street.   Tel: 339 8594/6
Seating capacity: 1200
    Principal location for concerts in Glasgow, the City Hall, built partly
above a large market, is host to the Scottish National Orchestra when it is
performing in its home town, as well as to the many visiting orchestras and
soloists who regularly appear here.

The Fore Hall (see University of Glasgow)

Kelvin Hall
Kelvingrove Park.   Tel: 334 1185
    Large exhibition building, it is used for concerts of the National Orchestra,
the BBC Scottish Symphony and visiting groups.

King's Theatre
335 Bath Street.   Tel: 221 0298
Seating capacity: 1643   Box Office Tel: 248 5125

The King's Theatre is one of the three "legitimate" theaters of Glasgow and the place where many pre-London dramatic touring productions tryout. It is listed here because, in the absence of a suitable opera house, it is the home of that extraordinary infant of Scotland, the Scottish Opera, when it performs on home territory in Glasgow. (For further details concerning this ten-year-old company, see pp. 161–162.)

Randolph Hall (*see University of Glasgow*)

Stevenson Hall
The Royal Scottish Academy of Music and Drama
St. George's Place   Tel: 332 4101/2
    The concert hall of the Academy in which musical performances by students as well as faculty and invited artists are given. An annual *Programme of Musical Events,* available from the Academy upon request, gives details of all the events scheduled at Stevenson Hall as well as the Athenaeum Theatre and other locations where Academy-sponsored musical events are held. Mid-day concerts (1:10 PM) are held free of charge at Stevenson Hall and constitute a regular feature of Glasgow musical life.

University Chapel (*see University of Glasgow*)

University of Glasgow, Department of Music
14 University Gardens, The University.   Tel: 339 8855, ext. 571
    As part of the myriad activities of this very active music department, there are innumerable concert series, discussed in greater detail elsewhere, held regularly in one of the many halls of the University. Bute Hall is used whenever the services of an organ are required; Randolph Hall for solo and small chamber recitals; Fore Hall for lecture recitals; and the University Chapel for music of a sacred nature with or without use of organ. The Hunterian Museum (see below) is the site of exhibitions often related to musical activities. (For further details, see p. 159.) Important musical events of a religious nature are held at the Glasgow Cathedral, Paisley Abbey, and St. Mary's.

Libraries and Museums

Glasgow Museums and Art Galleries
Department of Archaelogy, Ethnography and History,
Art Gallery and Museum, Argyll Street.   Tel: 334 1134/5/6

Hours: daily 10:00 AM to 5:00 PM. Sunday, 2:00 PM to 5:00 PM.

Collection: in the Department of Archaeology, et al., there is a sizable collection of musical instruments, both European and non-European, comprising the following collections: the Dyer collection of Japanese instruments; a collection of European musical instruments lent to the Museum in 1941 by the Scottish National Academy of Music; the Glen Instrument Purchase (1942) of European musical instruments and the Farmer Purchase (1945) of European and non-European instruments.

Mitchell Library, Music Room [Ben. 43]

Glasgow Public Library, North Street.   Tel: 248 7121

Hours: daily 9:30 AM to 9:00 PM; Sunday, during October to February, 2:00 PM to 8:00 PM.

Collection: approximately 50,000 volumes including extensive reference collection; Moody-Manners collection of orchestral scores; Gardiner collection on European folk music; Turnbull and Sheard collections; Kidson collection of seventeenth- and eighteenth-century British vocal and dance music.

Founded in 1874, the Mitchell Library is the largest public reference library in Scotland and one of the most important in Great Britain.

Royal Scottish Academy of Music and Drama Library [Long 357]

58 St. George's Place.   Tel: 332 4101

Hours: Monday to Friday, 9:30 AM to 7:30 PM.

The well-appointed Library contains excellent reference sections with appropriate reading rooms, as well as an extensive lending-library for the use of students only. The Orpheus Room contains a gramophone section and soundproof studios, as well as a large collection of recordings. Permission for outsiders to use the collection may be obtained upon request to the Senior Librarian.

Trinity College Library [Ben. 44]

Lynedoch Place.   Tel: 332 2080

Hours: Monday to Friday, 9:30 AM to 5:00 PM. Closed Christmas, New Year's, and ten days at Easter. Also for one month, usually August, during the summer.

Collection: music in the general library collection is chiefly liturgical. Includes the Mearns hymnological collection.

People's Palace (Old Glasgow Museum)

Hours: Daily, 10:00 AM to 5:00 PM; Sunday, 2:00 to 5:00 PM. Tel: 554 0223

An early nineteenth-century house containing a collection of portraits, documents, and a selection of early musical instruments.

Hunterian Museum and Library

University Avenue.

Hours: Monday to Friday, 10:00 AM to 5:00 PM; Saturday, 10:00 AM to noon.

The museum contains the collection of coins, medals, and surgical appliances bequeathed to it by its benefactor, Dr. William Hunter. In the library, there is a large collection of illuminated manuscripts, early printed books, religious musical scores and manuscripts and a portrait of Mozart's wife.

University of Glasgow. The following are all part of the University:

Euing Musical Library, University of Glasgow [Ben. 41]

The Library.   Tel: 339 8855

Hours: Monday to Friday and Saturday morning. Closed Christmas, New Year's and about two weeks from late June to early July.

Admission: special permission, apply in writing to the University Librarian.

Collection: the Euing collection of approximately 5,000 volumes forms the core of this separate department in the University Library. Many *unica*, including early theoretical works, sacred and liturgical music, and collections of English broadside ballads of the sixteenth to eighteenth centuries.

Glasgow University Library [Ben. 42]   Tel: 334 2122

Collection: contained within the general University Library are extensive musical collections aside from those in the Euing Musical Library. They include the following: The Drysdale, Farmer, Lamond, MacCunn, McEwen, Zavertal, Hunterian, Ferguson and 1883 bequests of Thomas Stillie, Glaswegian critic who contributed 760 volumes of full scores and operas.

Hague Collection of Wind Instruments

Department of Music, 14 University Gardens.

The collection of single and double flageolets, flutes, oboes, clarinets, bassoons, and brass instruments, originating between 1790 and 1890 may be seen in the music department between 10:00 AM and 7:45 PM during term.

Scottish Music Archive

University of Glasgow, 7 Lilybank Gardens.   Tel: 334 6393

Hours: Weekdays 9:00 AM to 5:30 PM; Saturday from 9:30 AM to 12:30 PM. Also open on Monday and Wednesday evenings. Closed during August and during the week between Christmas and New Year's.

Admission: no special credentials necessary.

The Archive was established in 1969 for the documentation and study of Scottish music of all periods.

Conservatories and Schools

The Royal Scottish Academy of Music and Drama
58 St. George's Place.   Tel: 332 4101
One of the principal colleges of music in Great Britain, equivalent to the
Royal Academy or the Royal College of Music in London. Offers degree or
degree-equivalent courses. Teaching and performing diplomas. A limited
number of places are available for students from overseas. For information
apply to The Secretary, address above.
The Academy publishes a *Programme of Musical Events* annually, in which
school-sponsored concert activities for the season are listed. In addition to
mid-day concerts by students and faculty, there are recitals by invited artists
and cooperative ventures with the music department of the University of
Glasgow and the Scottish BBC Orchestra.

University of Glasgow, Department of Music
14 University Gardens.   Tel: 339 8855
Offers undergraduate as well as Master's and higher research degrees in
music. The music department publishes a brochure annually, entitled *Music
in the University of Glasgow,* available upon request from the department of music
at the address above. The extent of the concert activities run and paid for
by the University and open to the public is impressive indeed. In addition
to concerts of medieval and Renaissance music, solo recitals, orchestra and
chamber orchestra concerts, popular music concerts and novelties of a highly
engaging nature, there are many interesting series such as the McEwen Bequest,
a triennial series made possible by a bequest from Sir John Blackwood McEwen
for the promotion and performance of chamber music works by composers
of Scottish race and descent. Traditionally the series takes place late in April.
Musica Nova takes the form of a public forum devoted to rehearsal, discussion,
and performance of new works. It takes place on five successive days at the
end of April and is held predominantly on campus with one or two large-scale
concerts at the City Hall. A new University group, Cantilena, has recently
been formed for the performance of Renaissance and Baroque Music.

Musical Organizations

BBC Scottish Symphony Orchestra
Broadcasting house, Queen Margaret Drive.   Tel: 339 8844
The BBC Scottish Symphony Orchestra was founded in 1935 as the BBC

Scottish Orchestra. Though most of its activities are confined to broadcasts from the Glasgow studios, it appears from time to time at the Edinburgh International Festival, the London Proms, and it tours Scotland.

The Scottish National Orchestra
150 Hope Street.   Tel: 332 7244

The Scottish National Orchestra may trace its ancestry to the group formed solely to provide accompaniment for the first Glasgow performance of Handel's *Messiah* given in the City Hall in 1844. It was not until 1873, however, that interest in orchestral music was sufficiently stimulated to warrant mustering a professional orchestra to be based in Scotland with a view to providing both orchestra and choral concerts on a regular seasonal basis. A Guarantee Fund was established (this practice survived until 1950), an orchestra was formed and engaged for a set number of weeks on a full-time salaried basis, and it was planned to give concerts all over Scotland.

In 1891 the Scottish Orchestra Company Limited was formed in competition with the Glasgow Choral Union, which was still running its concerts in Glasgow and Edinburgh. The new Scottish Orchestra, with a strength of seventy-one, was conducted by George Henschel. It embarked on a twenty-five-week season with concerts every two weeks—thirteen classical and fourteen popular concerts in addition to six chamber concerts. The first concert was held on October 30, 1893. An amalgamation of the Orchestra with the Choral Union finally took place in 1898. By 1916, the orchestra gave about sixty concerts each season: fourteen Tuesday and fourteen Saturday night concerts in Glasgow; fourteen Monday concerts in Edinburgh, and the rest in Dundee and several other cities and towns.

A parade of conductors reading like Who's Who in Orchestra Music held posts with the Scottish Orchestra, which was quite unpredictable from one season to the next in quality and personnel. The Scottish National Orchestra Society Limited was registered in response to a nationwide desire to establish a symphony orchestra which would perform in Scotland throughout the entire year. The new company took over the job of organizing such as a series, and issued a prospectus. Today, under the leadership of Alexander Gibson, the Scottish National Orchestra strongly challenges the supremacy long held by the Hallé Orchestra in technique and musical response. It has, by a common acknowledgment, extended its scope far beyond the provincial confines of Scotland to the world of music at large. The repertory is wide and the programming imaginative. Its tours are extensive and its season extended. Its full personnel currently is ninety-six and its duties include playing for the Scottish Opera.

Scottish Opera Ltd.
39 Elmbank Crescent.   Tel: 248 4567

Since its foundation by Alexander Gibson in 1962, Scottish Opera has established itself as one of the most exciting and rapidly expanding companies in the United Kingdom. Its reputation has been built up through a series of enterprising, exciting, and often brilliantly successful productions which have attracted the attention of press and public both in Britain and abroad. By 1969 it had developed to the point that the *New Statesman* was able to say in a review of *The Trojans,* that Scottish Opera "at its best is unsurpassed by any other opera company in Western Europe." The basic performance plan provides for a main spring season consisting of two weeks in Glasgow at the King's, two in Edinburgh (also at the King's Theatre), one in Aberdeen (at His Majesty's Theatre), and, recently, one in Perth as well. The company promotes works by Scottish composers (Robin Orr's *Full Circle* and John Purser's *The Undertaker,* for example) and participates in the Opera for All program by touring throughout Scotland and England.

The Business of Music

Instruments: Manufacture, Repair, and Distribution

Bradley Music Ltd. (Retail sale of musical instruments)
    69A West Regent Street.   Tel: 332 1830
J. D. Cuthbertson & Co. (Repair of electric organs and pianos)
    21 Cambridge Street.   Tel: 332 5382
Wm. Hill & Son and Norman and Beard (Pipe organ builders)
    66/70 McCullock Street.   Tel: 429 6336
Grainger & Cambell (Bagpipes)
    1103 Argyle Street.
A. Smilie & Sons. (Violins)
    368 Great Western Road.

Retail Music Shops

Alexander Biggar Ltd. (Music, records, instruments)
    271–275 Sauchiehall Street.   Tel: 332 1830
Chisholm Hunters (Music, records)
    27–29 Trongate.
J. T. Forbes Ltd. (Music, records, instruments)
    122 West Nile Street.   Tel: 332 1016
Glasgow Music Centre (Music and books on music)
    164 Buchanan Street.

Gramophone Shop (records)
    1017 Argyle Street   Tel: 248 6410
McCormack's Music Ltd. (Music, records, instruments)
    29–33 Bath Street.   Tel: 332 6644
Mozart Allan (Music, wholesale and retail)
    84 Carlton Place.   Tel: 429 0274
Whylie and Lochhead Ltd. (Music and instruments)
    45 Buchanan Street   Tel: 221 3880

EDINBURGH (Midlothians)   Tel. prefix: (031)

Edinburgh is the capital of Scotland, a city which is also a county and a royal burgh. It stands on the southern side of the Firth of Forth; its seaport is Leith, which is about two miles northeast of the center of the city. It is 44 miles northeast by east of Glasgow and 373 miles north by northwest of London. To its south stand the Pentland Hills; to the east, Edgebucklin brae and Musselburgh (long famed for its mussels, and the distich: "Musselburgh was a burgh when Edinburgh was nane/Musselburgh'll be a burgh when Edinburgh's gane"), and on the west flows the Almond River. Edinburgh is spectacular in its natural beauty, rich in romantic adornment and fascinating in its historic and literary associations. It offers the strongest of contrasts: at its heart is the castle which dominates the city. It is perched on a rock that juts out 443 feet above sea level and the building itself towers 270 feet above the street. This has been a fortress site since the seventh century. In front of the castle stands the Old Town; the witch's hat shape of the turrets of the buildings give the overall look of a medieval burgh, with sinuously winding cobblestoned streets. In truth, most of the buildings date back only to the sixteenth century. North of the main thoroughfare, Princes Street, however, is the Georgian New Town—with its eighteenth-century buildings of grey stone, its wide streets. The showpiece of this area is Charlotte Square, designed by Robert Adam in 1791, spacious, with terraces, crescents, and Georgian urbanity.

    The history of the city may be traced back to a hill fort in the sixth century, but real documentation only begins with the reign of Malcolm III in the eleventh century. Of all the events connected with Edinburgh, none compares in intensity and operatic improbability with the period in which Mary Stuart, Queen of Scots, figured. Both the palace and the abbey of Holyrood are to this day closely associated with the tragic queen.

    Edinburgh has long been the cultural center of Scotland. Here the youngest of her universities adds luster to urban life with its internationally-respected schools and fabulous libraries and collections. The Edinburgh International Festival (see pp. 178–179), since its establishment in 1947, has focused attention on the beautiful city for the three event-packed weeks each year when the diversity and excellence of its presentations bring flocks of tourists and music lovers from far and wide to the city. However, there is an active music life all year long. The Scottish National Orchestra, which is based in Glasgow, performs the programs in Edinburgh on Friday evenings, which it then repeats in Glasgow on Saturday evenings all season. The Scottish Opera divides its season evenly, in three equal parts, between Glasgow, the capital, and the rest of Scotland. In addition to the normal measure of visiting and touring artists who find their way to this urban center, there is a concentration of offbeat and experimental musical events around the Reid School of Music and its faculty and student body (see p. 169). There is, in addition, a tradition of pageantry which plays a significant role in the musical life of Edinburgh. Also, during the summer, the great parks and gardens of the city—of which there are proportionately more than in any other city in the United Kingdom— abound with outdoor entertainments such as Scottish dancing and bagpipe playing, military bands, and special orchestral concerts of great variety.

Guides and Services

City of Edinburgh Tourist Information and Accommodation Service
1 Cockburn Street.   Tel: 226 6591

Scottish Tourist Board
2 Rutland Place, West End.   Tel: 229 1561

What's On in Edinburgh

Published monthly by the City of Edinburgh Public Relations Department from April to October. Available free in hotels or at the Information Bureau, City Chambers, High Street. Diary of events and entertainments in the city with programs, locations, times, and prices.

Opera Houses and Concert Halls

Assembly Hall
8 North Bank Street.   Tel: 225 6028
    Used for chamber recitals.

Church Hill Theatre
Morningside Road.   Tel: 447 7596
Seating capacity: 379   Box Office Tel: 447 7597
    Small chamber hall used for solo recitals and special concerts all season long as well as during the International Festival.

Freemasons' Hall
George Street.   Tel: 225 5304
Seating capacity: 500   Box Office Tel: 225 2424
    Used during the Festival as well as for musical and non-musical events throughout the year. Chamber music, solo recitals, etc.

Gateway Theatre
41 Elm Row.   Tel: 556 2883
    Used primarily for recitals and chamber music events. In use during the Festival for daytime concerts.

King's Theatre
2 Leven Street, Tollcross.   Tel: 229 4840
Seating capacity: 1485   Box Office Tel: 229 1201
    During May and December, the Scottish National Opera presents its Edinburgh season in this theater, which is otherwise used for legitimate theater or visiting ballet companies. Used extensively for staged productions during the Festival.

Leith Town Hall
Ferry Road.   Tel: 554 7295
Seating capacity: 1442
    Somewhat outside the center of the city, the Leith Town Hall serves the area of Leith, the port city of Edinburgh. Symphonic and orchestral concerts as well as choral groups and special visiting performers are usually seen here. Used during the Edinburgh International Festival for daytime concerts.

Reid Concert Hall
The University, Teviot Place   Tel: 667 1101, ext. 2573
Seating capacity: 314

Royal Lyceum Theatre
Grindlay Street.   Tel: 229 4353
Seating capacity: 1292
    Predominantly a legitimate theater, their all-year-round season of dramatic productions is often supplemented by a short season of visiting opera company or ballet performances.

St. Cecilia's Hall
Niddry Street, Cowgate.   Tel: 667 1011
    Built in 1792 by Robert Mylne, who modeled it after the Teatro Farnese in Parma, it was used by the Musical Society of Edinburgh until 1802. In 1960, it was purchased by the University to serve as a concert hall and to house part of the Raymond Russell Collection (see p. 168).

Usher Hall
Lothian Road.   Tel: 229 7607
Seating capacity: 2752
    This is the Edinburgh home of the Scottish National Orchestra, where it presents its regular season on Friday evenings throughout the year. It is, as well, the location for symphonic concerts by visiting groups. During the International Festival season, Usher Hall is occupied every evening with the major musical event of the Festival, be it a visiting orchestra from London, Amsterdam, New York, or Bournemouth.

    Music of a liturgical nature is frequently performed at the Cathedral Church of St. Mary and at the Cathedral Church of St. Giles.

Libraries and Museums

Edinburgh Public Library [Ben. 34, Long 140]
Central Library, George IV Bridge.   Tel: 225 5584
Hours: Monday through Friday, 9:00 AM to 9:00 PM; Saturday to 1:00 PM. Closed
    regularly for September holidays, January 1 and 2, Good Friday, and
    Christmas.
Collection: the music holdings include the Edinburgh Musical Society Archive,
    the Marr bequest (eighteenth-century music), the Cowan and Niecks
    bequests and a substantial collection of Scottish music.

National Library of Scotland [Ben. 36, Long 285]
George IV Bridge.   Tel: 225 4104

Hours: Monday to Friday, 9:30 AM to 8:30 PM; Saturday from 9:30 AM to 1:00 PM. During July, August and September, closed Monday, Tuesday, and Friday at 5:30 PM. Closed Christmas day, January 1 and 2, Good Friday.

Collection: the music holdings include late nineteenth-century British prints as well as the Handel collection of A. J. Balfour, the Berlioz collection of Hopkinson, the Glen & Inglis collection of Scottish music, the Cowan collection of psalters and hymnals, the Julian Marshall library of Handel scores and librettos. The manuscript department holds early Scottish music, especially for bagpipe, as well as Percy Grainger manuscripts.

The National Library, founded in 1682 as the Library of the Faculty of Advocates, is one of the four largest libraries in Britain, containing something over three million books as well as a large collection of manuscripts. It is the national copyright library and is a depository for all publications printed in Scotland. A reader's ticket is essential in order to use this reference library. It is obtainable by application to the special bureau set up in the library for that purpose. Foreigners need passport identification.

National Museum of Antiquities of Scotland
1 Queen Street. Tel: 556 5984
Hours: weekdays from 10:00 AM to 5:00 PM; Sunday from 2:00 PM to 5:00 PM.

Situated in the same building as the Scottish National Portrait Gallery, the National Museum of Antiquities contains the most comprehensive collection in existence of the history and everyday life of Scotland from the Stone Age to the present. Established in 1781 by the Society of Antiquaries of Scotland, the collections include a representative range of instruments made in Scotland (wind, string, and keyboard), in addition to those which belonged to well-known Scots, and traditional instruments.

New College Library [Ben. 37, Long 141]
The University, Mound Place. Tel: 225 8400
Hours: Monday to Friday, 9:00 AM to 10:00 PM. Closed on January 1.

Separate theological section of the University of Edinburgh Library, formerly the Free Church College or United Free Church College Library, it is primarily for the use of the divinity faculty, the ministers in training for the Church of Scotland, or doing post-graduate work. For admission, apply to the Library. Credentials are necessary.

Reid Music Library [Ben. 38, Long 142]
Alison House, Nicolson Square. Tel: 667 1011, ext. 2471
Hours: Monday to Friday, 9:30 AM to 5:00 PM; Saturday 9:30 AM to noon in term. For admission, apply to the Librarian.

This is the library for the faculty of music of the University and its students. Approximately 50,000 volumes, including the bequests of Sir Donald Tovey, the Niecks bequest, and the Beethoven collection donated by the late Prof. P. Weiss. There is also an interesting collection of stringed, keyboard, and wind instruments on display at the Library. They hold the General John Reid collection of flutes.

Royal Scottish Museum
Chamber Street.   Tel: 225 7534
Hours: Monday to Friday, 10:00 AM to 6:00 PM; Saturdays 10:00 AM to 5:00 PM;
    Sundays 2:00 PM to 5:00 PM.
    Situated to the west of the Old College of the University of Edinburgh, the Royal Scottish Museum, founded in mid-nineteenth century, combines collections of exhibits which reflect human endeavor not only in Scotland, but in other countries. It is the largest comprehensive museum of science and art (excluding painting) in the British Isles. Among its many collections, it holds a fine group of keyboard, woodwind, and stringed instruments.

The Russell Collection
St. Cecilia's Hall, The University of Edinburgh.
    This extraordinary collection of early keyboard instruments was presented to the University of Edinburgh in 1964. The instruments are representative of most significant countries and periods. A catalog was published in 1968, prepared by Newman and Williams.
    The collection is housed in four separate places: the hall designed by Robert Mylne for the Musical Society of Edinburgh in 1762 and used until the end of the century. This is a first-floor hall, originally oval, with a large room below; the Freemason's Room, adjoining the hall on the first floor and built in 1812; the adjoining small premises to the north thrown in during the nineteenth century; and the premises beneath the 1812 room. There are twenty-eight instruments in all on display, including a pentagonal spinet dated 1585, an Italian harpsichord of 1600, a Hitchcock bentside spinet of circa 1705, and a Ruckers harpsichord of 1637, to name but a few.

Scottish United Services Museum
The Castle.   Tel: 225 2533
    The only museum in the United Kingdom dealing with all three services in all periods of their history. The displays of uniforms, headdresses, arms and equipments, military musical instruments, medals, engravings, and prints housed in the castle, illustrate the history of the armed forces of Scotland.

Signet Library [Ben. 39]
Parliament Square.   Tel: 225 6138
    Originally called the Library of the Society of Writers to the Signet, it is

a law library today with a small collection of theoretical and historical works on music and a small collection of Scottish airs.

University of Edinburgh Library [Ben. 35]

George Square.   Tel: 667 1011

Hours: Monday through Saturday. Closed the last week in June and public holidays. For admission, apply to the Librarian.

The Library has a small but excellent collection contained within the general University library holdings. There are approximately 5,000 titles, including early Scottish manuscripts, early eighteenth-century French music books and Marjorie Kennedy-Fraser's recordings of Gaelic songs.

Conservatories and Schools

University of Edinburgh, Faculty of Music

Old College, South Bridge.
The Reid School of Music, Park Place.
Alison House, 12 Nicolson Square.
Tovey Memorial Room, 18 Buccleuch Place.

Offers undergraduate as well as graduate and higher research degrees in music.

Heriot-Watt University

Chambers Street.

Modern, fee-paying school dispensing a curriculum of musical education.

Musical Organization

Scottish National Orchestra, (see p. 161).

Although the SNO is officially and physically based in Glasgow, its annual season is divided roughly into three equal parts: Glasgow, Edinburgh, and miscellaneous engagements in such places as Dundee, Aberdeen, Ayr, etc. The same concert which is presented on Friday evening at Usher Hall in Edinburgh is again performed on Saturday evening at Town Hall, Glasgow. Separate booking arrangements are maintained for the Edinburgh season and are handled as follows:

Box Office: Edinburgh Bookshop, 57 George Street.   Tel. 225 4296

Bauermeister Booksellers, 19 George IV Bridge.   Tel: 225 7236
Season tickets available only at the Edinburgh Bookshop, but single seats may be obtained at either shop.

The Educational Institute of Scotland
46 Moray Place.   Tel: 225 6244
Member organization of the National Music Council of Great Britain.

The Saltire Standing Conference on Music
483 Lawnmarket.   Tel: 225 7780
The Saltire Society devotes itself to questions concerning Scottish musical culture. It provides a clearinghouse for information and ideas concerning the future and the direction which Scottish music is taking and the problems basic to the cultivation and preservation of the Scottish traditions in music.

Scottish Arts Council
19 Charlotte Square.   Tel: 226 6051
As the Scottish branch of the Arts Council of Great Britain, it is the function of this organization to develop and improve the knowledge, understanding, and practice of the arts; increase the accessibility of the arts to the public throughout Scotland; and to advise and cooperate with Government departments, local authorities, and other bodies on any matter concerned with the aforementioned objectives.

The Business of Music

Instruments: Manufacture, Sale and Repair

Henry Carter Pianos, 15 Gilmore Place.	Tel: 229 4066
J. T. Forbes Ltd. (Instrument sale)	
62 South Clerk Street.	Tel: 667 4407
William Sinclair & Son Ltd. (Bagpipes)	
1 Madeira Street, Leith.	Tel: 554 3489
Mev Taylor (Instrument sale)	
9 Clifton Terrace.	Tel: 337 5951
Henry Wills & Sons Ltd. (Pipe organ builders)	
City Organ Works, 80a Pleasance.	Tel: 667 5306

Retail Music Shops

Hi-Fi Corner, 1 Hadington Place.	Tel: 556 7901
Rae, Macintosh & Co. Ltd. (Music, records, instruments)	
39 George Street.	Tel: 225 1171
Pete Seaton Ltd. (Music and instruments)	
18 Hope Park Terrace.	Tel: 667 3844
Gordon Simpson Ltd. (Records and instruments)	
6–8 Strafford Street.	Tel: 225 6305
Wilson and Son (Music, instruments, records)	
121 Nicholson Street.	Tel: 667 1748

Cities briefly noted:
ABERDEEN (Aberdeenshire)   Tel. prefix: (0224)

Concert Halls

His Majesty's Theatre
Rosemount Viaduct.   Tel: 27467
Seating capacity: 1820   Box Office Tel: 28080

There is an annual one-week spring season by the Scottish Opera and an occasional autumn and winter season of even shorter duration. The theater is also used by visiting ballet and opera groups.

Music Hall
Union Terrace.   Tel: 23456
Seating capacity: 1775

One of the finest buildings in Union Street, it was designed with a six-column portico by Archibald Simpson in 1820 as the Assembly Rooms, to which the Music Hall was added in 1858–9 by James Matthews. It is used regularly by the Scottish National Orchestra for its Tuesday evening concert series.

Tickets may be obtained from Munro's Tourist Agency, 130 Union Street.
Tel: 29373

Church concerts are given at St. Machaars Cathedral in the Great Northern Road and at The West Church at Hyde Park Corner.

Libraries and Museums

Aberdeenshire County Library [Long 3]
14 Crown Terrace.   Tel: 23444
Hours: Monday to Friday, 9:00 AM to 5:30 PM; Saturday 9:00 AM to 12:30 PM.
   Important music collection of reference books and gramophone records.

University Library, King's College [Ben. 1, Long 2]
High Street, Old Aberdeen.   Tel: 40241
Hours: Monday to Friday, 9:00 AM to 11:00 PM; Saturday 9:00 AM to 5:00 PM;
   Sunday noon to 5:00 PM.
   Music in general library. Approximately 9,000 titles, books and music.
Collection includes libraries of Gavin Grieg and Forbes Leith as well as the
Taylor psalm collection. Library founded in 1494.

Aberdeen University Anthropological Museum
Hours: weekdays 10:00 AM to 5:00 PM.   Tel: 40241
   Housed within the University compound, the Anthropological Museum
contains an excellent collection of early Scottish musical instruments, including
a dulcimer serpent, Highland and Lowland bagpipes, harps, flutes and other
winds.

Schools

Aberdeen University
Department of Music, Powis Gate, College Bounds,
Old Aberdeen.   Tel: 40241
   Undergraduate degree as well as Mus.M.A. and ordinary M.A. offered.

The Business of Music

C. Bruce Miller & Co. Ltd. (Music, instruments, records)
   51–53 George Street   Tel: 20278/9

DUNDEE (Angus)   Tel. prefix: (0382)

Concert Hall

Caird Hall
City Square.   Tel: 22399
Seating capacity: 3,080
   The Scottish National Orchestra gives a regular Wednesday night series every season, repeating the program which they do on Tuesday evenings at Aberdeen. Caird Hall also houses the occasional performances by the Scottish Opera and touring ballet companies and guest orchestras.
   Tickets may be obtained from Larg & Sons Ltd., 16–24 Whitehall Street, Dundee.   Tel: 26061

Libraries and Museums

City Art Gallery and Museum
Albert Institute, Albert Square.   Tel: 25492
   The Museum contains, in addition to an excellent archaeological collection, Scottish silver, rooms devoted to Egyptology, and the Simpson collection of keyboard instruments.

Dundee Public Libraries [Long 129]
Central Library, Albert Institute, Albert Square.   Tel. 24938/9
Hours: Monday to Friday, 10:00 AM to 9:00 PM; Saturday 10:00 AM to 5:00 PM. Closed during legal holidays.
Collection: folksong collection in reference library; music books and scores in Central Lending Library. Approximately 5,000 volumes. Holdings include the Wighton collection of national music, some 600 volumes printed chiefly in the early nineteenth century, concerning Scottish music almost exclusively.

Dundee University Library [Long 130]   Tel: 23181
Hours: Monday to Friday, 9:00 AM to 10:00 PM. (to 5:00 PM in vacation); Saturday 9:00 AM to noon.

Admission: students and faculty except at the Librarian's discretion.
Collection: working library, including the Carnegie edition of *Tudor Church Music.*

Schools

University of Dundee
    Originally incorporated with the University of St. Andrews (see p. 175), Dundee attained independent status in 1967 and now offers an arts degree in music.

The Business of Music

J. T. Forbes Ltd. (Musical instruments)
    89 Methergate.   Tel: 23353
Larg & Sons Ltd. (Music, instruments, records, concert tickets)
    16–24 Whitehall Street.   Tel: 26061

SAINT ANDREWS (Fife)

Concert Halls

Buchanan Hall
The University.   Tel: St. Andrews 4411
Seating capacity: 400

Town Hall
2 Queens Gardens.   Tel: St. Andrews 2301
Seating capacity: 364

Younger Graduation Hall
The University.   Tel: St. Andrews 4411
Seating capacity: 1000

Libraries and Museums

St. Andrews University Library [Ben. 90, Long 363]
South Street.   Tel: St. Andrews 4333
Hours: Monday to Friday, 9:00 AM to 9:00 PM; Saturday, 9:00 AM to 12:15 PM.
    during term. During vacations, Monday to Friday, 10:00 AM to 4:00 PM.
    Closed Christmas, New Year, Good Friday.
Collection: general music collection in the university library. Acquired the Finzi
    collection of manucripts dating from the eighteenth century and earlier
    in 1966.
    The University Library was founded in 1611 and incorporates the Library
of Saint Andrews College which had been established in 1500.

Conservatories and Schools

University of St. Andrews, Department of Music
Kennedy Hall.   Tel: St. Andrews 4343
    Degrees granted include MA (Honours) as well as an ordinary MA in
music.
    The University of St. Andrews is the oldest in Scotland, having been
founded in 1410.

Scottish Amateur Music Association Summer School
John Burnet Hall and Kinnessburn Hall.
    Each year, for one week in July, the Scottish Amateur Music Association
sponsors a summer school session at St. Andrews. There are three courses given:
an instrumental course, vocal course and an opera workshop.
    For information, address all correspondence to Scottish Amateur Music
Association, 7 Randolph Crescent, Edinburgh EH3 7TE.

SCOTLAND, GENERAL

Miscellaneous Concert Halls Not Previously Mentioned

Motherwell (Lanarkshire)

Civic Centre
Windmillhill Street.
Seating capacity: Concert Hall, 1200
                    Theater, 400   Tel: 0698 66166
    Opened in December 1970, the new Civic Centre design was the result
of a national competition for the best arts complex plan. The Centre contains,
in addition to offices, public buildings, and shops, a concert hall and theater
fully equipped to the most modern standards.

Stirling (Stirlingshire)

MacRobert Centre
University of Stirling.   Tel: 0786 61081
Seating capacity: 500
    The MacRobert Centre was opened in September, 1971. It is at the center
of the new University overlooking the Airthrey Loch and the Ochil Hills. It
is regularly used for concerts, and for the annual two-week Festival held in
mid-May, as well as the two-day seminar held in June and organized by the
Composer's Guild of Great Britain (Scottish branch).

Libraries and Museums

Blair Atholl (Perthshire)

Blair Castle and Atholl Museum
Hours: weekdays, 10:00 AM to 6:00 PM; Sundays from 2:00 to 6:00 PM from
    May to October. Also open Easter weekend, Sundays and Mondays in
    April.
    Situated in beautiful surroundings, this large whitewashed mansion dates

from 1269 and contains magnificent collections of china, pictures, furniture, lace, Jacobite relics and musical instruments, including a positive regal (reed organ) by Loosemore dated 1650, Highland and Lowland bagpipes from 1800, and a North Highland shepherd's Pipes of Pan.

Schools and Conservatories

Dalkeith (Midlothian)

Newbattle Abbey College.   Tel: (031) 663 1921
    Offers weekend programs in April for beginning and intermediate recorder players.

Dunferline (Fife)

Carnegie Music Institute
Holyrood Place.   Tel: 0383 23786
    A school of music offering a degree-equivalent course of study or a degree.

Musical Organizations

Scottish Country and Western Music Appreciation Society
Bicknell, Victoria Street, Dumbarton.   Tel: 0389 2315

Traditional Music and Song Association of Scotland
29 Sunnyside, Strathkinnes, Fife.

The Business of Music

Music shops of every variety flourish in every town and village above a certain size in Scotland. We will mention only one business establishment, more because of the rarity of its operation than for any other reason:

Waverley Piano Co. (Repairs antique instruments and
manufactures piano rolls)
   55 Balmoral Road, Galashiels, Selkirk.   Tel: 0896 2308

Festivals

Aberdeen *(Aberdeenshire)*

Aberdeen Festival
St. Nicholas House, Broad Street.   Tel: 0224 23456
Dates: two weeks in mid-June.

Dunfermline *(Fife)*

Carnegie Festival of Music and the Arts
Abbey Park House, Abbey Park Place.   Tel: 0383 23638/9.
Dates: one week in April.

Edinburgh *(Midlothians)*

Edinburgh International Festival of Music and Drama
Festival Offices: 21 Market Street.   Tel: (031) 226 4001
Dates: three weeks in late August to early September.
Performance locations:
   King's Theatre, Leven Street, Tollcross
       (cap. 1485)   Tel: (031) 229 4840
   Usher Hall, Lothian Road (cap. 2752)   Tel: (031) 229 7607
   Freemasons' Hall, George Street (cap. 500)   Tel: (031) 225 2424
   Leith Town Hall, Ferry Road (cap. 1442)   Tel: (031) 554 7295
   St. Cecilia's Hall, Cowgate
   Royal Lyceum Theatre, Grindley Street
       (cap. 784)   Tel: (031) 229 4353
   Church Hill Theatre, Morningside Road
       (cap. 379)   Tel: (031) 447 7596
   The Gateway, 41 Elm Row
   Haymarket Ice Rink, Haymarket Terrace
   The Castle, Esplanade
Box Office: program brochure available from April on. Mail orders begin early
   May, in-person booking from the end of June on. Box office hours:

weekdays 9:45 AM to 4:30 PM. Saturday 9:45 AM to noon. From mid-August on, tickets for the King's and Lyceum Theaters on sale at their respective box offices only. After August 21 or the beginning of the Festival, the Festival box office hours are: weekdays 9:45 AM to 8:00 PM; Sunday 10:00 AM to 8:00 PM.

Housing Accommodations: apply to The City of Edinburgh Tourist Accommodation Service, 1 Cockburn Street.

Opera by visiting companies as well as by the resident Scottish Opera, presenting rare and unusual works, as well as rare and unusual performing groups; theater and ballet; choral and orchestral concerts by as many as six internationally prominent groups; chamber music recitals; film festival; exhibitions; Military Tattoo and fringe programs of plays, reviews, ballets, etc. by amateur and professional companies.

Undoubtedly the most comprehensive festival of its kind in the world, the Edinburgh Festival will be celebrating the twenty-seventh year of its existence in 1973. During the three weeks of the Festival, the quiet city of castles, cathedrals, precise gardens, and cobblestoned streets comes alive for an unparalleled cultural orgy. The atmosphere is ideal for international contact. Note well the mini-festival, called the Fringe Festival—where many very interesting and experimental productions are launched. Although there are always one or two focal points around which some of the Festival activities are organized (such as music from Czechoslovakia or Poland, or music by younger artists, or music in Italy from the sixteenth century to the present), there is a largely freewheeling policy which encourages excellence and variety.

Pitlochry (Perthshire)

Pitlochry Festival Theatre ("Scotland's Theatre in the Hills")
Knockendarroch House.   Tel: Pitlochry 128
Dates: end of April to the end of September.
Box Office: 10:00 AM to 6:30 PM, Monday through Saturday. For Sunday concerts, box office open only from 7:00 PM to 8:00 PM. Mail order bookings from March 22. Counter booking from April 19. Seating capacity of the theater is 502.   Tel: Pitlochry 233
Authorized agents in Dundee (Larg & Sons Ltd), Edinburgh (Rae Macintosh & Co. Ltd), Glasgow (Arbuckle Smith & Co. Ltd), and Perth (Grampion Travel Ltd.).

Repertoire of five or more plays per season; Sunday celebrity concert series; art exhibitions.

Dress is casual except for opening nights or galas when black-tie is optional but customary.

Competitions

Glasgow

International Competition for Junior Violinists
Annual. June.
Age limit: 12–18
For information apply to: Iain Turpie, 12 Washington Street, Glasgow G3.

Ian Whyte Award
Orchestral work.
Triennial: 1978, 1981, etc.
Age limit: 34
For information apply to: General Administrator, Scottish National Orchestra, 150 Hope Street, Glasgow G2.

Periodicals

Scottish Folk Notes
quarterly
Published by the Glasgow Folk Centre, 45 Montrose St., Glasgow C1

Scottish Opera Magazine
three times a year
Published by the Scottish Opera Club, Glasgow.

Wales

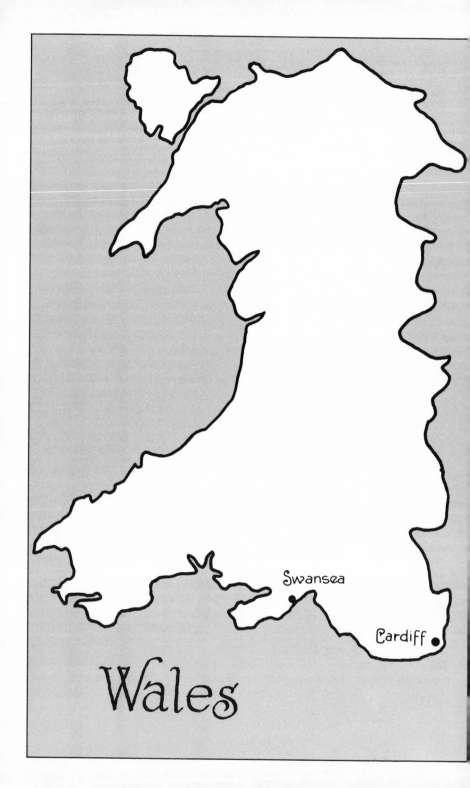

Swansea

Cardiff

Wales

Wales

CARDIFF (Glamorganshire)

In slightly more than one hundred and fifty years, Cardiff has grown from a good-sized village to become the capital of Wales, a major seaport, and a university city. From the point of view of the economy of Wales, Cardiff is its most important city by far, providing employment for hundreds of thousands of Welshmen in enterprises connected with the bustling Cardiff docks. Away from the centers of commercial activity, the city is beautiful. Both the Llandaff Cathedral and Cardiff Castle (see below), as well as the National Museum, Cathay's Park, and the civic center of the city with its fine municipal buildings, help to create an ambience that is at once unique and typical. The population of the city now numbers 286,000 and continues to grow. Complete with skyscraper (twenty-three stories opposite City Hall), shopping centers, and museums, the urban life of the community approximates that of any of its important sister cities in the British Isles.

The abundance of concert halls and musical events gives proof of the basically musical nature of the people. However, the enormously strong folk- and religious-music appetites which may be especially characteristic of the Welsh, have been groomed and curried in recent times to assume a more sophisticated aspect. The Welsh National Opera, which is based in Cardiff, is the pride and joy of the entire nation and receives the warmest of welcomes as it tours the principality offering performances of *Carmen* and *Simon Boccanegra*. The festivals which are not *Eisteddfodau* are beginning to proliferate in increasing numbers. (This is not to denigrate the folk festivals, which are unique and exciting, but merely to emphasize that the Welsh musical scene has recently developed new facets giving it a less parochial nature.) The establishment of university degrees in music and music conservatories of international standing has also done much to put Cardiff in the forefront of Welsh musical culture today. And the physical setting of the city, the delightful, unscarred Vale of Glamorgan with its charming towns and unexpected antiquarian treasure troves, supplies the additional fillip for enjoying this animated and enthusiastic community to the fullest.

Guides and Services

City of Cardiff, Information Bureau
Greyfriars Road.   Tel: 31033

Wales Tourist Board (Bwrdd Croeso Cymru)
Welcome House, High Street, Llandaff.   Tel: 566133-7
Information Centre, 3 Castle Street.   Tel: 27281

Events in Bristol and Cardiff
Monthly publication available at the City Information Bureau. Lists community events, theater and opera schedules, concert schedules with programs, activities of local societies, sport events, etc. The brochure is divided into two sections, one covering Bristol (see p. 54), and the other concerning Cardiff, on the other side of the Severn.

Opera Houses and Concert Halls

The New Theatre Cardiff
Park Place.   Tel: 23431
Season: September through June.
Seating capacity: 1430   Box Office Tel: 32446
The New Theatre Cardiff is a well-situated and attractively-designed opera house of Victorian design with excellent backstage facilities and ample space for the countless operations upon which any stage production depends. It is the home of the Welsh National Opera Company (see p. 187), although they share this home with other forms of theater: visiting London repertory companies, visiting ballet groups such as the London Festival Ballet, and touring musical comedies. The acoustics of the house are excellent as are the public areas, providing adequate and accessible cloakrooms and carefully designed seating. There is plenty of parking space immediately outside the theater.

Assembly Rooms
City Hall.   Tel: 31033
Seating capacity: 800
Commonly known simply as City Hall, the Assembly Rooms are the principal site for concerts in Cardiff center. Here solo and chamber recitals, band and choral concerts, are regularly scheduled. In use all year round.

Pavilion
Sophia Gardens.   Tel: 27657/8
Seating capacity: 2000
Located in the park known as Llandaff Fields, the Pavilion is used for large-scale popular events. In the summertime, the Pavilion is also used for visiting orchestras and concerts by famous personalities.

Reardon Smith Theatre
Cardiff University, Park Place.   Tel: 26241
Seating capacity: 475
The Reardon Smith Lecture Theatre is the site of the Cardiff International Recitals as well as innumerable events, both University-sponsored and not. It is one of the five halls used for the Llandaff Festival (see p. 196) each June.

Other Locations Used for the Presentation of Concerts and Related Events

Broadcasting House
Llandaff.   Tel: 564888
Regional headquarters of the BBC. Used for public concerts of the BBC Welsh Orchestra (see p. 187).

Llandaff Cathedral
Cathedral Road, Llandaff
Used extensively for organ recitals, concerts of religious choral music, etc. Regular evensong services at 6:00 PM on Monday, Tuesday, Thursday, Friday, and Saturday. The cathedral dates back to the twelfth century.

Cardiff Castle
Dating back to the late twelfth century, Cardiff Castle was given to the city by the Marquis of Bute. Part of it is used today as a college of music and drama (see p. 187). It has beautifully decorated public rooms in which special musical events are held from time to time. It is regularly used, for example, during the Llandaff Festival, for special events which combine a concert with a tour and supper (see p. 196).

Libraries and Museums

Cardiff Public Libraries, Central Library [Ben. 28, Long 84]
The Hayes.   Tel: 22116
Hours: Monday to Friday from 11:00 AM to 6:00 PM; Saturday 10:00 AM to
     6:00 PM. Closed on bank holidays. For permission to use special collections,
     write to the City Librarian.
Collection: approximately 10,000 volumes in separate music department of
     public library. Special collections include the Theodore Aylward collection
     of English and sacred music; the Bonner Morgan collection of seventeenth-
     and eighteenth-century music prints collected by Sir Henry Mackworth;
     extensive collection of Welsh folk music; and works by Welsh composers.

National Museum of Wales, Welsh Folk Museum
St. Fagans, near Cardiff.   Tel: 71357/8
     St. Fagans is five miles west of Cardiff and the Welsh Folk Museum is
contained in a sixteenth-century house which is surrounded by old buildings
moved from their original locations for the purpose of recreating a traditional
seventeenth-century Welsh community. Included in the various collections of
artifacts and period furnishings are groups of keyboard, string, and wind
instruments, both folk and art, of Welsh origin.
Note: A delicious Welsh tea may be purchased on the premises which features
     the popular Welsh "bakestone."

University College of South Wales and Monmouthshire,
The Library [Ben. 29, Long 425]
Cathays Park.   Tel: 44211
Hours: Monday to Friday, 9:00 AM to 10:00 PM; Saturday 9:00 AM to 1:00 PM.
     Closed for one week at Christmas, Easter, and the first week of August.
     For permission to use Library, write to Librarian in advance.
     Music collection is contained in the University general library.

Welsh College of Music and Drama, Music Library [Long 440]
The Castle.   Tel: 28307
Hours: Monday to Friday, 1:30 PM to 2:15 PM.
Admission: students and faculty only.
Collection: working library of books, scores and records.

Conservatories and Schools

University College of South Wales and Monmouthshire at Cardiff, The Music Faculty
Cathays Park.   Tel: 44211
Degrees offered: B.Mus.; B.A. in Music; general B.A.M. Mus. and Ph.D in research; M.Mus in instruction; M.A. in instruction.

Welsh College of Music and Drama
The Castle.   Tel: 28307
Cardiff Castle was presented to the city in 1947 by the Marquis of Bute and it is now a school for one thousand students. Courses of study in all forms of music are offered.

Musical Organizations

BBC Welsh Orchestra
BBC Broadcasting House, Llandaff.   Tel: 564888
The 44-man orchestra gives concerts, both public and broadcast, from Broadcasting House as well as City Hall. The Mid-Day Prom Series, broadcast weekly from City Hall, 12:15 PM to 2:05 PM, is very popular.

Welsh National Opera Co. Ltd.
John Street.   Tel: 40541/5
Season: eighteen weeks per year.
Resident House: New Theatre, Cardiff.
The Welsh National Opera Company's first seasons were played in Cardiff and Porthcawl in 1946, with little outside financial assistance. The early repertoire relied heavily on the Company's remarkable amateur chorus, but with the growth of the producing and administrative organization and the addition of a strong, fulltime chorus (see below), more contemporary works such as Berg's *Lulu,* were successfully essayed. The company now gives nearly one hundred performances annually, divided equally between Wales and England. In addition, they participate in the Opera for All (see p. 37) program, and have set up a training scheme which was initiated in 1962. Set up more or less along the lines of an apprenticeship rather than an academy, it avails the opportunity to train to a number of aspirants every year, and the result is that the company is kept supplied with fresh, well-trained personnel.

Welsh Philharmonia Orchestra
Welsh National Opera, John Street.

A fifty-man orchestra which performs with the Welsh National Opera, but also has an independent symphonic season of its own. Established in 1970.

Welsh Arts Council (*Cyngor Celfyddydau Cymru*)
Holst House, Museum Place.   Tel: 43055

The Council devotes a good proportion of its music expenditure to arranging a season of concerts throughout Wales by visiting orchestras. They also give support to composers, both direct and indirect. The Council gives grants to the Welsh Amateur Music Federation (founded in 1969) to assist mixed choral societies, male choirs, brass bands, folksong and dance groups. They sponsor the triennial Young Welsh Singer's Competition, with a concert held as part of the Llandaff Festival, offered as first prize. They support the Welsh festivals (Llandaff, Cardiff, Swansea, etc.) directly and offer financial assistance to a number of music clubs and societies for the presentation of chamber music performances by professional artists. Planning conferences are held to help these organizations in arranging programs. Tours by Opera for All, Ballet for All, and the Welsh National Opera Chorus are also assisted.

The Business of Music

Retail Music Stores

Crane & Sons Ltd. (Musical instruments)
    7–13 Castle Arcade.   Tel: 20859
Gamlin Pianos
    55 St. Mary Street.   Tel: 20828
Steve & Olive Gibson Ltd. (Music and instruments)
    35 Castle Arcade.   Tel: 26045
A. Donald Glew (Instruments)
    29 Pontcanna Street.   Tel: 30517
J. Glough & Co. Ltd. (Recording equipment)
    148–154 North Road.   Tel: 28473
A.M. & R. Grand Ltd. (Musical instruments)
    19 Castle Arcade.   Tel: 25136
F. M. Henderson & Sons Ltd. (Musical instruments)
    24 Wyndham Arcade.
Howell (Records and recording equipment)
    St. Mary Street.   Tel: 31055
Rowlands Music and Book Store Ltd.
    19 High Street Arcade.   Tel: 26935

SWANSEA (Glamorganshire)   Tel. prefix (0792)

The city of Swansea, population 170,000 stands on the neck of the Gower Peninsula, marking the end of the industrial region along the South Wales coastline. It is a university town, a resort and holiday area, a town which grew into a city in 1970. In addition to the renowned Swansea Festival (see p. 197), there is an active concert life all year long, with one major event monthly.

Guides and Services

Wales Tourist Board
Principality House, 64/65 The Kingsway.   Tel: 50622

Opera Houses and Concert Halls

Arts Hall
Swansea University College, Singleton Park.   Tel: 21231
  Used for concerts and recitals, including performances during the Swansea Festival (see p. 197).

Brangwyn Hall
Guildhall.   Tel: 50821
Seating capacity: 1496
Box Office: 9:30 AM to 5:00 PM daily, except Saturday (closed). Located in the Collection Hall of the Guildhall.
  Brangwyn Hall, which is part of the Guildhall, is the largest concert hall in Wales. The stage and platform accommodate the largest choirs and orchestras. There is also a four-manual Willis organ on the stage. Concerts are held here throughout the year, with the most concentration during the Swansea Festival (see p. 197). The Brangwyn Panels, work of Sir Frank Brangwyn, may be seen daily between 10:30 AM and 5:30 PM, except on Saturday, Sunday and legal holidays when the Guildhall is closed.

Grand Theatre
Singleton Street.   Tel: 55141
Seating capacity: 1124
  This Victorian horseshoe-shaped theater was built in 1897 and completely

renovated in 1969. A variety of programs are presented here, ranging from opera and ballets to events of the Swansea Festival.

Libraries

Swansea Public Library [Long 408]

Alexandra Road.   Tel: 54065/6

Hours: 9:30 AM to 1:00 PM and 2:30 PM to 4:30 PM, except Saturday (closed).

Collection: extensive collection of gramophone records, in addition to standard reference materials including a special collection of the poetry readings of Dylan Thomas, a native of Swansea.

Wales University, University College of Swansea [Long 427]

University College Library, Singleton Park.   Tel: 25678

Hours: Monday to Friday, 9:00 AM to 10:00 PM (vacation 5:00 PM or 6:00 PM; Saturday 9:00 AM to 5:00 PM (vacation—noon); Sunday 2:00 PM to 6:00 PM (term only).

Collection: Deffett Francis collection of eighteenth- and nineteenth-century music, including some scores.

Schools

Bach Week

University College of Swansea, Department of Extra-mural Studies

Berwick House, 6 Uplands Terrace.   Tel: 57168

Date: one week in mid-April.

Activities: lectures and recitals held at Clyne Castle. Each year there is a theme around which all the events are built. The course includes lectures on performing traditions and authenticity, construction of instruments. The recitals are related to the theme and to the lectures as well. A choir and orchestra rehearse daily and weekends with an informal concert of the works studied during the course.

Accommodation: formerly called Clyne Castle and now called Neuadd Gilbertson, a hall of residence for men at the University College of Swansea, it is situated in a woodland overlooking Swansea Bay. A baronial-style building, it has been extensively modernized and adapted to the requirements of a university hall.

Closing Date for Applications: end of January.

The Business of Music

Retail Music Stores

Bishop's Piano Works	
10 Victoria Terrace.	Tel: 57097
Duck, Son and Pinker Ltd. (Music, instruments, recordings, etc.)	
11 Union Street.	Tel: 55337
Sidney Heath Ltd. (Booking office)	
Beau Nash House.	Tel: 50741

Open daily, except Thursday, from 9:30 AM to 5:00 PM; Thursday 9:30 AM to noon.

Picton Music (Music, instruments, recordings, etc.)	
9–15 Picton Arcade.	Tel: 55608
Snell & Sons Ltd. (Music, instruments, recordings, etc.)	
8 Craddock Street.	Tel: 50518
Wilks Music Stores Ltd. (Instruments)	
60 Oxford Street.	Tel: 55952
Welsh Teldisc (Manufacturers of phonograph records)	
139 Walter Road.	Tel: 59854

WALES, GENERAL

Miscellaneous Concert Halls

Aberystwyth (Cardigan)

Great Hall
Penglais, The University.   Tel: 0770 2711
Seating capacity: 1300

Concerts requiring large forces (orchestral, oratorio, etc.) are regularly given in this late-nineteenth-century hall.

Bangor (*Caernarvon*)

Pritchard Jones Hall
University College.   Tel: 0247 4371
Chamber music recitals, opera and concerts are held in this interesting room.

Harlech (*Merioneth*)

Coeleg Harlech Theatre
Seating capacity: 365   Tel: 076673 363

Llandudno (*Caernavon*)

Pier Pavilion
Pier Head, Great Orme.   Tel: 0492 76258
Situated at the end of a pier, this handsome concert hall is the setting for opera, chamber music, and symphony concerts.

Libraries and Museums

Aberystwyth (*Cardiganshire*)

National Library of Wales (*Llyfryell Genedlaethol Cymru*) [Ben. 2]
Tel: 0970 3816/7
Hours: Monday to Friday, 9:30 AM to 6:00 PM; Saturday 9:30 AM to 5:00 PM.
Closed Christmas, Boxing Day, and Easter. No admission restrictions. For permission to use special collections, see Librarian.
Founded in 1909, the Library houses a large collection of books and documents relating to Wales. The music collection specializes in manuscripts and documents concerning Welsh music and musicians.

University College of Wales, Library   Tel: 0970 2711
Hours: Monday to Friday from 10:00 AM to 5:00 PM during term. Saturday 10:00 AM to noon.
The music collection contained within the general University Library,

specializes in Welsh music and composers. There is a well-known collection of Mendelssohn letters and autographs here.

Brecon (Glamorganshire)

The Brecknock Museum

Glamorgan Street.   Tel: Brecon 2218
Hours: weekdays 10:00 AM to noon and 1:00 to 4:00 PM except for Monday afternoons.

Originally the chapel where Adelina Patti (1843–1919) was married in 1898, it has been turned into a museum displaying items of local interest, including a fine collection of musical instruments. Among the instruments may be found flutes, harmonium, harps, Welsh harps, and a three-valve horn.

Merthyr Tydfil (Glamorganshire)

Cyfartha Castle Art Gallery and Museum   Tel: 0685 3112

Hours: April to September, weekdays from 10:00 AM to 6:30 PM; October to March from 10:00 AM to 5:00 PM. Weekly admission free. Sunday 2:00 PM to 5:00 PM. Closed Good Friday, Christmas Day, Boxing Day.

Cyfartha Castle is the neo-Gothic nineteenth-century manor house belonging to a wealthy family of ironmongers, the Crawshays. They presented the Castle to the community to be used as an art gallery and museum. There is a collection of musical instruments here.

Schools and Conservatories

University College of Wales, Department of Music

Aberystwyth, Cardigan.   Tel: 0970 2711
Offers undergraduate degrees in music. Also M.Mus. and Ph.D.

University College of North Wales, Department of Music

Bangor, Caernarvonshire.   Tel: 0247 5201
Offers B.Mus. and B.A. in music as well as an M.A. and Ph.D. in research subjects.

Musical Organizations

Almost all the important arts societies and professional associations are quartered in Cardiff or Swansea with the exception of The Guild for the Promotion of Welsh Music. The mailing address of this group is 10 Llanerch Pathm Fairwater, Cwmbran, Monmouthshire. For information concerning activities, contact the Secretary at that address.

On the other hand, in the area of amateur performing groups, especially vocal groups of all kinds, there is an *embaras de richesse* which would make a listing of the active performing groups of Wales read like a telephone directory of the country. From the Barry and District Choral Society, to the Cor Dogre'r Aran (The Choir at the Foot of the Aran Mountain of Bala and Llanuwchllyn on Bala Lake in County Merioneth), the singing societies proliferate and the choral groups multiply almost daily. In the teeth of modern technology and the forcible decline of the Welsh language through unavoidable economic dependencies, the singing tradition of Wales is kept alive in almost every town and valley of North, Middle and South Wales.

Note: the distinction between competitive festivals and festivals, made on p. 145, must be carefully redrawn when discussing such activities in Wales. Throughout the summer there are festivals of music and art called *Eisteddfodau.* We will describe some of the more important ones. They are a uniquely Welsh combination of competitive festivals and professional festivals. They offer to the visitor a rare opportunity to hear the very best of Welsh singing performed by competing choral groups from all over the country. They also feature professional concerts and recitals which would qualify in any category as bona fide festival fare.

Festivals

Bangor (Caernarvonshire)

The Royal National Eisteddfod of Wales
Eisteddfod Office, Garth Road, Bangor, Caernarvonshire.   Tel: 0247 4491
Dates: one week early in August. The Royal National Eisteddfod rotates between Bangor in odd-numbered years, and Haverfordwest in even-numbered years. The Southern office is located at: 2b Dark Street, Haverfordwest, Pembrokeshire.   Tel: 0437 2742
Box Office: tickets are sold on a weekly or daily basis. There are Class 1 and

Class 2 reserved seats, as well as field and unreserved seats. The halls chosen for these occasions seat approximately 7,000 persons.

In addition to the daily competitive sessions, which are divided into categories such as Chief Choral Competition, Children's Competitions, Youth Competitions, Solo Competitions, Youth Blue Riband Competition, Male Voice Choirs, there are choral and orchestral concerts, guest artists, dramatic performances, and concerts by professional folk artists which are held every evening in the hall being used.

The huge annual Royal National Eisteddfod is one of the most picturesque and moving ceremonies in Wales. Presided over by white-robed druids with attending blue-robed bards, the *Eisteddfod* gathers the singers and poets of Wales for this tournament. At a finale ceremony, the winning poet is chosen, and the results of a national baseball game, football match, or soccer game could not be more attentively awaited than the announcement from the *Eisteddfod* is in Wales. The Royal National Eisteddfod offers the visitor a unique opportunity to hear the Welsh sing and it will offer the visitor all the explanation he will ever need to have for the international reputation the Welsh guard as the greatest singing people in the world.

Caerphilly (Glamorganshire)

Caerphilly Festival
Caerphilly Urban District Council Offices,
Mountain Road.   Tel: 044722 266
Dates: last week in October.
Performance Locations: Town Chapel, Van Road Congregational Church, Caer-
    philly Boys Grammar School, St. Martin's Church, the Workman's Hall,
    Abertridwr.
Box Office: Festival booking offices open from September 30. The Cash Office,
    Caerphilly U.D.C. Offices, address and phone number above.

Solo and chamber recitals, choral and orchestral concerts, varied light entertainment, and some theater.

Cardiff (Glamorganshire)

Cardiff Festival of 20th-Century Music
Department of Music, University College of South Wales and
Monmouthshire, Cathays Park.   Tel: 0222 44211
Dates: two weeks in mid-March.
Box Office: The Music Center, Castle Arcade.   Tel: 0222 24186

The program consists primarily of evening concerts held in the specially-designed concert hall of the department of music at University College (New

Hall). In addition, there are lunch time concerts held at the National Museum of Wales, and seminars on musical topics in the University. Performers of the caliber of Peter Pears, Barry Tuckwell, Ruggiero Ricci, and ensembles such as the London Symphony Orchestra, the BBC Welsh Orchestra and the Pendyrus Male Voice Choir are on the concert schedule. The seminars feature such names as John Culshaw, Hans Keller, and Moelwyn Merchant.

Cowbridge (Glamorganshire)

Llandaff Festival

The Festival Secretary, The Well House, Penylan Newton, Cowbridge.

Tel: 04463 2395

Dates: ten days in early June.

Performance Locations: New Theatre, Cardiff (Tickets available at this theater only for opera events of the Festival being held here.), Llandaff Cathedral, National Museum of Wales, Reardon Smith Lecture Theatre, Cardiff Castle.

Concerts begin either at 7:30 PM (for the most part) or occasionally at 8:00 PM. Afternoon events begin at 1:00 PM.

Box Office (except for New Theatre as noted above): booking begins in mid-May at Crane & Sons, Ltd. 7/13 Castle Arcade, Cardiff.

Opera, choral groups, piano recitals, symphony orchestra concerts, chamber music.

Vale of Glamorgan Festival

Old Rectory, Cowbridge.   Tel: 04463 3334

Dates: two weeks from the end of August into September.

Since it was established in 1961, this festival has combined two arts in one occasion: music and architecture. The concerts are given in famous homes, churches, and manors of the area, such as Llanharen House and St. Donat's Castle.

Fishguard (Pembrokeshire)

Fishguard Festival

Sycamore Lodge, Hamilton Street.   Tel: Fishguard 2813

Dates: one week late in August.

Featuring the Festival Orchestra under William Mathias, as well as the North Pembrokeshire choir, the events take place in the hall of Fishguard School, St. Mary's Church Hall, the Festival Club, and St. Peter's Church in Goodwick. This young festival, begun in 1970, strives for a high level of excellence coupled with a diversified program featuring invited artists of prominence as well as artists of promise.

Llangollen (Denbighshire)

Llangollen International Musical Eisteddfod
Plas Hafod.   Tel: 097886 2236

Dates: one week in early July, annual.

Singers and dancers from more than thirty countries compete in this event. Specific choral "test pieces" required. The performances, at a uniformly high level, include folksong and dance groups, vocal and instrumental soloists, and choral groups in all combinations. A major and very Welsh event.

The evening concerts for the most part usually consist of a national folk opera or ballet company and performances by winning groups of former years.

Machen (Monmouthshire)

The Lower Machen Summer Festival
9 The Gardens, Machen near Newport.   Tel: 0600 2390

Dates: one week, end of June to early July.

The Festival seeks to present a balanced and broad repertoire using many media and presenting works from the seventeenth century to the twentieth. Encourages young artists and performs Welsh music.

Swansea (Glamorganshire)

Swansea Festival of Music and the Arts
Guildhall.   Tel: 0792 57168

Dates: from the second week to the end of October.

Performance Locations: Brangwyn Hall (capacity 1600), Grand Theatre (capacity 1000), Arts Hall, University College, Dragon Hotel Ballroom, Swansea Little Theatre.

Box Office: Guildhall, Rates Hall. Tel: 0792 50821. Hours: Monday to Friday from 9:00 AM to 1:00 PM and from 2:15 PM to 5:00 PM.

Housing Accommodation: apply to the Publicity Department, Principality House 64/65 The Kingsway, Swansea SA1 4NT.

Concerts, recitals, theater, ballet, art exhibitions.

This is Wales's most international festival, featuring a wide range of artists from many countries and offering sophisticated urban fare. Every festival includes at least one commissioned work by a contemporary Welsh composer.

Periodicals

Welsh Music (Journal of the Guild for the Promotion of Welsh Music)
34 Mountain Road, Caerphilly, Glamorgan.
quarterly
> Contains articles on Welsh music, both folk and art, on Welsh music resources, on performances, music reviews, record reviews, and notes on Welsh musical personalities.

Soundings (A music journal)
Department of Music, University College, Cardiff.
annual
> Scholarly journal founded in 1970. Contents on a very high intellectual and international level; articles written by reputable authors dealing with theoretical, analytical, and historical problems.

Ireland

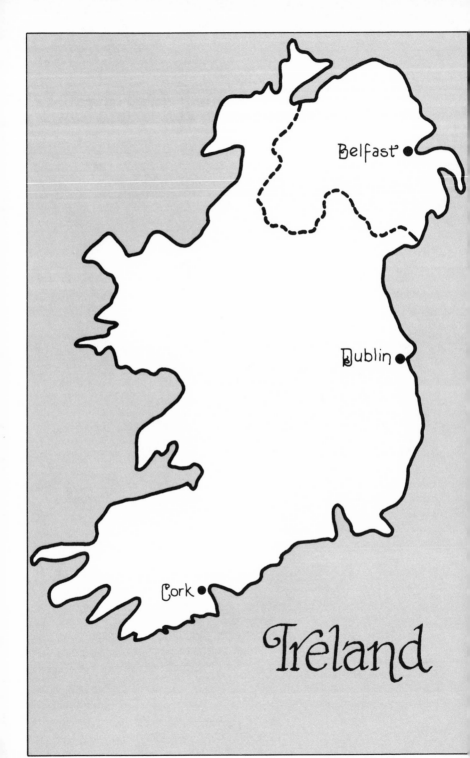

Ireland

Ireland's most important musical achievements have been in folksong and in early medieval sacred music. As early as the very early Middle Ages, Irish monks were adapting Gregorian chant and investing it with enthusiasm and fervor. On the secular side, the first references we have to Irish music are reliefs of instruments vaguely resembling harps (lyres ?) on stone crosses of the eighth and ninth centuries. From this beginning evolved the Irish national instrument and her heraldic symbol (the *clarsech*).

Aside from Dowland and Purcell, who are alleged to have been of Irish descent, there have been very few Irish composers of prominence other than those referred to on p. 203, and even they can hardly be called influential or even consequential. This is understandable when one admits that Irish art music is, to this day, struggling to be born. These efforts are being officially aided and abetted by the various art councils appropriate to each of the two official political states into which Ireland today is divided: Northern Ireland (the six counties in northeast Ulster—Antrim, Down, Londonderry, Armagh, Tyrone, and Fermanagh—which remained part of the British Empire and now enjoy her largesse and share her cultural programs in return for their somewhat less than autonomous status), and Eire (the twenty counties which are totally self-governing). As elsewhere, the universities have entered prominently into the picture as patrons of contemporary music and supporters of its creators and protagonists. Much of the encouragement for modern music is found in the academic institution. The methodical and systematic ordering of folk material and its traditional practice is carried on, to a greater or lesser degree, in both parts of Ireland. There is, of course, an emphasis on colorful and picturesque performances in order to titillate the tourist trade, a titillation sometimes paid for in authenticity. But when traditions are kept alive, even the distortions which current practice bestow on them have some justification.

It would be a gross exaggeration to say that Ireland is a musical country in the sense that England with its traditions and its institutions is musical or in the way that Germany with its history and overwhelming cultural inheritance is musical. But one can surely say that the Irish folk tradition is being kept alive and a new art tradition is being carefully nurtured on both sides of the "lace curtain."

DUBLIN (County Dublin)   Tel. prefix (0001)

Dublin, the capital of the Republic of Ireland, is one of the most beautiful cities in Europe from the point of view of architecture and layout. It has, in addition, good libraries, theaters, museums, and art galleries, as befits a city with a distinguished tradition in the arts and letters. Dublin's earliest monument is a 4,000-year-old-prehistoric burial site in Phoenix Park. The site must have been very important in Celtic times, lying, as it did, at the mouth of the River Liffey in a natural harbor. The town was actually founded by Norse sea-rovers who established a settlement there in 841. The Normans seized the town in 1170, constructing a strong wall and a castle to secure it against future attack. The remains of this medieval part of the city have been largely rebuilt in recent times. The Reformation, the wars of the seventeenth century, and years of neglect left all of Dublin in a sadly decrepit and impoverished state. The first 40 years of the eighteenth century were to bring about a remarkable transformation in the city and its people—an expansion and prosperity culminating in the squares and houses of the Georgian era which grace Dublin to this day and contribute to its unique charm. The splendor of the eighteenth century dimmed as famines and land clearances in the nineteenth century took their toll. Only in our own time, as a result of social and political revolution, has this process of decay been arrested, and that only after Dublin has already lost many of her treasures.

The roll call of eminent Dubliners will give us a clue to the role which music has traditionally played in modern Irish history. A list of her men of letters includes Jonathan Swift, Edmund Burke, Richard Brinsley Sheridan, and Oscar Wilde, as well as John Millington Synge, George Bernard Shaw, James Joyce, and Sean O'Casey. But the art of music can muster up only three names and all three could hardly be placed in the ranks of the great:

John Field (1782–1837), Michael William Balfe (1808–70), composer of *The Bohemian Girl,* and Sir Charles Villiers Stanford (1852–1924), who wrote operas, songs, chamber music, and symphonies that are rarely, if ever, heard today. Furthermore, although modern-day Dublin possesses two Church of Ireland cathedrals, five large theaters, and miscellaneous halls used for myriad purposes, it does not have a concert hall suitable for the large-scale performances of symphony orchestra with choral forces, for example. This is not a new situation. As far back as 1742, when Handel's *Messiah* was performed for the benefit of Mercer's Hospital, the New Music Hall in Fishamble Street, long Dublin's largest public hall, held only 700 persons. Unhappily, even the Music Hall is not available to today's Dubliner, for Kennan's Ironworks occupies the site where Handel returned in 1748 for the first performance of *Judas Maccabaeus.* Efforts have been made to raise funds for the erection of a new concert hall, but as of this writing, nothing has come of them. The musical life of Dublin goes ahead, making do with the various public halls available for musical events, and the city has an interesting and active schedule. The isolation from Great Britain and the political tensions brought about by the recent terrorism have made the abortive efforts of the sixties toward reciprocity and exchange of musical resources come to naught. It is hoped that this situation will change and the geographic proximity and cultural mutuality of the several nations will allow them to engage in the enrichment of each other's musical life.

Guides and Services

Irish Tourist Board (*Borde Failte*)
Information Bureau, Baggott's Street Bridge.   Tel: 65871
Mailing address: Borde Failte, P.O. Box 273, Dublin.

Ireland: Calendar of Events
    Published annually by the Irish Tourist Board and available free of charge at the Information Bureau of any of the Irish Tourist Board branch offices. Also available at hotels and major airport and railroad stations. Details of musical and theatrical events are not given. For these, it is necessary to consult the local newspapers or the nearest Tourist Information Office. Festivals broadly noted as well as regular seasons indicated.

Dublin Tourist Office
14 Upper O'Connell Street.

Opera Houses and Concert Halls

Examination Hall (also called the Theatre)
Trinity College, Parliament Square.   Tel: 772941

The theater was built in 1779 and has one of the finest interiors in the College. The Hall is the center for most musical activity in Dublin and presents concerts by visiting companies, orchestras, and chamber music ensembles. Regular programs are given here by the Radio Telefis Eirann Orchestra (see p. 209), the Trinity College Choral Society, and the Palestrina Choir of the Pro-Cathedral.

The Gaiety Theatre
South King Street.   Tel: 771717

Grand opera, ballet, symphony concerts, and musical comedies are regularly presented in this theater.

The Olympia Theatre
72 Dame Street.   Tel: 770907

Primarily a legitimate theater, the Olympia is used for ballet, musical reviews, and visiting performances employing choral as well as orchestral forces.

St. Francis Xavier Hall
Upper Sherrard Street and Gardiner Street.   Tel: 41775

During the summer months, visitors can enjoy concerts here given by the Radio Telefis Eireann orchestras. Admission is free and tickets may be obtained at the reception desk of the radio station (see p. 209). A schedule is available at the Tourist Information Service Office.

Queen's Theatre
Pearse Street.   Tel: 774455

Some Saturday afternoons, there are concerts held here for want of a more suitable hall. It is not exactly an innovative use of this theater, since we know that Paganini played here during a music festival in 1831.

Royal Dublin Society Concert Hall
Merrion Road, Ballsbridge.   Tel: 689645

During the winter months, concerts and recitals are presented in this hall.

Church Concerts

Christchurch Cathedral
Christchurch Place.

Concerts held every Friday evening from mid-June to September featuring music and poetry of Ireland. There are also organ recitals and choir concerts.

St. Bartholomew's Church
Clyde Road.
Sacred concerts given here regularly.

St. Catherine's Church
Thomas Street.
Presents a regular monthly program featuring Italian and French Baroque music in addition to weekly organ recitals.

Summer Concerts

St. Stephen's Green.
Open air concerts are held during the summer months in Dublin's oldest and largest square. The buildings around the square present a diversified facade of eighteenth and nineteenth-century exteriors. The concerts are announced at the Tourist Information Service Office and at concert bureaus.

Libraries and Museums

Archbishop Marsh's Library (or Marsh's Library, or Library of St. Sepulchre) [Ben. 2]
St. Patrick's Close. Tel: 753917
Hours: Monday, and Wednesday to Friday, 2:00 PM to 4:00 PM; Wednesday to Saturday, 10:00 AM to 12:30 PM. Closed from December 21 to January 1.
Collection: founded in 1707; primarily seventeenth century with a few pre-1600 and several post-1900 additions. Partbooks and manuscripts originally belonging to Narcisus Marsh, who became provost of Trinity College in 1687.

Christ Church Cathedral Library [Ben. 3]
Christchurch Place. Tel: 778099
Hours: Monday to Friday. Closed in August.
Admission: apply to the Cathedral Organist.
Collection: exclusively musical and predominantly nineteenth-century manuscripts.

Monteagle Reference Room

Royal Irish Academy of Music, 36 Westland Rowe.   Tel: 64412

Hours: Monday through Friday. Closed in August.

Collection: opened in 1939, the library has a good collection of scores and parts, Irish folk music in manuscript, and the library of the defunct Antient Concerts Society of Dublin.

National Library of Ireland [Ben. 4]

Kildare Street.   Tel: 65521

Hours: Monday to Friday from 10:00 AM to 10:00 PM; Saturday from 10:00 AM to 1:00 PM. Closed from July 20 to August 15.

Collection: music collection is contained in the general library, which serves as a depository for all books published in Ireland since 1927. The musical portion of this collection consists of extensive holdings in Irish songbooks and country dances, eighteenth-century music such as ballad operas, songsheets. Contains some of the Royal Dublin Society Library, as well as the bequests of Dr. J. Joly, the library of George Noble, and the collection of Count Plunkett.

The National Museum

Kildare Street.   Tel: 65521

Hours: Tuesday to Saturday, 10:00 AM to 5:00 PM. Sunday 2:00 PM to 5:00 PM. Closed on Monday.

Collection: musical instruments include an extensive collection of harps, bagpipes, Dublin-made harpsichords, and pianofortes.

Royal Irish Academy Library [Ben. 5]

19 Dawson Street.   Tel: 62570

Hours: Monday to Friday, 9:30 AM to 5:30 PM; Saturday 9:30 AM to 1:00 PM. Closed during August, as well as four days at Christmas and Easter. For admission, apply to the Librarian.

Collection: music is contained in the general library collection, which is famous for the extent and rarity of its Irish manuscript collection. Included in this collection are rare medieval musical manuscripts and some printed works. The Society was founded in 1783 and is Ireland's foremost learned society, recruiting membership from the entire island.

St. Patrick's Cathedral Library [Ben. 7]

St. Patrick's Close.   Tel: 754817

Trinity College Library

Library Square.   Tel: 77291, ext. 337

Hours: Monday to Friday, 10:00 AM to 5:00 PM; Saturday from 10:00 AM to

1:00 PM. Closed for five days at Christmas, two weeks in July. For admission, apply to the Deputy Librarian or the Reading Room Superintendant.

Collection: music collection is contained within the general library. Manuscripts and early prints available for research purposes. Public reference library with some restrictions on use. Contains collection of Ebenezer Prout, which is kept in the Long Room. Also a fine medieval Irish harp (Brian Boru's harp).

University College, Dublin (National University of Ireland),
Music Library [Ben. 9]
Earlsfort Terrace.   Tel: 752116
Hours: Monday to Saturday. Closed for one week at Christmas and Easter, and from July 1 to 15. For admission, apply to Librarian.

Collection: separate music library for the music department. Approximately 3,000 volumes including the special collections of Arnold Bax manuscripts, John McCormack bequest, and the copyright collection of Irish music publications.

Conservatories and Schools

National University of Ireland, University College,
Department of Music
Earlsfort Terrace.   Tel: 752116
Offers both the B.Mus. and the Mus.D in addition to undergraduate degrees in music. Department of Irish Folk Music established in 1951.

University of Dublin, Trinity College, Department of Music
Parliament Square.   Tel: 772941
No official music course is as yet provided. B.Mus. and Mus.D. offered.

Royal Irish Academy of Music
36–38 Westland Row.   Tel: 64412
The Royal Irish Academy of Music, founded in 1856, occupies the old townhouse of Lord Conyngham. Reconstruction of the facade and interior took place in 1963. In addition to the regular conservatory program, there is a summer school of two weeks duration available to senior students over 16.

Summer Schools

Dublin University International Summer School
Trinity College.   Tel: 772941

Course of Study: either two weeks or four weeks.
Areas of Instruction: Irish history and culture, including folk and modern music; Anglo-Irish literature.

For further information, write to: The Registrar, Summer School, Trinity College, Dublin 2.

Institute of Irish Studies
5 Wilton Place. Tel: 63276
Course of Study: two weeks in July-August.
Areas of Instruction: aspects of Celtic Ireland, comprising language, literature, mythology, archaeology, history, music, and drama.

Musical Organizations

Arts Council (An Comhairle Ealaíon)
70 Merrion Square. Tel: 62615
Coordinates and advises on all cultural projects under official support in Eire.

Folk Music Society of Ireland
35 Bóthar Ardpháirce, Ath Cliath 6.
The Folk Music Society of Ireland came into existence in 1971. Its objects are to preserve traditional music, to promote the study of it and to encourage an informed interest in it. The Society enters into relations with other organizations having national and international status, as well as local, with similar objectives. They hold meetings and conferences, arrange for performances of folk music, and publish an annual journal.

Irish Folklore Commission
82 St. Stephen's Green. Tel: 752440
Established in April 1935, to replace the Irish Folklore Institute, the Folklore Commission is supported by a substantial grant from the government to safeguard Irish traditions through the use of sound recordings and commitment of folk music to manuscript.

Music Association of Ireland
11 Suffolk Street. Tel: 770976
Founded in 1949 for the encouragement of Irish composers, the organization of concerts, and the dissemination of information concerning Irish music and its creators.

Radio Telfís Eireann (*Irish Radio and Television*)
Henry Street.   Tel: 42981

    The Radio has a very active role in the musical life of Eire, much in the same way as broadcasting companies do in the rest of Europe. In addition to the scheduling of a great deal of Irish folk and contemporary art music, the Radio supports several active performing organizations.

Dublin Grand Opera Society
Gaiety Theatre, South King Street or
11 S. Leinster Street.   Tel: 771717

    Since its 1941–2 season, The Dublin Grand Opera Society has held two seasons of opera annually at the Gaiety and one in the provinces. The orchestral support is usually supplied by the Radio Telefís Eireann Symphony Orchestra and it is not unusual for the Society to import an entire cast from a European opera company for a specific production. Both a sponsoring and a performing organization.

The Business of Music

Musical Instruments: Manufacture, Distribution and Repair

Danfay Distributors Ltd. (All musical instruments)
    61 Drury Street.   Tel: 775176
Gerards Music Stores (Pianos, sale and repair)
    159 Parnell Street.   Tel: 744447
Harmonic Strings Ltd.
    10 N. C. Road.   Tel: 778531
Henry Willis & Sons Ltd. (Organ builders)
    45 St. Columbanus Road.   Tel: 982176

Record Shops

Disc Finder (Rare and foreign records and tapes)
    146 Lower Baggot Street.   Tel: 760429
    Hours: 9:30 AM to 6:30 PM and 8:00 PM to 11:00 PM.
The Gramophone Store,
    6 Johnstons Court.   Tel: 777856
Murray's Record Centre
    23 Ormond Quay.   Tel: 776001

Retail Music Shops

Thomas Brown and Switzers (Concert tickets available at
ticket bureau)
    15 Grafton Street.   Tel: 776861
McCullough Piggott Ltd. (Pianos, musical instruments,
concert information, and tickets)
    11 Suffolk Street.   Tel: 773161 or 773138
Brendan Dempsey (Music, instruments) 218 Parnell Street.   Tel: 44877
V. J. Nordell & Co. Ltd. (Records, sheet music, pianos, organs)
    4–7 Cathal Brugha Street.   Tel: 49643

BELFAST (Antrim)   Tel. prefix (0232)

Belfast, the capital of Northern Ireland since the partitioning of Ulster in 1921,
lies at the mouth of the River Lagan where it meets the Belfast Lough (lake).
Blessed with one of the finest natural settings in Europe, it is ringed with
hills—from the Castlereagh Hills to the loftier Black Mountain range—which
form an amphitheater around the city. It is 101 miles north by northeast from
Dublin and 74 miles east by southeast from Derry. It is Ireland's greatest
seaport and commercial and manufacturing center. It is the seat of the General
Assembly of the Presbyterian Church in Ireland as well as the cathedral city
of the Catholic dioceses of Down and Connor. The name Belfast—*Béal Feirsde*
(mouth of the sandspit or approach to the River Lagan crossing)—first appears
in the late fifteenth-century references to a Clannaboy O'Neill castle com-
manding the Lagan crossing. It belonged to the Chichester family, who later
were designated the Earls of Donegall. On the accession of the fifth Earl of
that name, in 1757, a program of town improvement was systematically begun.
By 1770 the town was beginning to show signs of what its future industrial
development would bring and it became the center of a social-political reform
movement among the Ulster Protestants. The expansion and activity in the
burgeoning city resulted in the establishment of Queen's College—now Queen's
University—in 1845. By 1888, Belfast had achieved city status.

    Today it is a modern urban community dominated at its center by a great
Renaissance-style City Hall. There are theaters and concert halls, museums
and art galleries, and a large-scale exhibition area in the King's Hall at
Balmoral. The city is ringed with a series of splendid parks—Hazelwood,
Bellevue, and Victoria—and facilities for shopping, visiting, and taking excur-
sions out of the center of the city are well-organized and convenient. Belfast
understandably enough supplies the main setting for the majority of musical

activity in the province. Concerted efforts on the part of the conscientious Arts Council of Northern Ireland to encourage musical activity in all parts of the province have had happy results. The touring activities of the Studio Opera Group were very much welcomed. Naturally, the musical activities of Belfast receive the fullest attention and support from the Arts Council, not only in encouraging native musicians, but in sponsoring guest artist appearances on a reasonably regular basis.

Guides and Services

Northern Ireland Tourist Board
River House, 48 High Street. Tel: 31221

The Tourist Board publishes a booklet called *Coming Events in Northern Ireland*, which lists the major national, international, sporting, and cultural events of the year. It is available from the Board without charge.

On a monthly basis and in cooperation with the Arts Council of Northern Ireland, the Tourist Board also publishes a guide called *"What's On,"* which provides more detailed information, programs, addresses, prices, etc. This is available from the Board, from the Arts Council, and at major hotels throughout Northern Ireland.

Opera Houses and Concert Halls

Grand Opera House
Great Victoria Street. Tel: 230951
Seating capacity: 2,237 Box Office Tel: 22903

Grosvenor Hall
Glengall Street. Tel: 41917
Seating capacity: 1850

King George VI Youth Centre
20 May Street. Tel: 23805
Seating capacity: 800 Box Office Tel: 23554

Ulster Hall
Linenhall Street. Tel: 21341

The city's largest public hall and the scene of the major portion of Belfast's concert life, Ulster Hall also serves as the home of the Group Theatre, visiting repertory and ballet companies, as well as occasional visiting symphonic groups. An 1861 Hill organ in original condition graces the auditorium.

Wellington Hall
Wellington Place.   Tel: 25945
Seating Capacity: 1500

Whitla Hall
Queens University, University Road.   Tel: 45133
Seating capacity: 1250
Built in 1949 from designs by J. McGeagh, it is part of the University compound. Together with Ulster Hall, it is the symphony hall used most widely by the Ulster Orchestra and visiting orchestras. In the University, concerts are also given in two smaller halls used widely for chamber and solo recitals: the Harty Room and Elmwood Hall.

Concerts are also given in the Ulster Museum and in the Members' Rooms of King's Hall, Balmoral. This latter, belonging to the Royal Ulster Agricultural Society, is most usually used for fairs and horsing events, but it is also the traditional place for the Summer Proms, featuring the Ulster Orchestra, in June and August.

Church Concerts

Both St. Anne's Cathedral and St. Peter's Church on Antrim Road are used for concert series by the Ulster Orchestra, as well as for choir concerts, oratorio performances, and the like.

Libraries and Museums

Belfast Public Libraries
Central Library, Royal Avenue.   Tel: 43233
Hours: Monday, Wednesday, Thursday, Friday, 9:30 AM to 8:00 PM; Tuesday 9:30 AM to 5:00 PM; Saturday 9:30 AM to 1:00 PM.
Admission: no restrictions. Ticket available upon request to the Librarian.
Collection: included in a general collection are the Sam Henry collection of Irish folk songs; Bunting, Hardebeck, and O'Neill collections of Irish music; collection of broadside ballads; and a run of the *Journal of the Irish Folk Song Society.*

Queen's University, Main Library

University Square.   Tel: 45133, ext. 249

Hours: Monday to Friday from 9:00 AM to 11:00 PM and on Saturday from
    9:00 AM to 1:00 PM. Closed on St. Patrick's Day, from Good Friday to
    Easter Monday, the last full week in June, July 12, and from December
    24 to January 1.

Admission: borrowing facilities are limited to staff and students of the University.
    Graduates and outside readers, admitted at the Librarian's discretion, may
    borrow on payment of a deposit, or may simply consult books at no charge.

Collection: the music collection, which includes reference works and periodicals
    of a comprehensive standard order, also holds the Sir Hamilton Harty
    autograph scores and his marked orchestral scores used in Hallé per-
    formances. Also the Bunting collection of Irish folk tunes from before the
    nineteenth century in manuscript.

Ulster Museum

Stranmillis.   Tel: 668259

Hours: Monday to Saturday, 10:00 AM to 6:00 PM. Wednesday 10:00 AM to
    9:00 PM.

Located in the Botanic Gardens adjacent to the University, the Ulster
Museum houses an art gallery as well as interesting archaeological, natural
history, technological, and historical collections, including a general collection
of musical instruments.

Conservatories and Schools

Queens University, Music Department

University Road.   Tel: 45133

Grants B.Mus and M.A. as well as a combined A.B. in music and English.
Catalogue available from Admissions Office.

City of Belfast School of Music

99 Donegall Pass.   Tel: 22435

A gigantic school of music divided into three sections: day schools which
reach 68,000 pupils; Saturday morning sessions in all combinations imaginable
for the performing of music; and the evening tuition. Class instruction, as well
as inservice courses for teachers; concerts and recitals.

The Ulster College of Music

45 Windsor Avenue.   Tel: 688141

Individual training. Private instruction.

Musical Organizations

Arts Council for Northern Ireland
Bedford House, Bedford Street.   Tel: 41073

The Arts Council undertakes to encourage and support the arts in Northern Ireland, and works to develop and improve the knowledge, understanding, and practice of these arts. Cognizant of the special problems relating to Northern Ireland, the Council subsidizes performing groups, amateur organizations, and performing societies, and attempts to help maintain high standards of music and musical performance.

British Broadcasting Corporation, Northern Ireland
Broadcasting House, 25–27 Ormeau Avenue.   Tel: 27411

The Northern Ireland Opera Trust
26 Stanmillis Road.   Tel: 667756

In 1969, the Grand Opera Society, a venerable organization which witnessed much of Belfast's history and was part of most of it, was succeeded by the Northern Ireland Opera Trust, which has been acting primarily as a producing organization. The Trust uses local talent (including the Ulster Orchestra) whenever possible, also important soloists, and imports productions when necessary. With the help of the Arts Council, the Opera Trust has, since its beginning, presented three operas each season, preferably one in English. A small amount of local touring is undertaken by each production. Due to the bombing of the Opera House during the recent difficulties, the 1971–1972 season was presented at the Grove Theatre, where standards were maintained despite the difficulties. Although the audiences, perforce, were smaller, there was no decrease in enthusiasm. The weekly season traditionally takes place in May.

The Studio Opera Group
30 Rosetta Park.   Tel: 642992

In addition to giving regular performances in Belfast, this chamber opera group does extensive tours of opera in English by Mozart and Britten.

The Ulster Orchestra
26–34 Antrim Road.   Tel: 749201/2

A professional orchestra of thirty-nine players working in full association with the Arts Council of Northern Ireland. Has extensive season both in Belfast and throughout Northern Ireland. Acts as accompanying orchestra for the Northern Ireland Opera Trust, and since its formation in 1966, has been fundamental in the province's musical life.

The Business of Music

Arts Council Booking Office

Bedford House, Bedford Street.   Tel: 44222
Hours: open Monday to Friday from 10:00 AM to 5:00 PM.

In Belfast, the box office at a concert hall opens one hour before the concert only. Tickets for Arts Council-affiliated events are available at the Arts Council booking office one month in advance of the concert.

Instruments: Manufacture, Distribution and Repair

Crowther & McArthur (Pipe organ builders, repair of all
keyboard instruments)
    7 Tamar Street.   Tel: 656825
Matchetts Musical Instruments Ltd.
    6 Wellington Place.   Tel: 26695
Marcus Musical Instruments
    30 Gresham Street.   Tel: 22871

Retail Music Shops

Stanley Coppel Ltd. (Music, musical instruments)
    30 Gresham Street.   Tel: 22871
Hart & Churchill Ltd. (Music, records, instruments)
    24 Wellington Place.   Tel: 27868
Music Centre, 16 Grosvenor Road.   Tel: 28964
Tughan Crane Music Ltd. (Music, instruments)
    45 Fountain Street.   Tel: 21908
R. Young & Co. (Music, instruments)
    42 Bedford Street.   Tel: 22402
Edmund R. Curry (Music, musical instruments)
    42 Bedford Street.   Tel: 22402

CORK (County Cork)   Tel. prefix (021)

Third largest city in Ireland, Cork is situated in the Lee valley, 161 miles southwest of Dublin. It is an important seaport and an industrial center of note. It is also a cathedral city of the Catholic diocese of Cork and the seat of a constituent college of the National University of Ireland.

Guides and Services

Southern Regional Tourism Organization Ltd.
P.O. Box 44, Monument Buildings, Grand Parade.   Tel: 23251

Opera Houses and Concert Halls

The Opera House
Emmet Place.   Tel: 20022
                                                    Box Office Tel: 226701

The Opera House is a new theater in which the Grand Opera Society (see below) in cooperation with the Dublin Grand Opera Society sponsors an annual season of opera in April and May. It is also used for visiting performers and performing groups and touring repertory and ballet.

City Hall.   Tel: 21731
Concerts as well as competitive festivals are held in the City Hall. In good part, these concerts are sponsored by the Cork Orchestra Society (see below).

Group Theatre and Arts Centre Club
40 South Main Street.   Tel: 226371

Intimate theater where one-man shows, recitals and dramatic reading are presented regularly. During the month of July, there is a special season of Irish drama, poetry and music.

Summer Concerts

During the summer, there are open-air concerts held regularly in Fitzgerald Park. Further information may be obtained from the Tourist Information Bureau office or the Southern Regional Tourism Association in Cork.

Libraries

University College, Music Library
Western Road.   Tel: 26871
Hours: Monday to Friday, 2:30 to 5:30 PM. During holidays, Tuesday through
    Fridays, 2:30 to 4:30 PM. Open to the general public.

Collection: open to the general public with collection of approximately 5,000 volumes including the Johnson, Lloyd and Bax collections. Scores and standard reference works. Recordings of orchestral works, opera and folk music. Irish music collection.

Conservatories and Schools

University College, Music Department   Tel: 26871
Catalogue or brochure available upon request to the Registrar.

Crawford Municipal School of Music
Emmett Place, Union Quay.   Tel: 20076

Summer School

Summer Course in Traditional Music
Music Department, University College, Cork.

The course consists of lectures, practical demonstrations and recitals by leading fiddlers, pipers, singers, dancers and opens with a Corlan Tercentary Concert by Sean O Riada. For further information apply to the Secretary, Summer Course, Music Department, University College, Cork.

Musical Organizations

Cork Orchestral Society
Munster Arcarde, Patrick Street.

Arranges and sponsors concert activity in Cork. The Cork Symphony Orchestra, founded and conducted by the Chairman of the Orchestral Society, serves as the performing arm of this organization, but the concerts that are advanced by the society are not necessarily restricted to performances by the Orchestra.

Grand Opera Society
"Montrose," Linaro Avenue, College Road.

Sponsors and promotes opera season in Cork at the Opera House annually. Brings opera groups from Dublin and from many European and British centers.

The Business of Music

Music Shops

T. Crowley & Sons (Musical instruments, sale and repair)
  10 Merchants Quay.   Tel: 22446
Patrick Griffin (Pianos, bought, sold and repaired)
  St. Cecilias, Tory Top Road.   Tel: 26379
William E. Roycroft (Piano sales, tuning and repair)
  The Haven, Rossa Ave, Bishopstown.   Tel: 42855
Reginald P. Wade (Instrument repair)
  9 Belmont Park.   Tel: 32350

Record Shops

Leek
  62 Oliver Plunkett Street.   Tel: 26696
Ursula's Record Shop
  33 Oliver Plunkett Street.   Tel: 23455

IRELAND, GENERAL

Festivals

The reader's attention should be called to two important facts which helped shape the list of festivals which follows: 1. We have taken a timeless and lofty position—and united Ireland. The words "Northern Ireland" appear whenever they apply; otherwise one may assume that what is not Northern Ireland is Eire. 2. We have not identified the innumerable and delightful folk gatherings which dot the countryside and the calendar (for example, the Pan-Celtic Festival at Killarney or the An Fleadh Nua [feast of international music and dancing] in Dublin, or the Tionol Choeil [weekend get-together of traditional musicians and music-lovers] at Gormanston College in the county of Meath), nor have we provided details concerning the competitive festivals which abound here as in Britain (i.e., the Oireachtas na Gaeilge in Dublin, the International Song Contest in Castlebar, the Monaghan Band Festival for Pipe Bands, Brass and Accordian competition, or the Fleadh Cheoil nah Eireann, Ireland's annual gathering of traditional musicians in formal competition, held in a different location each year).

The festivals included in the short list below conform to some degree at least to those international standards by which we have defined "festival" throughout the present volume.

Avoca (County Wicklow)

Avoca Melody Fair
Dates: two weeks from the middle to the end of July.

Music in the lovely valley made famous by the poet, Thomas Moore.

Belfast (Northern Ireland)

Queen's University Festival
Festival House, 20 Malone Road.   Tel: 0232 667687
Dates: Held annually for two weeks in November.

Since its origin in 1964, the aim of the Queen's University Festival, Belfast, has been to provide a wider public platform for the indigenous culture of Northern Ireland, particularly for its traditional music, poetry, and fine art, while at the same time creating the opportunity to present artists from Great Britain, Ireland, and Europe who might not otherwise be seen here.

Festival events will take place in Whitla Hall (see p. 212) as well as recital and lecture rooms of Queen's University. Exhibitions, poetry readings, lectures, late-night entertainments, and clubs all form part of the Festival's many activities. Brochures and schedules available from the Festival House, address above.

Celbridge (County Kildare)

Festival in Great Irish Houses
Castletown House, Celbridge, Kildare.   Tel: Dublin 288252
Dates: one week in mid-June.

Begun in 1970, the Festival has proved an attractive and popular event. Both foreign visitors and local residents are charmed by the combination of music and the magnificent surroundings of some of Ireland's finest houses.

Concerts are held in the Pompeian Long Gallery, Castletown House (seating capacity 300), and at Headfort near Kells, some forty miles away. Both are eighteenth-century houses with splendid furnishings and elaborate gardens.

The music of the Festival is organized around the Tortelier family. Composers of the eighteenth century dominate the schedules, with a dollop of contemporary music for good measure.

Castletown is about one hour's drive from Dublin. A combination of public and private transport is available. A reception is held at Castletown after the final performance.

Address requests for programs, schedules, information to The Festival Secretary at Castletown House.

Cork (*County Cork*)

Cork International Choral and Folk Dance Festival
City Hall, Cork.

Dates: one week at the beginning of May.

Leading choirs from Europe and Ireland in competition, and a seminar of contemporary choral music. The activities take place at the City Hall and at University College.

Information from Cork City Tourist Information Office, 109 Patrick Street.

Tel: 021 23251

Dublin (*County Dublin*)

Dublin Arts Festival
7 Templemore Avenue.

Dates: one week to ten days early in March.

Music (pop, folk, jazz, classical), poetry, and theater; lectures, discussions, round tables held in that section of Dublin which is mostly medieval (i.e., the Christchurch Cathedral area, commonly known as The Liberties).

Dublin Festival of 20th Century Music
Music Association of Ireland, 11 Suffolk Street.   Tel: 0001 770976

Dates: one week late in June.

Performances of works by leading contemporary Irish and international composers. First performances are a special feature.

Galway (*County Galway*)

Seoda (*a traditional entertainment comprising folksongs, choruses, dances, instrumental performances, and drama*).
Taibhdhearc na Gaillimhe (The Galway Theatre).   Tel: 091 2024

This is a very well-known theater usually devoted to plays in Gaelic. Many famous Irish theatrical personalities have been associated with this institution.

From July to September, on Tuesdays, Thursdays, and Fridays, there are Seoda at the Galway Theatre. Information: Galway City Arus Failte (Ireland-West House)   Tel: 091 3081

Killarney (*County Kerry*)

Bach Festival
Dates: one weekend at the end of July.

Orchestral concerts are held in the Town Hall; organ recitals in St. Mary's Cathedral. Information: Town Hall, Killarney.

Tralee (County Kerry)

Siamsa (an Irish folk pageant to music and mime dance, displaying the changing seasons of North Kerry. Choral as well as solo singing predominates.)
Ashe Theatre, Tralee.
Dates: June to September on Monday and Thursday evenings.

Pageant performed by the Siamsoiri Na Riochta, a nationally known folk-theater group. For information, dates and times, apply to the Tourist Office, Tralee.

Waterford (County Waterford)

Waterford International Festival of Light Opera Ltd.
7 Barker Street.   Tel: Waterford 5437
Dates: two weeks at the end of September.

Amateur companies from England, Wales, and Ireland stage light operas on a competitive basis. All performances open to the public.
Performance Location: Theatre Royal, The Mall.   Tel: 051 4402
Box Office: in City Hall. Hours 10:00 AM to 5:00 PM from early August.
Seating capacity: 800

Formal dress for opening and closing performances. Optional at all other times.

Wexford (County Wexford)

Wexford Festival Opera ("Wexford Festival")
Theatre Royal, High Street.   Tel: (053) 22240
Dates: two weeks at the end of October.
Seating capacity: 444

Performs rare and unusual works of opera; also concerts and plays, as fringe activities.
Box office: located on first floor of the theater. Open daily from 10:00 AM to noon and from 2:00 PM to 6:00 PM. There is no standing room allowed. Authorized agent: McCullough Pigott, 11/13 Suffolk Street, Dublin.

Since it was started in 1951, the name of Wexford (a small country town and ancient port in the southeast corner of Ireland, about seventy miles south of Dublin), has become synonymous with first-class music and opera throughout the music world. Here little-known operas may be heard with relatively unknown young performers achieving the highest standards attainable. The Festival offers good company, lively discussion, marvelous ambience, and the friendliest hospitality. In the words of Anthony Lewis, reporting on the Festival to the *New York Times:* "On the last night of the opera festival, the audience links arms and sings 'Auld Lang Syne.' It is that sort of affair."

The eighteenth-century theater in which the performances are held is very small. Therefore, applications for tickets are accepted from mid-June and it is advised to get these in very early.

Transportation: opera trains leave Dublin Pearse Station (Westland Row) at 5:30 PM on evenings of performances.

Periodicals

Béaloideas (Official publication of the Commission, devoted to Irish Folklore in Irish and English.)
An Cumannie Béaloideas
c/o Irish Folklore Commission, 82 St. Stephen's Green,
Dublin 2.   Tel: 0001 52440
annual

Ceol
A Journal of Irish Music
47 Frascati Park, Blackrock, Dublin.
quarterly

Counterpoint
Music Association of Ireland, 11 Suffolk St., Dublin 2.
monthly

New Spotlight Weekly
Botanic Road, Glasnevin, Dublin 9.   Tel: 0001 302233

Treoir
6 Sraid Fhearchaiv, Dublin 2.

The Arts in Ireland
48 Raglan Lane, Dublin 4.
quarterly review
> Information concerning tax relief for writers, artists, and museums from the Government.

Appendix

Several organizations with offices in New York City and others with offices abroad can be of service to those intending to spend several months or a year studying in Europe. They include the following:

Institute for International Education
809 United Nations Plaza, New York 10017

Council on International Educational Exchange
777 United Nations Plaza, New York 10017   Tel: (212) 661-0310
(Paris address of the CIEE: 49 rue Pierre Charron, Paris VIII)

Institute for American Universities (under the auspices of)
University of Aix-Marseille, 27 Place de l'Université, 13,
Aix-en-Provence, France

Some organizations can provide assistance in locating employment abroad. These include:

International School Services, Educational Staffing Program
392 Fifth Avenue, New York 10018

American Association of Colleges for Teacher Education
Associate Secretary for International Relations
One Dupont Circle, Suite 610, Washington, D.C. 20036

U.S. Government, Committee on International Exchange of Persons
Senior Fulbright-Hays Program
2101 Constitution Avenue, N.W., Washington, D.C. 20418

Recruitment and Source Development Staff,
Office of Personnel and Training
U.S. Information Agency, Washington, D.C. 20547

Finally, two additional organizations that can help you if you intend to stay abroad for a considerable length of time:

Sabbatical Year in Europe
265 Maple Avenue, Morton, Pennsylvania 19070

This organization provides information on special rates for sabbatical flights, establishes contacts with Europeans who are willing to advise you on your sabbatical, and helps make available an exchange of apartments for its members.

Vacation Exchange Club
663 Fifth Avenue, New York 10036

This group helps to arrange an exchange of homes or apartments for those who need it.

For additional information on living in various countries of Europe during a sabbatical year, consult *Shoestring Sabbatical,* edited by Harold E. Taussig (Philadelphia, Pa.: Westminster Press, 1971).

It is advisable when writing to any of these organizations to state your reasons for going abroad and to ask for practical as well as professional advice for your visit. In the United States, send along a stamped, self-addressed envelope. When writing to foreign organizations, send an International Reply Coupon, available at most local post offices. This added courtesy should assure you a more prompt reply.

Reference Books for the Student or Scholar Going Abroad

European Library Directory: A Geographical and Bibliographical Guide. Lewanski, Richard C. Florence: Olschki, 1968.
Fellowship Guide for Western Europe, published by the Council of European Studies, 213 Social Sciences Building, University of Pittsburgh, Pittsburgh, Pennsylvania 15213.

The *Fellowship Guide* is intended for American graduate students, faculty, and researchers in the social sciences and humanities who need funds for study or research in Western Europe. Included is information about those fellowships which permit an extended stay abroad (usually one academic year), either in residence at a specific foreign university or for independent research.

Guide to Study in Europe. Shirley Herman. New York: Four Winds Press, 1969.

Handbook on International Study for U.S. Nationals. New York: Institute of International Education, 1970.

International Library Directory: A World Directory of Libraries, 3rd ed. Wales, A. P. London: The A. P. Wales Organization, 1969–70.

Performing Arts Libraries and Museums of the World. Veinstein, André. Paris: Editions du CNRS, 1967.

Study Abroad. Paris: United Nations Educational, Scientific and Cultural Organization, 1969.

Subject Collections in European Libraries: A Directory and Bibliographical Guide. Lewanski, Richard C. New York: Bowker, 1965.

Youth Travel Abroad: What to Know Before You Go. This pamphlet is issued by the State Department and is designed to help young Americans abroad. It is available for 20 cents from the U.S. Government Printing Office, Washington, D.C. 20402.

Additional Information
for Student Travelers

A *Student Travelpack* put together by the Council on International Educational Exchange includes information on discounts available to students, intra-European charter flights, youth fares, student tours, etc. It can be obtained free from the Council at 777 United Nations Plaza, New York, N.Y. 10017.

The Council also issues to eligible students, at a cost of $2.00, the *International Student Identity Card* (for college undergraduate and graduate students) and the *International Scholar Identity Card* (for high school and other non-university students). These are accepted throughout Western Europe for discounts on intra-European air, train, and bus travel, low-cost tours, student lodgings, and meals in student restaurants. Several cities will give student rates for concerts and opera performances if one presents an I.S.I.D. card, although this does not apply to all theaters in those cities. Museums often give discounts too. The cards are valid from October 1 of one year to December 31 of the following year.

International Student Exchange

Europa House, University of Illinois, 802 West Oregon,
Urbana, Illinois 61801   Tel: (217) 344-5863

This organization arranges study trips in Europe.

The Institute of European Studies

The John Hancock Center, 875 North Michigan Avenue,
Chicago, Illinois 60611   Tel.: (312) 944-1750

The Institute offers American college students a variety of programs in six
European cities: Durham, Freiburg, Madrid, Nantes, Paris, and Vienna. The
Institute offers its own courses taught in many fields by European professors,
but it also encourages students to take regular European university courses for
which they have satisfactory preparation. Only the Vienna and Nantes programs offer courses in music. The Extension Division of the Institute provides
services for a complete range of tours, workshops, and professional programs for
the American musician—students and professionals alike. In addition, the
Institute sponsors music festivals from time to time. For complete information,
write to the above address.

International Postal Abbreviations for European Countries
(For Intra-European Mail Only)

These abbreviations are to be used *only* when writing from one European
country to another. For example, when writing to the Palais des Beaux-Arts in
Brussels from Paris, the address of the Palais should be: Rue Ravenstein 23,
B-1000 Bruxelles. (The "B" stands for Belgium.) When writing to the Palais
from Brussels or anywhere else in Belgium, the address is simply Rue Ravenstein 23, 1000 Bruxelles. (The "B" is unnecessary within the country.) However,
when writing from the United States to Belgium, be sure that the address has
1000 Bruxelles *as well as* Belgium indicated on the envelope.

Austria = A	Great Britain = GB
Belgium = B	Italy = I
Denmark = DK	Netherlands = NL
Finland = SF	Norway = N
France = F	Sweden = S
Germany = D	Switzerland = CH

Index